T0322355

The Great
Épinal Escape

The Great Épinal Escape

Indian Prisoners of War in German Hands

GHEE BOWMAN

The
History
Press

First published 2024

The History Press
97 St George's Place, Cheltenham,
Gloucestershire, GL50 3QB
www.thehistorypress.co.uk

British Library Cataloguing in Publication Data.
A catalogue record for this book is available from the British Library.

ISBN 978 1 8039 9500 7

Typesetting and origination by The History Press
Printed and bound in Great Britain by TJ Books Limited, Padstow, Cornwall.

Trees for LYfe

Dedicated to Alex and Hans: With thanks for all you've taught me.

The names of men who really make history are often kept out of it.

Mohan Singh,
Mohan Singh Soldiers' Contribution to Indian Independence
(New Delhi: Army Educational Stores, 1974), p.337.

Contents

List of Illustrations

Map

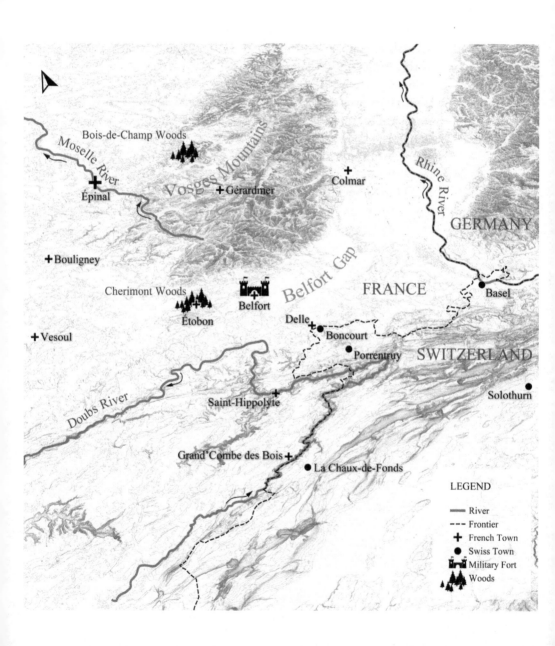

LEGEND

━━━ River
- - - Frontier
✚ French Town
● Swiss Town
🏰 Military Fort
🌲 Woods

Indian Army Ranks

Throughout the text, soldiers are identified by the rank they held during the war, although many of them rose to a higher rank later.

Viceroy's Commissioned Officers (VCOs)

Rank	Used in Which Service?	UK Equivalent
Jemadar	All	Lieutenant
Subedar	Infantry	Captain
Subedar-Major	Infantry	Major
Risaldar	Cavalry	Captain
Risaldar-Major	Cavalry	Major

Non-Commissioned Officers (NCOs)

Rank	Used in Which Service?	UK Equivalent
Dafadar	Cavalry	Sergeant
Havildar	Infantry, artillery	Sergeant
Naik	All	Corporal
Lance Dafadar	Cavalry	Corporal
Lance Havildar	Infantry, artillery	Corporal
Lance Naik	All	Lance Corporal

Privates

Rank	Used in Which Service?
Ambulance Sepoy	Indian Army Medical Corps
Driver	Royal Indian Army Service Corps
Armourer	Indian Army Ordnance Corps
Fitter	Indian Electrical and Mechanical Engineers
Gunner	Artillery
Pioneer	Pioneer Corps
Labourer	Pioneer Corps
Rifleman	Gurkhas
Sapper	Sappers & Miners
Sepoy	Infantry
Sowar	Cavalry, Army Remount Depot

Followers and Tradesmen

Rank	Used in Which Service?
Barber	All
Bellows boy	RIASC (Animal Transport Company)
Blacksmith	RIASC (Animal Transport Company), IAOC
Bootmaker	All
Carpenter	RIASC, IAOC, IAMC
Cook	All
Dhobi (washerman)	All
Farrier	RIASC (Animal Transport Company)
Groom	RIASC, ARD
Hammerman	RIASC (Animal Transport Company)
Mess servant	All
Saddler	RIASC, IAOC
Servant bearer batman	All
Sweeper	All
Tailor	All
Water carrier/bhisti	All

Glossary

ARD	Army Remount Depot
ATC	Animal Transport Company
Axis	Those countries fighting against the Allies: principally Germany and Austria, Italy, Japan
Baccu	Shelter built in the woods
BBC	British Broadcasting Corporation
CSDIC	Combined Services Detailed Interrogation Centre
FFI	*Forces françaises de l'Intérieur* – the name for the French Resistance after D-Day
Gurdwara	A Sikh place of worship
Guru Granth Sahib	Sikh holy book
Halal	Permitted for Muslims (especially used for food)
Heer/Wehrmacht	German Army
ICF	Indian Comforts Fund
ICRC	International Committee of the Red Cross
INA	Indian National Army
IOM	Indian Order of Merit – the second-highest medal awarded during the Second World War, after the Victoria Cross
Kriegie/Kriegsgefangener	POW
Kriegsmarine	German Navy
Lagergeld	Camp money
Lascar	Sailor from Asia in British Merchant Navy
Lazarette	Hospital attached to a POW camp
Legion Freies Indien/ Azad Hind Fauj	Free Indian Legion or Free Indian Army

Luftwaffe	German Air Force
Maquis	French Resistance in rural areas
MI9	That part of British Military Intelligence responsible for POW camps
Marlag und Milag Nord	German POW camp for sailors and merchant navy
NCO	Non-commissioned officer
Oflag	German POW camp for officers (*Offizierlager*)
POW	Prisoner of war
RAF	Royal Air Force
RAMC	Royal Army Medical Corps
Reich	Empire
Reichsmark/ Rentenmark/*pfennig*	German currency
SHAEF	Supreme Headquarters Allied Expeditionary Force
Stalag	German POW camp for other ranks (*Stammlager*)
USAAF	United States Army Air Force
VCO	Viceroy's Commissioned Officer – a series of ranks between NCO and officer, particular to the Indian Army
Vichy	The collaborationist French government between summer 1940 and summer 1944
YMCA	Young Men's Christian Association

Prologue: An Unknown Story

The memories of my experience during World War II have been my constant companions. They are as fresh in my mind today as they were decades ago[1]

London, Sunday, 21 May 1944, morning. The city is awake, in its fifth year of war, the weather is cloudy but dry.[2] The invasion of Western Europe and the opening of the Second Front is on everyone's mind. The previous day, *The Times* had published a short article entitled 'The Tragedy of Stalag Luft III', which detailed the shooting of forty-seven Allied officers who had escaped from that air force camp.[3] London is tense, expectant, on edge.

At 8 a.m. at the War Office, the building opposite Horseguards, where the Household Cavalry stand vigil, a telegram marked 'Secret' arrives. It comes from the Swiss capital, Berne, and was written the previous evening in code on a One Time Pad, using a random secret key. The message is from Henry Antrobus Cartwright, the British Military Attaché in the Swiss capital, and is short – sparse even. Addressed to MI9, the part of the War Office responsible for prisoners of war, it reads:

> Swiss internal authorities inform me that up to midday today 186 Indian prisoners of war who escaped from camp near Epinal as a result of recent bombing there have entered Switzerland and are at present being kept in Porrentruy district. One man was killed by Germans when swimming a river on the frontier and his body was recovered by fellow escapers.[4]

Three days later, after considerable press speculation, a further telegram arrives from Berne, based on information gleaned from escapers. This message gives the names of some of the prisoners, details the bombing by the Americans and the loss of life, and relates some of the circumstances of the journey to the neutral frontier. The total number of escapers in Switzerland has reached 278, and that number will continue to rise over the next few weeks. Although not all the information in the telegram proved to be completely accurate, the core of it was true: this was a mass escape unlike any seen before.

The escapers included Barkat Ali from Punjab, who is buried in a cemetery at Vevey beside Lake Geneva. There was also a Gurkha called Harkabahadur Rai, who escaped and joined the French Resistance in a fierce battle in the mountains south of Belfort. Their comrade A.P. Mukandan was a postman by trade, captured at Mersa Matruh in Egypt in 1942. He escaped from Épinal but was recaptured, and wrote of his experience in a fascinating and detailed account. They were assisted along their way by hundreds of French people ready to guide, feed and support, among them the blacksmith-farmer Jules Perret in the village of Étobon.

The story of the escapes, and the support given in France, is completely unknown. No film has been made, no book written, no article exists on the internet or in an academic journal.[5] The Stalag Luft III escape, however, is well known – it would go on to become a book and later the film, *The Great Escape*, made memorable by Steve McQueen jumping over barbed wire on a motorbike.[6] In fact the Great *Épinal* Escape involved many more escapers, and many more successes, but as the escapers' faces were brown not white, and as they were not officers, their experience has languished in the pool of the unremembered for eighty years.[7]

This book will tell their story in full.

This book will also tell the wider story of the 15,000 Indian Army prisoners who went through German hands during the war.[8] They were Sikhs, Muslims, Hindus, Indian Christians and Gurkhas from right across South Asia, part of the 2.5 million-strong Indian Army, all volunteers. They had been taken prisoner in North Africa, France, Italy, Greece and Ethiopia, and on the high seas. They endured up to five long years behind barbed wire, making music, learning languages, grumbling about the food and praying to God.

Some of these men got free of the walls and the barbed wire and found their way to safety, helped by generous French peasants and welcomed by the multilingual people of Switzerland. During a period of the worst of humanity, a period marked by brutality, bloodlust and fascism, ordinary people were able to demonstrate the best of humanity: resilience, support and a warm welcome. Ultimately, this is a story of hope.

Part I

Background

Background

1

The Indian Army in Africa and Europe

Lo! I have flung to the East and West
Priceless treasures torn from my breast,
And yielded the sons of my stricken womb
To the drum-beats of duty, the sabres of doom.[1]

Barkat Ali came from Punjab and Harkabahadur Rai from Nepal, two of the traditional British recruiting grounds. British recruitment was based on the so-called Martial Race Theory, the widely held belief that some people were inherently good at fighting – it was 'in their blood'.[2] Europe in the 1930s and 1940s witnessed the historical high point of racism. Nazism was an attempt to make racism the dominant world order. It failed.

But racism was not restricted to Germany. It was built into the British imperial system and built into the Indian Army as part of that imperial system. Young men from Punjab – Sikhs and Muslims – were praised as warriors and targeted for the army. Meanwhile, young men from Bengal were seen as weak, effeminate '*babus*', who were good only for clerical work and could never fight. Pressure on numbers throughout the Second World War would see the abandonment of that prejudice, from necessity rather than principle, and the 2.5 million men who served came from across the subcontinent, as did the 15,000 who became prisoners of the Germans.

This was an army in transition, from a country in transition. Indian opinions about the war were divided – talking of 'Undivided India' at the time is an illusion. The politicians, the people, even the type of government varied enormously across India. While Sikandar Hayat Khan's Unionist Party in Punjab was all-out in favour of the British and Jinnah's Muslim League took a broadly pro-British stance, the Congress Party took an altogether different line.

With the idea of independence firmly in their sights, Mohandas K. Gandhi and Jawaharlal Nehru – although both anti-fascist in outlook – were not prepared to support the British war effort unless and until independence was secured. For Churchill and the British Viceroy, everything else was secondary to winning the war. For Gandhi and Nehru, it was the reverse: independence came first and 'All other issues are subordinate'.[3]

Yet another view was held by many, led by Subhas Chandra Bose, previously President of the Congress Party. Bose – known as '*Netaji*', or respected leader – saw Britain as the enemy, and with the irrefutable logic of 'my enemy's enemy is my friend', sought to find ways to enlist Indians in armies that would fight against Britain and on the side of the Germans and Japanese.

Indian soldiers – even fellow Bengalis – had mixed feelings about Bose. A young army medical officer called Dutt, although a nationalist, 'was conflicted … he didn't agree that Indians should join the Axis … you don't consort with evil to get something done … he decided he would fight on the side of the right'.[4]

The men in Épinal and the other European prisoner-of-war (POW) camps came from across this spectrum, sometimes with loyalties that changed more than once.

Some of the future recruits to Bose's forces were already officers in the Indian Army, men like Mohan Singh of the 1/14th Punjabs, with five years' experience under his belt. He wrote later that soldiers of free nations 'fought because freedom of their country is their first duty, whereas the Indian soldiers fought because they were paid for it by our alien rulers'.[5]

This view of the Indian Army as being essentially composed of mercenaries is at least partly true. The motivations that brought young Indians to the recruiting officer were of course a mixture, as are those of any soldier. Unlike in Britain and the White Dominions, there was no conscription in imperial India, so historians sometimes talk of the 2.5 million men as 'the largest volunteer army ever'.[6] The word 'volunteer' carries overtones of volition or choice, but many sepoys had little choice. They joined up because it was expected of them; because their forefathers and cousins had joined; because it was tradition. They could look at the old soldiers back in the village with their medal ribbons and their strips of land and know that this was a way to secure the future prosperity of their family, as well as the immediate fullness of their belly. Every Indian soldier sent back money to his family, and many villages in Punjab and Nepal owed most of their income to these remittances. An anonymous Épinal escapee reflected on his experience of soldiering as a career move, years later in Switzerland:

> All Indian soldiers are volunteers. I signed up when I was 16 years old … In peacetime there were many [of us], the English did not make us aware that there could be war. Englishmen, also Indian officers, led our training, which was not very strict. Once a night march lasted until 2 a.m., then we were brought in on trucks to the barracks. We shot for a week a year with our guns and machine guns. We also got trained for transport vehicles. We had vacation for 3 whole months a year, plus 10 days at Christmas. Once there was a 3-day field service exercise, but there was no live shooting.[7]

That sentence, 'the English did not make us aware that there could be war', is significant. Despite the evidence of history, many of these young men had no idea that they would be transported in ships around the globe, be shot at by other uniformed men and spend years behind barbed wire.

Some of the Indian Army prisoners were officers, and some of those were Indians. By 1939, the Indian Army was deep into a process of 'Indianisation': the gradual replacement of the old white British officer class with indigenous Indians, a process that was massively accelerated over the following ten years of war and independence. Many of the senior-most officers of the post-Partition Indian and Pakistani armies had been trained by the British in the 1920s and 1930s; men like Kodandera Madappa Cariappa, the first Indian Commander-in-Chief of the Indian Army, and Muhammad Akbar Khan – with the Pakistan Army No. PA1 – were among the very first Indians to receive a King's Commission, training together at Indore in 1919.[8] There were also many Indian medical officers, even one in the British Army itself, and the medical needs of many POWs – Indians and others – were met by doctors from India.[9]

As well as the officer ranks that would have been familiar in any army, the Indian Army featured some strange ranks that would prove difficult for the Germans to delineate and would lead to tension in POW camps. These were the Viceroy's commissioned officers, or VCOs – jemadars, subedars and risaldars – situated between non-commissioned officers (NCOs) and King's commissioned officers (KCOs). VCOs were men who had come up through the ranks, often after many years of service, and commanded a platoon or troop. Before the Indianisation process, this was as high as an Indian could get in the Indian Army.

Besides reducing the need for white British officers in a regiment, their job was in some ways that of cultural and linguistic interpretation – helping the men to understand the British and the officers to understand the Indians. The Germans were confused over the VCOs' status and requested clarification from the British via the Red Cross.[10] The British preference was that they should be treated as equivalent to officers and housed in the same camps, and the Germans duly went along with this.

An additional complication was the status of Indian warrant officers, who were accustomed to being treated the same as VCOs in India.[11] In fact, they were transferred around from officers' camp to privates' camp, and a group of eleven of them wrote a letter of complaint to the Swiss authorities about this upgrading and downgrading, eloquently pointing out the advantages of the officers' camp.[12]

One officer POW was Santi Pada Dutt, from Dhaka in East Bengal, who had been a newly trained doctor aged 25 when the war started. His daughter described his first meeting with a Briton called Masters – the Adjutant of the 4th Gurkha Rifles, his new regiment:

> My father walked into his office. Masters greeted him.
> 'What's your name?'
> He gave him his last name.
> 'What's your Christian name?'
> My father stopped and said, 'I don't have a Christian name.'
> 'Don't waste my time!'
> 'I'm not a Christian, I'm a Hindu. I don't have a Christian name! I do have a middle name and a first name.'
> Masters had a long history with India – to my surprise something as basic as this hadn't occurred to him.
> Masters then spoke to Colonel Wheland and said, 'I think this chap is a good egg – he will do well for our medical officer'.[13]

Dutt was captured at the Battle of the Cauldron in June 1942 and imprisoned in Italy. He was later awarded the Military Cross for his heroism in continuing to treat wounded Gurkhas while being bombarded by German artillery and then overrun.[14] Later, Dr Dutt said of his decision to remain with the troops, 'How could I leave them? They were my boys.'[15]

Among the very first Indian 'boys' to become prisoners of the Germans were those who were not soldiers, nor even military men, but lascars – sailors of the Merchant Navy. Trade was the lifeblood of empire, and the ships of the Merchant Marine were the blood vessels. The size and scale of the docks in London and Glasgow – as well as their counterparts in Calcutta and Cape Town – testify to the central importance of ships to the imperial project, with grain, raw materials and cotton arriving in Britain and manufactured goods going out.

To facilitate that process and increase the workforce, Europeans had been using Indian sailors since Vasco Da Gama hired an Indian pilot from East Africa in 1498.[16] British ships employed Indians in increasing numbers from the eighteenth century, and such sailors formed part of the first Indian communities in Britain. Not only were they cheap – earning around a sixth of the rate of Europeans – they were also 'good, efficient sailors'.[17]

In time of war, Indians were used as crew on merchant ships that had released their European sailors for the Royal Navy. Such lascars (the name was applied to men from anywhere east of the Cape of Good Hope) formed an increasingly large proportion of the Merchant Navy as the twentieth century advanced. By 1938, more than a quarter of the Merchant Navy workforce was Indian – around 50,000 men.[18] Muslims from Sylhet and Punjab could be found in the engine room, Hindus were employed as deckhands, while stewards and catering staff – in daily contact with European officers – tended to be recruited in Goa and Cochin.[19]

The lascars sailed all round the world and many of them landed in Britain – around 55,000 every year in peacetime.[20] Hostels had been established in port cities for many years, and some had settled in the UK, notably in Cardiff, London and South Shields. Ison Alli, a Fireman and Trimmer on board SS *Iceland*, lived in Swansea and was married to a woman called Iris – he would spend many years behind bars.[21] As soon as the war started, merchant ships were targeted by the German navy, and many of their crew suffered a similar fate. The very first Indians interned by the Germans, in fact, were Indian crew on German ships like the *Trautenfels*. Some 238 such men were immediately imprisoned at the start of the war and released in February 1940 via Rotterdam.[22]

The first Indian soldiers to be imprisoned were also in the business of delivering supplies and were captured in France. The 22nd Animal Transport Company of the Royal Indian Army Service Corps were captured on 25 June 1940, at Gérardmer, not far from Épinal.[23] These men would go on to become the longest-serving Indian prisoners of the war, passing through many camps. They included one Indian commissioned officer – Captain Anis Ahmed Khan. By the next summer, most of them were in Stalag VIIIB in Poland – Lamsdorf – a camp that would house many Indians over the next few years.[24]

The next Indian officer to be taken prisoner was probably Shaukat Hayat Khan, caught up in the campaign in East Africa, where the Italians had occupied Ethiopia in 1936 and attacked British Somaliland in August 1940.[25] Shaukat was part of the 5th Indian Division in East Africa, and was captured in his first day of battle. With four other officers, including a South African, a Rhodesian, an RAF pilot and a Welshman, he dug a tunnel 150ft long from the camp at Adi Ugri. This was a 'back-breaking job', digging naked, using tools shaped from metal bedsteads, while being harassed by rats. The air supply was provided via a pump made from empty tins and shoe leather, and comrades up above made a non-stop musical show to cover the noise – classic Stalag antics. One day before they were ready to break out, in March 1941, the Italians pulled out and the POWs were released. Khan was immediately taken to hospital and then rejoined his regiment.[26]

Khan's 5th Indian Division went from East Africa to North Africa, becoming a key part of the fabled 8th Army. The Middle East held a paramount importance for Britain, forming the central body – together with India – of the Empire. Egypt served as the base camp for the whole region, from which the British sought to crush the nascent Italian empire, maintain naval supremacy in the Mediterranean and keep trade routes open.[27] Hitler understood the strategic importance of the region, and planned to push through in 1942, seize the Suez Canal and link up with the Japanese advance from the east.[28] India therefore assumed a crucial importance to both sides, but much of its army was away from home, defending far-flung territories of the Empire.

The 8th Army became one of the most multicultural in the world, with troops from across Africa, Palestine and the White Dominions, as well as many from India. The 4th Indian Division had been the first in Egypt, arriving in September 1939 and featuring in an early propaganda film shown in Indian cinemas.[29]

Many famous Indian regiments were to be tested in the sand and sun of Egypt, Libya and Tunisia. Over a period of two years – from September 1940 till November 1942 – the pendulum of success in the desert swung repeatedly east and west: the final eastward swing being in 1942, when the Axis reached El Alamein. After the protracted defensive battle there, the Allies advanced inexorably, all the way to Tunisia, until finally pushing the Germans and Italians out of North Africa in May 1943.

The first substantial loss of Indian soldiers as prisoners came in April 1941, at an obscure Turkish stone fort near Derna in Libya. This was El Mechili, which had been captured by Commonwealth forces during the first successful advance in January 1941. Three months later, the whole garrison of around 3,000 men was surrounded and captured by the Italians. They included a young man of 30 years called Beant Singh Sandhu. He is something of a rarity among sepoys in that we have a named photo of him, taken in Switzerland in 1944, after his successful escape from Épinal.[30]

He was a Sikh from Montgomery district in Punjab, now Sahiwal in Pakistan. His father – Fauja Singh – was a decorated veteran of the First World War, who had risen to the rank of Subedar Major, so Beant was one of the many Punjabis who joined as part of family tradition. By 1941, he was a dafadar in Prince Albert Victor's Own Cavalry, also known as PAVO. In 1941, the PAVO – together with the 2nd Royal Lancers and the 18th King Edward's Own Cavalry – were part of the 3rd Indian Motor Brigade, going through the process of converting from horses to tanks. By this stage, the men were transported by lorry and Bren Gun carrier, armed only with 2-pounder anti-tank guns and 3in mortars.[31]

Those taken prisoner in the uneven fight at El Mechili included half the PAVO and 459 men of the 2nd Royal Lancers – three-quarters of their strength.[32] The historian of the Lancers called this a 'crippling loss' to a regiment of regulars who 'from officer down to sowar had worked and lived together for years'.[33] The impact of imprisonment was wide – on families and communities at home, but also on regiments and their *esprit de corps*. In fact, the prisoners of the 2nd Lancers had a high escape rate, including men whose story will be told in the next chapter, part of which may be accounted for by that very strong sense of connection to the regiment and to each other.[34]

The next haul of prisoners was in December 1941, when two companies of the 5th Mahratta Light Infantry were 'overwhelmed by the enemy during the night' at Bir El Ghabi, south of Tobruk in Libya.[35] This was a heavy loss, but only the first of many. The following month, over 200 men of the 4/16 Punjabs were taken at Benghazi in Rommel's counterattack.

The year 1942 was the peak for Indians taken prisoner in North Africa. As Rommel's Afrika Korps swept eastwards, forts and towns and defensive boxes fell, and many of the experienced pre-war regular soldiers who had been in the army for many years were snapped up.

In May 1942, Indian soldiers were involved in the crucial battle of Bir Hakeim, another old Turkish fort at a desert spring. The Arabic name means 'Well of Wisdom', and the name is usually remembered as Bir Hacheim in South Asia. This battle is especially well remembered in France, representing the first major encounter of the Free French forces, who held off the Axis forces for several days, buying valuable time. The Indian 3rd Motor Brigade was also involved, and the 2nd Lancers lost a further 122 men as POWs.[36]

The greatest loss of Indians, however, was to the 1st Regiment of Indian artillery, which 'suffered so heavily that it had to be broken up temporarily'.[37] On 27 May, they were attacked by two German Panzer Divisions and the Italian elite *Ariete* Division. The artillery acquitted themselves well, destroying eighty tanks with their 25-pounder guns, earning many medals. Some 400 men were killed or captured and twenty-four officers taken prisoner, including Indians like Naravane and Kumaramangalam, who would go on to the most senior posts after the war.[38] Winston Churchill praised the Motor Brigade in the House of Commons, and the battle is remembered in the regiment to this day as 'a legend that will never die'.[39]

Shortly afterwards, more Indians were taken prisoner at the so-called Cauldron, a series of minefields near Bir Hacheim. More than 500 men of the 4/10 Baluch Regiment, over 600 of the 2/4 Gurkhas and half a battalion of the 13 Frontier Force Rifles were surrounded and captured by the Germans.[40] Among the Gurkhas was Dr Dutt, and among the Baluchs was the Punjabi Siddiq Khan, an Épinal escaper.

One regiment of the Indian Army that was particularly unlucky during the war was the 18th Royal Garhwal Rifles, among them Rifleman Bhopal Sing Negi. In 1931, Bhopal Sing Negi had been just 19. Like other boys of the high country, he was interested in advancing his career, earning some money and getting out of the valley. So, he walked the 7 miles down the zigzag paths to the river and found transport from Augustmuni to Lansdowne, headquarters of the Garhwal Rifles. Medical tests, aptitude, fitness – all went fine – so on 23 October, he signed up to the colours, joining the regiment's 3rd Battalion.[41]

The region in which young Bhopal lived – now part of Uttarakhand – is in the northern, mountainous fringe of India, butting up against Tibet and Nepal. The people look somewhat like the folk of Nepal, the climate is milder, reminding the Britishers of 'Blighty'. India's second-highest mountain – Nanda Devi – rises there, blessing the land with streams which form the headwaters of the Ganga, the most holy river in the country.[42] This is a special country, with forests of chestnuts, black-barked pines and deodar trees – timber of the gods, widely used for furniture – climbing up the mountainsides, which teem with flowers, colourful birds and small mammals. Going from such lush hills to the dry, flat deserts of the Middle East must have been a considerable culture shock to Bhopal when he left in the monsoon season of 1940. This would not be his last culture shock, however.

Having joined up in peacetime in 1931, Bhopal served the customary seven years with the colours, married Sobati Devi and was put on the reserve list in November 1938, ten months before war broke out. Having returned his kit in February, he received it all back again in November, when he was recalled to prepare for a war between European empires. In September 1940, the 3rd Battalion embarked at Bombay and sailed off westwards across the Indian Ocean. Past Aden, through the straits at Bab al Mandab (or Gate of Lamentation), and into the Red Sea. At Port Sudan, they unloaded and drove cross-country, joining the small Commonwealth force at Gallabat, on the border with Italian-occupied Abyssinia. They fought with distinction there – Gallabat Day is still a regimental celebration – and went on to be part of the Commonwealth victory at Keren, where the first Indian Victoria Cross of the war was won by Premindra Singh Bhagat of the Sappers and Miners. By the summer of 1942, the men of the Garhwals had been posted around the region, in Sudan, Eritrea, Egypt, Palestine, Jordan, Syria, Iraq and Cyprus, winning many medals.

At this stage, the Germans and Italians had their tails up. The Commonwealth 8th Army were in retreat, trying to stem the flow of Rommel's Afrika Korps, and the 3rd Garhwalis were just the latest unit to get in their way. On 18 June, the Garhwalis' retreat brought them to Gambut in eastern Libya, where they found themselves surrounded by tanks of the German 15th and 21st Panzer Divisions. The Indians tried to break away southwards into the desert, but only five vehicles made it through. On this terrible day, nearly the whole battalion – 555 officers,

VCOs, NCOs, riflemen and followers – were captured, among them 30-year-old rifleman Bhopal Sing Negi, who would reach Switzerland two years later.[43]

This was to be the last of the Axis advances eastwards across the desert, taking them all the way to an obscure Egyptian railway station called Two Flags – El Alamein in Arabic – where their advance would falter and grind to a halt. On the way to that halt was one of the great Axis victories of the woeful year of 1942, the fall of Tobruk. During the previous year, this coastal city had held out against the Axis forces for 246 days, with the Commonwealth defenders – among them the 18th Indian Cavalry – becoming known as the Rats of Tobruk.[44]

All that was to change in June 1942. There were four brigades dug in, in defence, three from South Africa and the 11th Indian Brigade, which comprised the Cameron Highlanders, the 2/7 Gurkhas and the 2/5 Mahrattas.[45] The Mahrattas and Gurkhas were posted to the eastern perimeter of the defence lines. On 20 June, they were overrun by massive tank attacks and all the Mahrattas and Gurkhas became prisoners.[46]

As well as the infantry, large numbers of Indian support troops became prisoners at Tobruk. The 18th Field Company of the Bombay Sappers & Miners – who had invented the Knotted Cord Drill for detecting mines – were taken, along with large numbers from the RIASC.[47] There was also a Field Post Office – postmen in uniform – who were to show up later at Épinal.[48] A total of 33,000 Commonwealth troops marched away westwards into captivity from Tobruk.

Famed for their *kukri* knives and their *terai* slouch hats, the 7th Gurkha Rifles were one of ten Gurkha regiments in the Indian Army at that time. Although not actually part of the Raj, Nepal was a uniquely important part of the army, with over a quarter of a million men serving in the Second World War, doubling the pre-war total. They sustained 32,000 casualties and won ten Victoria Crosses.[49] After Partition, they were divided, with six regiments staying as part of the new Indian Army and the other four joining the British Army, a last vestige of the old Indian Army tradition that continues still today. Perhaps it is this post-war ongoing service that has led to the Gurkhas being so well remembered in a positive light in the UK, unlike most of their contemporaries. As one ex-officer put it:

Gurkhas are a product of the past. If they did not exist no one would now invent them. They have survived by achieving standards higher than those the modern world normally sets itself ... never has a nation had such loyal and good soldiers for so long at so cheap a price.[50]

Featuring large in the army as they did, Gurkhas were also found in proportion in German and Italian POW camps – 936 in number, being around 10 per cent of the total.[51] One of those captured at Tobruk was Harkabahadur Rai. He came from the mountainous region of Okhaldunga in eastern Nepal, not far from *Sagarmāthā* – Mount Everest in English. Harkabahadur was no mountaineer, however; he was a soldier of the King Emperor and keen to fight for his regimental honour. After a few years in the army, he had risen to the rank of havildar. With hundreds of his comrades, he was captured on the outskirts of Tobruk on 21 June, going on to become one of the Épinal escapers two years later.[52]

Alongside the 7th Gurkhas were the 5th Mahrattas. Recruited in the south-western parts of India – the Konkan and Deccan – the Mahratta Light Infantry were the inheritors of a long military tradition.[53] They claim descent from Shivaji, who established the Mahratta Empire in the seventeenth century with a combination of diplomacy and military victories, and their war cry is still 'Sri Chhatrapati Shivaji maharaj ki jai!' ('Victory to Maharaja Shivaji').[54] As light infantry, they march at 140 paces per minute, but this was not enough to escape the German tanks in June 1942.[55] Among their number was a clerk called Ganpatrao Tawde, who would go on to be awarded the Military Medal for his work after the escape from Épinal.

The great Commonwealth victory at El Alamein was a turning point in the desert, and in the war overall. Winston Churchill later wrote, 'Before Alamein we never had a victory. After Alamein we never had a defeat', and the bells in British churches rang for the first time since the start of the war.[56]

That victory came in November, but before that, the first battle in the summer entailed stopping the Axis advance and holding them. On the first day of the battle – 1 July 1942 – the inexperienced 18th Indian Brigade held the line at Deir El Shein. Two thirds of the men of the 4/11 Sikhs, 2/3 Gurkhas and 2/5 Essex were taken prisoner, with the Sikhs losing over 540 men, as well as ancillary services like the Bengal Sappers & Miners.[57] In due course, many of the ordinary soldiers were released as their captors had insufficient supplies of water to keep them, but the officers and VCOs were transported away from the front line.[58]

Before these better-known battles in North Africa, however, some few hundred Indians were to fall victim to a lesser-known contribution to a little-known campaign. Following the unsuccessful drawn-out campaign by Italy against Greece, which had started in late 1940, the Germans got involved, attacking Yugoslavia and Greece simultaneously on 6 April 1941. The British had already agreed to reinforce the Greeks, sending two Australian and one New Zealand divisions, plus an English Armoured Brigade.

The Germans overran the Allied defences with remarkable rapidity, the Greek government fell, and large numbers of Commonwealth troops were evacuated by sea, but 12,000 became prisoners.[59] Among those were around 120 men of the Army Remount Department, all Punjabi Muslims, who had come from India escorting 832 mules intended for supply work in the mountains.[60] A later report tells us:

> After handing over their animals at Kalamata, they returned to their vessel, which was lying off the coast; but before they could sail the ship was bombed and the unit had to return to land in boats. They remained in the vicinity of Kalamata for a few days, but the whole unit, together with some 200 lascars, were captured by the Germans on 29 April 1941.[61]

Their mules would prove useful to the Germans in their attack on the Soviet Union a few months later, but the men would have to endure up to four years of captivity before they would be free again. The conditions for these POWs in Greece were particularly bad. Clive Dunn – later famous in the UK as Corporal Jones in *Dad's Army* – was then a trooper of the Hussars and wrote of a camp in Corinth where 'thousands of British, Indians, Yugoslavs, Palestinians and others were in the process of being subjugated by means of bad conditions and fairly ruthless behaviour from the SS guards'.[62] A photograph in the German Historical Museum shows several sepoys sitting in the heat of a courtyard, staring blankly at the camera.[63] The grooms, cooks, farriers and sweepers must have wondered what they had let themselves in for when joining the army.

The lascars who joined them included sailors from SS *Clan Fraser*, which had been bombed and sunk at Piraeus in January 1941. Their Indian quartermaster was named Mohd Alli, and he displayed courage and resourcefulness at the time, as reported by one of the British officers later, 'The wounded were got off the burning vessel by dragging them through the water on a line made fast to an overturned crane by a plucky Indian quartermaster who swam ashore with it.'[64]

A German correspondent called Grossmann, working for the propaganda magazine *Signal*, was at Corinth and wrote a report focusing on the 'mixture of races'. Grossmann interviewed and photographed an unnamed lascar, who said:

> We have been in Britain's service for many years. We were still children when we began. We cooked for the officers and cleaned their boots. No, we did not know where we were going. We do not understand English. We travelled for a very long time. When land was in sight, our ship went down. We were below deck and just managed to get out before the boat sank. We are all good swimmers. I think we ran into a mine, or it may have been a bomb. Nobody told us anything. I am ... an old man. I have never had such a good time as I am having now. I am unaccustomed to the food here, but there is nobody ordering us to do this that and the other, or to go here or go there. We need not do anything.[65]

A remarkable picture of captivity as luxury and leisure. That impression would not last, with the next few years taking their toll on the health and well-being of these men.

Two years later, another small group of Indians were captured in the eastern Mediterranean. After the Italian capitulation of September 1943, the Germans moved rapidly to occupy the Dodecanese Islands.[66] A British brigade landed on Cos and Leros to head them off – later fictionalised in the film *The Guns of Navarone*. The British force included the 9th Field Company of the Madras Sappers & Miners. Two complete platoons were captured, except for three sappers who escaped by boat to the nearby Turkish coast and rejoined their unit by crossing the full breadth of Turkey to the Syrian border.[67]

The commanding officer of the Remount men captured in 1941 was Lieutenant Colonel Denehy, a 43-year-old decorated First World War veteran and a well-known horse breeder in the Indian Army. Denehy family legend says that the Germans were so pleased to capture the mules and their loads of ammunition at Kalamata that they told Colonel Denehy he could run away, but he refused, as the troops could speak no English or German and 'I need to be there to look after them'.[68]

In fact, these men were more than capable of looking after themselves – eight of them successfully reached Switzerland from Épinal
in the summer of 1944. One of those – Allah Ditta from Jhelum –
earned a Mention in Despatches for his previous unsuccessful escape
attempt from Stalag VC at Offenburg, and six are buried in Greece
and Germany.[69]

It would be easy to see these men from Punjab as victims, transported
thousands of miles without any understanding of what was happening
to them. Some of them, however, were not prepared to sit around and
wait for what would happen next but were willing and able to take
responsibility for their fates, even if they died in the attempt.

Many Rivers to Cross

We can only guess the level of bewilderment in the German officer's question – what was a brown man doing in white men's war?[1]

Many new prisoners captured in North Africa took an early opportunity to escape. Among the many medal recommendations in the UK National Archives is the story of Shriniwas Raghavendra Kulkarni, a clerk in the Mobile Workshop Company of the Ordnance Corps. Captured during the great German advance in June 1942, he escaped two weeks later in a group of six, who 'walked barefoot to make no noise and headed SE by the Pole Star. They skirted all camps and spent the next day hiding in a *wadi*'.[2]

He was recaptured but escaped again soon afterwards and took refuge in an Arab village, but 'had very cut feet, so spent a month in this village being looked after by the Arabs. He had to change his abode every day to avoid detection and busied himself with [learning] Arabic.'

After a few weeks he felt his Arabic, disguise and feet were ready, so he moved on eastwards, gleaning information by selling eggs and tomatoes to Italians and Germans. He fell in with a Gurkha rifleman, also disguised, and they made themselves fake passes, as used by the local Arabs to get past the Italian Carabinieri. When they were stopped by Italian troops, they pulled out their passes and said 'they were looking for a lost camel', to no avail. The Italians interrogated them and a colonel pulled out his pistol, saying, 'I know you are British and if you don't confess now I will shoot'. Kulkarni called his bluff, repeated that he was an Arab and a Muslim and not afraid to die. The colonel was convinced, and Kulkarni escaped again.

By this time, the Allies were advancing into Libya, having defeated the Axis at El Alamein, and he was picked up by New Zealand troops soon after. This clerk in a military workshop learnt fluent Arabic, fooled the Italians and stood up to physical and mental tribulations in what an MI9 colonel described as 'a most excellent performance', and was awarded the Indian Order of Merit.

The treatment for other new prisoners immediately after capture was often woefully inadequate, and POWs speak of being herded and treated like animals. Many POWs taken in North Africa spent time in a large camp at Benghazi, the capital of the Cyrenaica region. This was the site of much ill-treatment and many complaints. Prisoners were made to work without payment, in contravention of the Geneva Convention, their diet was insufficient, they were beset by lice and flies and there was frequent brutality.[3] One Gurkha reported there was so little water that 'our mouths dried and there was no need to empty our bladders'.[4] R.R. Dave was one of the postmen-soldiers of the 19 Field Post Office, captured at Tobruk. He wrote:

> It was a wretched existence. The whole day we were kept at back-breaking fatigues in the sun. Food was bad and meagre. We were usually given a loaf of bread for every five men. It was always a problem to divide the loaf between the recipients. The total quantity was so pitifully small that a slight inaccuracy in cutting it made a quarrel inevitable ... But to me these physical tortures were nothing compared to the mental anguish that I was undergoing. It was a new experience to be bullied, beaten and kicked about.[5]

Another havildar of the Post Office, A.P. Mukandan of 25 FPO, who later escaped from Épinal, wrote of his experience at Benghazi in great detail. He records their daily ration, which reflects the dietary habits of the Italians far more than those of Indians, including bread, tinned fish, coffee powder and sugar:

> The quantity of bread was not sufficient even for one meal. So we cut our bread into small pieces and mixed it with tinned fish to cook a paste which we called *rottiganji* [bread-porridge]. This was consumed at the main mid-day meal. In the morning and the evening we had to be content with a cup of coffee and the odd slice of bread kept back from the ration. For cups we used discarded tins and spoons we fashioned out of bits of wood. We formed a 'combine' out of five friends and managed to keep a small reserve from our rations for use on the days when bread rations were issued late in the evening ... Due to malnutrition, the men felt tired and exhausted and became giddy even with slight exertion. Nerves were frayed and quarrels flared up quickly. After many

representations to the Camp Commandant, one hot meal of rice and beans was ordered to be issued to us in the evenings.[6]

This situation was far worse than conditions later in camps in Italy itself and in Germany – at least until the winter of 1944 – and is reminiscent of what prisoners of the Japanese endured at Changi and other camps. Mukandan also reports that clothes were in short supply:

> Most of us had no change of clothes. For the first three months I managed with a pair of shorts, one shirt and one towel. As there was not even sufficient water to drink there was no question of washing the clothes. By October, in spite of infinite care, my shirt got torn in many places due to daily wear. As the nights began to cool and there was no hope of getting any clothes from the Italian quartermaster, I managed with the help of a friend to get an old but serviceable warm shirt in exchange for fifty cigarettes.

Keeping clean was always an issue. There was always a 'long nudist queue' for the shower, in which they could stand for two minutes, but the Sikhs, with their religious requirement to wear *kacchera* (undershorts) at all times, refused to stand naked in line.[7] Like POWs and civilians throughout the theatres of war, Mukandan was infested with *Pediculus humanus humanus* (the body louse):

> As soon as the sun came up each morning there would be crowds of men removing their shirts etc in search of these elusive and well camouflaged vermin. We used to call this operation 'reading the morning news'! As if the army of lice were not a sufficient plague we had to feed their allies the fleas which jumped all night between the blankets and the bodies. No amount of care for personal and tent cleanliness seemed to help as the whole place was full of these pests and there was no escape from friends and visitors.

After a few months of this torment, the majority of Indian POWs were taken to Italy by boat, although some officers were flown to Europe. Mukandan shipped out on 14 October with 1,500 other Indians:

> The ragged crowd marched to the harbour and was loaded into the hold of a German cargo steamer. The entrance to the top decks was

closed with heavy planks, leaving only a little open space for air and ventilation. The ship moved from the harbour at 1:30pm. The hold was littered with the breakages of the last cargo. Those who were lucky to go in first picked all the spilt flour that there was. The guards after shoving us inside, neither came down nor worried themselves as to how we were faring. Because of intense heat in the lower regions, there was a squabble for higher space. On top of it there was some trouble about colour prejudice. By the evening we all adjusted ourselves to whatever space was available. Every day we were doled out a ration of hard Italian biscuits with some tinned fish and water. But the greatest trial was the lack of toilet arrangements. A forty-gallon empty barrel was kept in one corner of each deck and it was a feat to balance over it for answering the calls of nature while the ship was tossing in the heavy seas. There was of course no privacy and only one person could use the barrel at one time. No light was provided and even during the day only occupants of the higher places could ever see sunlight. During the nights one could hear cries and curses, when men stepped over the limbs of others while groping their way to and from the nocturnal visits to the barrel. As the barrel also served as a urinal, it was full to the brim on the second day and the filth overflowed to a corner. On the third night the blankets etc of some of the men sleeping in the vicinity were soaked with excreta. This was a nauseating and sorrowful sight. Like pigs, we huddled together in filth and stench. To this misery was added the fear of allied air and undersea attacks as we approached Italy. Each one of us heaved a sigh of relief when the horrible voyage ended at Brindisi on 18th of October 1942.[8]

From the ports of Taranto and Brindisi, the POWs were taken to transit camps, where conditions were often very bad. Havildar R.P. Shirke of the Postal Service wrote about the camp at Bari:

It seemed that Man had jumped from the civilised 20th Century back to the Stone Age … Thousands of lice used to roam about freely on our bodies. These filthy insects had a comfortable abode in my beard, which had been unshaved for about three months. All sense of cleanliness seemed to have deserted us. Every mouth was giving out a filthy odour and every face looked as villainous as it could.[9]

But it wasn't only the Italians that treated these men badly. The VCOs at Bari were housed with British officers, who clearly didn't like them. Years later, many VCOs recalled an incident that occurred at roll call one morning. A senior officer 'shouted, "All Bloody Indians should go to the left!" This seems to have started the feeling that all British officers – or nearly all – looked down on the VCOs and were out to down them on every possible occasion.'[10]

Mukandan's experience started to improve when he arrived at Campo 51 at Altamura, where they were issued with new blankets and straw mattresses and 'our happiness was complete when Red Cross parcels and cigarettes were distributed to us. Though we had heard a lot about Red Cross food parcels, this was the first occasion on which we saw and tasted their contents. It was like manna from heaven.'[11]

By August of 1943 there were around 8,000 Indians in camps in Italy, including forty-three commissioned officers and over 300 VCOs, mostly in Aversa, with the other ranks mostly in Avezzano.[12] The majority of these would be transferred to Germany shortly afterwards, doubling the number of Indians in German hands. There were also large numbers of Italians in camps in India – men who had been captured in East and North Africa. The idea of reciprocity was always in German and Italian heads when they considered how to treat their prisoners.

Aversa – just north of Naples – was largely an officers' camp, and many of the Indian officers and VCOs taken in early 1942 spent time here. By all accounts, it was not a bad camp, especially after the privations of the camps in Libya. There were concerts, music and language classes, and Captain Naravane of the Artillery ran cookery lessons, which had to be what he called an 'imaginary exercise' as they had no ingredients.[13]

In the autumn, the Gurkhas celebrated the festival of *Dussehra* with goats, chicken, eggs and *vino*.[14] Santi Pada Dutt was the medical officer, and when an emissary from the Pope visited the camp, Dutt and the other non-Christians each received an album of Vatican stamps.[15] Some of the officers flexed their nationalist muscles, advocating the singing of Iqbal's nationalist poem '*Taranah-e-Hind*' in place of 'God Save the King'. After a discussion, both songs were sung by way of compromise – a harbinger of the shape of things to come after the war.[16]

Apart from that, this camp appears like a typical British officers' camp, with an escape committee led by Kumaramangalam, later Chief of Indian Army Staff, and three tunnels on the go at one time.[17]

Naravane, meanwhile, had a peaceful stay, 'Apart from the roll calls in the morning and again in the evening and a weekly hot bath, we were mainly left alone'.[18] By May 1943, post was running smoothly both ways and Subedar Balbir Rai wrote to his wife:

> My dear Subedarni. Many thanks for your sweet letters. I am quite well here by the Grace of God. I am very glad for Son try to next class this year. You are do not worry about me. My best wishes and DHOG to Father sister Brother. Love to you, Balbir.[19]

For these men, so far from home, and for their loved ones, letters like this were vital in keeping them sane.

The camp at Avezzano was situated about 100km east of Rome, in the mountains that run up the Italian peninsula like a snake's backbone. This was an entirely Indian camp, with around 700 prisoners in April 1942, under the leadership of Italian Commandant Tirole and Indian Man of Confidence (see Chapter 3 for more on this role), Subedar Samant.[20] At first, in the harsh Italian winter, conditions were poor here. R.R. Dave of the Field Post Office wrote of a 'sub-human existence … With our clothes in tatters, our feet innocent of shoes, we had to try conclusions with the Italian winter. Many of the men fell ill and some died.'[21] His fellow postman Mukandan arrived there on 5 December:

> The camp consisted of 40 wooden barracks and a brick building known as 'Zafferni' and was designed to hold four thousand prisoners. The conditions in the camp were unsatisfactory and did not start improving till February 1943. Water was scarce, rations were inadequate, food parcels were irregular, there was little outside work and the camp administration was unsympathetic. Many prisoners lost appetite and weight and became mentally lethargic. Winter was severe and our party, especially the Madrassis [from southern India], suffered much due to insufficient warm clothes and poor conditions of health. As there was no warm water for soothing our swollen toes and fingers, we had to use the morning coffee for this purpose. My biggest worry was the shortage of firewood … to cook the contents of the food parcels. With the advent of summer and the appeasement of hunger, the prisoners turned their minds in other directions to fight idleness and boredom. We had several entertainments, dinner parties, dances and dramas – the dancing of one young Gurkha attracted even the Italian

officers. The 'tinkers' excelled in 'tin bashing', making useful articles by reshaping used food tins. The finished articles had a ready sale in the camp. One of our craftsmen manufactured a violin. Between meals, many were engaged in outdoor and indoor games.

Even Cupid found a way to sneak into our camp. A few prisoners started making love from inside the camp to the Italian girls standing outside the fence. It was a funny sight to the onlookers but the participants seemed very earnest. The girls all wanted chocolates, cigarettes, soap etc in return for being claimed as ladyloves of amorous soldiers. There was the usual rivalry and jealousy. Once a vehement fight took place between two prisoners inside the camp over a girl standing yards outside the fence each claiming that she was his and the other fellow had no right to make signs to her![22]

Later, the officers were transferred there from Aversa, and Kumaramangalam set up another escape committee with other officers.[23]

Campo 57 was at Grupignano, north of Trieste, near the Yugoslav border, a camp mostly inhabited by other ranks from Australia and New Zealand, with a few Indians mixed in. At one stage, the Commandant Calcaterra decided to clamp down on beards among the prisoners and ordered that 'All prisoners will be shorn'. Some prisoners protested, and the Italians upped the ante, handcuffing prisoners and shaving them by force, then putting them in solitary confinement. The Anzacs made fun of the whole process, bleating like sheep after shearing. The Commandant wanted to prove that he was in power, and ordered the five Sikhs in the camp to also be shaved. Uncut hair, kept clean (*kes*) is one of the central pillars of the Sikh faith,[24] so Naik Harbans Singh took matters into his own hands, and confronted the Colonel:

> … grabbed him by the throat and glared at the guards. Singh, towering over six feet tall in his socks, enveloped the Colonel in a bear hug, thrust his black beard into the Colonel's face and glaring into those beady eyes, cried out in a loud voice that all would hear, 'Italian, you violate a single sacred hair of a Sikh – you die with us!'[25]

Calcaterra backed down, and Harbans Singh remained unpunished. Later, in Germany, there was a similar incident. Thirty-four Sikhs had their hair cut by force at Annaburg and wrote a letter of complaint to the Red Cross.[26]

After the successful Allied invasion of Sicily in July 1943, Mussolini was deposed, and the new government surrendered on 3 September. The Germans, however, had predicted this change of allegiance and brought in army units from France and the Eastern Front, ready to take over when the Italians laid down their arms.[27] At this stage, there were over 80,000 Allied POWs in camps in Italy, and on the day of capitulation, the Italian guards marched away, leaving the camp gates open and unguarded. R.R. Dave was one of many who decided to benefit and 'taking advantage of the general confusion, I made a bid for escape. I had not made any elaborate plans. Mine was the wild impulse of an excited man and soon afterwards I was retaken by the Germans.'[28]

Many POWs, however, stayed where they were, in obedience to an order from Montgomery passed into the camps by coded messages from MI9.[29] Monty was expecting a quick victory. In fact, it took twenty months until all of Italy was liberated. Many of those who escaped during that confusion were more successful than Dave.

An impressive total of ninety-six officers and 575 other ranks of the Indian Army reached the Allies between September 1943 and August 1944.[30] Most of them were looked after and fed by Italian peasants or sympathisers in Rome. R.G. Salvi and four of his comrades were sheltered by villagers in the mountains for nine months until the Allies reached them, and he wrote a book about his experience.[31]

Naik Mohd Khan of the Rajputs escaped while being taken to a train. He spent six months on the run, meeting many other escapees in the hills. He was recaptured and taken to Germany.[32] Gurkha Subedar Bilbir Rai was one of many who escaped from Avezzano in a small 'syndicate', or group. He joined the partisans and fought bravely near Monte Cassino, rejoining the Allies on 8 June.[33]

★★★

As well as the Indian prisoners in Germany and Italy, there was also the strange phenomenon of those held by the collaborationist Vichy French government in unoccupied France. In the summer of 1940, the Commonwealth soldiers in the south of France were brought together in Marseille, where they were billeted around the city and had to report every Monday to be accounted for – 'not quite prisoners, not quite free'.[34] Many were smuggled out of the country across the Pyrenees through the good offices of the Reverend Donald Caskie, previously the Scottish minister in Paris, among them Jemadar Jehan Dad of the RIASC.[35]

By the following summer, all these Commonwealth prisoners were in a camp at Saint-Hippolyte-du-Fort, near Nîmes. There were 205 British POWs there, including four Indians, all of whom had escaped from German camps in the occupied zone, crossed the line of control and been captured by the Vichy police.[36] *Picture Post* carried an article about the camp in September, designed to reassure the folks at home. The photos included group shots of 'The Boys from the Highlands' and 'The Boys from London', but none of the four boys from India.[37] Luckily, the Red Cross delegate snapped them in September 1941 – two smiling shyly at the camera, two looking slightly away.[38] These four Indians were almost certainly men of the RIASC, who had escaped from their camps in northern France. On 17 March the following year, they were transferred to Fort de la Revère, in the mountains above the sea between Nice and Monte Carlo.[39] Here, they received a monthly payment of 123 francs, paid by the US Consul in Nice, and by now they had been joined by two more unidentified escapees.[40]

As well as the escapees, camps in Vichy France also held Indian POWs who were severely ill or disabled. Mughal Khan of the 22nd Company wrote a letter from a hospital in Nice, which he described as 'a lovely place. A place where the sun never sets.'[41] Unfortunately, he died in 1943; he is remembered on the Dunkirk memorial.

A disabled British lance corporal called Uttley wrote to Mrs Bell on behalf of Dafadar Sirdar Khan, also of the 22nd Company, who reported that they listened to the BBC every Sunday morning, tuning in to the special radio programme for Force K6 men in the UK.[42]

This odd situation of detention by an erstwhile ally came to an end in November 1942. Following the Allied landings in French North Africa, the south of France was occupied by German and Italian soldiers, and the Vichy government lost all its territory.[43] Nice fell into the new Italian zone of occupation, so most of the Allied POWs in the Vichy zone were taken to Italy.

One of the 131 Indians who was part of that relocation was Driver Qasim Shah of the 22nd Animal Transport Company, a Shiite Muslim from Kamra Kalan, in Campbellpore, Punjab. Aged just 17 when he arrived in Marseille at the end of 1939, his travels would take him across the map of Europe over the five years until he reached Punjab again at the end of 1944.[44] After spending several months in Marseille loading and unloading ships and trains, he was posted with his fellow muleteers to the Maginot Line in the north of France, where they faced the Germans directly. After the blitzkrieg of May 1940, his company worked its way southwards along the River Moselle until their capture at Gérardmer in the Vosges Mountains. There followed a succession of camps in France and Germany, including Stalag V-A, near Stuttgart.

Brought back into France, Qasim Shah managed to escape, and spent time on the run in Lyon, Paris and Limoges, before being captured by the Vichy authorities. While at Fort de la Revère, he wrote to Lieutenant Colonel Kean in Oxford, saying, 'There are five other Indians here with me in this camp and we are all very well and not too unhappy'.[45] With the fall of Vichy, he was taken to Italy, spending time in Campo 73, near Modena, as well as Avezzano and Aversa, with another escape attempt along the way. After the Italian capitulation, he was sent to a camp in Austria, then to Germany and finally to Épinal, from which he reached Switzerland on 19 May 1944. In total, Qasim Shah was in at least nine camps in Europe, and a map of his travels would look like a snail shell traced around Europe.

Those prisoners who didn't manage to escape in September 1943, when the Italians marched off leaving the camp gates open, were to face the prospect of a long and arduous train journey in goods wagons through the Alps into the Reich. Mukandan traced a six-day route taken from Avezzano via Rome, Florence, Mantua, Vicenza and Udine, and then to the Austrian town of Markt Pongau. As there was no room in that camp, they were moved on again to Stalag XVIII-A, at Spittal, in Austria.[46]

A letter sent from Stalag VIIIB at Lamsdorf a little later listed twenty-one POWs who had died on the way, some of whom had been shot trying to escape.[47] Havildar Ramasharan Sahi of the Gurkhas was one of those who tried to escape while the train was in motion through the Alps. He was shot at and recaptured but reached Switzerland from Épinal nine months later.[48] Another havildar had less luck. Mohindar Singh of the 3/12 Frontier Force Rifles cut through the wooden floor of the wagon he was in, let himself down on to the tracks and lay motionless till the train had passed on. He went towards Switzerland but was recaptured after five days and taken back to imprisonment.[49]

As the 8,000 Indians arrived in camps across the Reich in the autumn of 1943, they went through the same bureaucratic routine that thousands of other newly arrived POWs had done. They were registered and photographed and issued with a German POW dogtag. Naravane recounts the next stage at Oflag 79:

> We were then taken to a delousing enclosure where we were made to strip and then taken in our birthday suits for a hot shower with the luxury of a disinfectant soap. In the meanwhile our clothes were labelled and sent for fumigation. It was with a wonderful feeling that we wore our deloused clothes after the soap bath.[50]

If this was their first camp, they were given a standard Red Cross postcard, on which they filled in their basic details. This was sent to Geneva, who in turn informed the Red Cross in Delhi, who then notified their family. With the administrative requirements completed and a bunk allocated, the prisoners spent their first night in the German Reich.

3

Stalags and Oflags

I saw a wounded bird
Its wings clenched
It was striking desperately
Again and again
Against the wall of the garden[1]

On 25 August 1941 at Stalag VIII-B Lamsdorf – the largest camp in the German empire – an Indian soldier called Mohamed Afzal sat down to write a letter to England. This is what he wrote:

Many thanks for your letter of 7th April, and also for one food or one clothing parcel. I am able to get letters translated quite easily, and some of our comrades are able to speak English, and there are also a lot of English here too. We are quite happy here, and feeding on Red X parcels, and the Germans also supply us with a special soup. We all think a lot about England and hope to be able to visit it when the time for repatriation comes, as we all hope, pretty soon. We are all quite fit, and indulge in various sports, including football. There is one general opinion about the [redacted] and that is that the [redacted] not to keep us in, but to keep the [redacted] out – so you see, really we are quite cheerful. The English here have a lot of concerts and various Bands, including a hot Dance band – led by a fellow called Jimmy Howe. Naturally we are invited, and we enjoy these evenings tremendously. Well, once again, I thank you for taking an interest in me, and hope to hear from you again soon.[2]

This letter serves as a useful summary of many aspects of imprisonment for Indian POWs in Germany. The importance of the Red Cross and its parcels to Mohd Afzal and his comrades is clear, and their function in augmenting the 'special soup' supplied by their captors. He has realised that keeping active and busy is key to mental and physical health, and that music will lift the spirits.[3] Like all letters from German camps, Afzal's letter has been through a censor's office, and the redacted section probably refers to a common joke among prisoners on the function of the barbed wire. It reads as if this letter was probably written by a scribe rather than Afzal himself.

There is very little about Mohamed Afzal in the archives. His name tells us that he was a Muslim and the records show that he was one of the 320 men captured in France in June 1940 and held for most of the war.[4] He was a member of the Indian Army Veterinary Corps attached to the 22nd Animal Transport Company, so his job was to look after the health of the mules themselves. Apart from this one letter, I have found nothing else by or about this soldier, except that he was recorded in 1944 as being a prisoner at Épinal.[5] He may or may not have escaped in May 1944, but his name is not recorded as having entered Switzerland. As his name is not on the Commonwealth War Graves Commission website, we can assume he survived his long imprisonment and made it back home to his family. This information vacuum is typical of the records for the Indian Army in the war. In fact, we are lucky that his letter has been preserved. Such is the nature of the sources for the sepoys in the Stalags.

Stalag VIII-B at Lamsdorf got its number from the strict system that the Germans used to organise and name their camps. The Reich was divided up into *Wehrkreise*, or military districts, numbered in Roman style – Wehrkreis III was around Berlin, Wehrkreis VIII was near Breslau and so on. Within each district there were several different types of camps. The most numerous were *Stammlagers*, abbreviated to Stalag, a standing camp for other ranks, usually with several *Arbeitskommando* – subsidiary work camps. Lamsdorf was the second camp for non-officers in District VIII near Breslau, so was numbered VIII-B. A Stalag *Luft* was for the air force. An *Oflag* was short for an *Offizierlager* for officers and VCOs plus their orderlies or servants. A *Dulag* was a transit camp, and a *Frontstalag* was a camp outside the Reich itself, usually in France or Poland, often used for colonial troops.

Prisoners were generally looked after and guarded by the same service as themselves: so RAF by the *Luftwaffe*, Royal Navy and Merchant Navy by the *Kriegsmarine*, and the Army by the *Wehrmacht*.[6]

Structurally, camps came in different types. Stalag Luft III of *Great Escape* fame is a classic example of the huts-in-the forest type: wooden buildings in rows erected for the purpose in a flat sandy area among thick layers of trees, with a double layer of barbed wire around. Microphones, guard dogs and watch towers complete the scene – the familiar currency of Hollywood and British movies. In other cases, POWs were kept in old castles – the classic example being Oflag IV-C at Colditz. Frontstalag 315 at Épinal was in an old French barracks, and *Arbeitskommando* could be anything from a factory to a zoo to a farm.

Large camps like Stalag VIIIB at Lamsdorf could feel like 'real towns, with streets, police, road maintenance and cleaning service'.[7] Every Stalag and Oflag had a camp leader and a Man of Confidence: two different roles which were vital for the smooth running of the camp and the health and well-being of the prisoners. The Camp Leader in an Oflag was usually the senior officer; in a Stalag, it was the senior NCO. The Man of Confidence, on the other hand, was elected by the prisoners: at Épinal it was Bhagat Ram, who witnessed the bombing and did his best to keep up the spirits of his fellow prisoners.[8]

The Stalags saw an unprecedented number of men passing through them. Of the 80 million men and women in military uniform around the world during the Second World War, perhaps as many as 35 million were captured at some stage.[9] France saw over 30 per cent of its mobilised forces end up in camps, while for the UK it was less than 3 per cent, with a similar proportion for India.[10] So Indian POW numbers are relatively small as part of those totals: the standard figure given for Indians in camps in Europe is around 15,000.[11] I have tracked down the names of over 12,000 of those men and compiled a database, which shows that Indian *Kriegsgefangene* were as diverse as any other group.[12]

Military systems see men in groups and blocks, but each soldier was – like any human being – unique. There were large numbers of Muslims, Sikhs and Hindus among the POWs in Europe, but also around 100 Indian Christians, and at least one Parsi – Lieutenant Jimmy Vakil of the RIASC.[13] Although perhaps half were from Punjab, most of the lascars were Bengali, and there were many from the south, as well as 1,000 Gurkhas from Nepal. There were even a few from outside British India, like Sarto Pacheco, who hailed from the Portuguese colony of Goa.[14]

These men came from all social classes and castes of South Asia. Captain Anis Ahmad Khan was the son of a Vice Chancellor of Aligarh Muslim University – from the top drawer of Indian society.[15] Many were farmers, with a small amount of land. Among the non-combatants were over 200 'sweepers' – men from the lowest caste of Indian society, whose job was to sweep up rubbish. One of these – named Bhundu from Meerut – reached Switzerland from Épinal.[16]

They also varied widely in age. Some were in their teens, like Qasim Shah, and many were in their twenties. Jemadar Ghaus Mohammed of the Veterinary Corps was described by the Red Cross delegate thus: 'His age is 53, but he appears much older.'[17] Just as the British Indian Empire was wide and varied, so too was the prisoner population that sprang from it.

In some ways, of course, Indian prisoners were distinct from their fellow captives. At the time, they were usually counted as part of the 'British' category – men from right across an empire covering a quarter of the world's population. But Indians were different – they spoke many languages as well as English, they included faiths not found in other groups of prisoners, their preferred diets were distinct from those of many other nations. For these reasons, it often became convenient for their captors to separate them out. Some South Asian writers also see ways in which they were unusual. The leader of the first pro-Japanese Indian National Army (INA) wrote, 'An Indian soldier is a remarkable character: he admirably studies each situation in his own way but when stumped helpless, he simply resigns to Fate.'[18]

Regardless of their background, captivity would prove to be something that Indians were capable of enduring – in large numbers and for long periods. The idea of being a prisoner of war was not a new one in India. Many sources from ancient India talk of the treatment of prisoners. In the ancient Indian epic *Ramayana*, Hanuman is taken prisoner by the evil demon Ravana but escapes with his tail ablaze, setting fire to the whole island of Lanka.[19] For Muslims, there is clear guidance within the Qur'an on the conduct of war and the treatment of captives. Sura 47, Verse 4 says in translation:

When you meet [in battle] those who disbelieve,
[let there be] smiting of their necks;
And then, when you have wrought havoc amongst them,
Make fast the bonds;
Then afterwards [let there be] grace or ransom,
Until war lays down its burdens.[20]

After the 1857 rebellion, the British perpetrated what would now be considered war crimes against prisoners, as at Kolhapur, where captives were tied to the mouth of a cannon, and 'according to eyewitnesses, the torsos vaporised, but arms, legs and heads fell into the crowds'.[21]

Within living memory, thousands of Indians had been taken prisoner in the 1914–18 war. The siege of Kut Al Amara in Mesopotamia led to the surrender of over 10,000 Indian troops to the Ottoman Turks. While the officers were generally treated properly, the other ranks endured a 600-mile death march.[22] Within three months, around 2,000 had died and the remainder were forced to labour in appalling conditions building the Baghdad Railway. Equally, many Indians had been locked up by the British authorities for anti-imperial activity. Gandhi said, 'We should consider it our good luck if we are sent to jail for the good of our country, for preserving our honour, for observing our religion.'[23]

There is of course a crucial distinction between a political prisoner like Gandhi, a criminal in jail, and a prisoner of war, and POWs were keen that their relatives should remember that their condition was an 'honourable' status.[24] As the men of the RIASC prepared to surrender in June 1940, their officers took pains to clarify their impending status and talked about 'the meaning of being a prisoner of war. It was, they explained, "Issati Walli Kaid" and not to be confused with ordinary imprisonment.'[25]

These men had committed no crime: their incarceration was not a result of any fault on their part, but a product of the ebb and flow of military fortune. Additionally, the POW knows not the length of their sentence, there is no predictable end point. The experience of being a POW almost becomes an occupation in itself; a job, a way of life. The day is structured around mealtimes and roll calls, darkness and light. Festivals came and went, and the passing of seasons was marked, even if there was no monsoon to wash away the dust of summer.

★★★

Indian prisoners were frequently moved around from camp to camp within the German empire. The Swiss protecting power remarked in 1944 that Indians were 'very particularly the object of frequent movements'.[26] At first, the German policy was to concentrate Indians together and then to try to recruit them for the German army. Those who refused then became part of the vast workforce needed to keep the machine of total war running.

The multiple moves that they were subjected to meant that they could find themselves reunited with old friends or neighbours. In late 1942, a Jemadar from Punjab wrote a letter from Germany listing eleven men from his village in two adjacent camps.[27] The vicissitudes of modern war could recreate a small section of their Punjabi village in Saxony.

Mohamed Afzal was writing from the largest camp that Indian POWs were sent to: Lamsdorf (now Łambinowice in Poland), 100km south of Breslau near the border with Czechoslovakia.[28] This camp was so vast it was like a town, its population reaching a maximum of 31,000, including the numerous dependent work camps.[29] There were six compounds in the sandy clearing in the forest, each housing a different nationality, most of whom wore British uniform.

The Indian compound peaked at around 300 prisoners, all NCOs and privates.[30] One of that number was Lance Naik T.D. de Cruz, part of a select group who knew about the camp radio. These crystal sets were kept in bully beef tins, hidden beneath the bricks in the floor. Every evening, the POWs tuned into the news from London, and the news was spread through the grapevine the next day.[31]

Probably the most famous German camp was Oflag IV-C at Colditz, between Dresden and Leipzig. At a castle perched on a hill above the town, the Germans locked up 'bad boys' – Allied prisoners who had attempted escape or were perceived as *deutschfeindlich* (anti-German) – from the Netherlands, France, Poland, the USA and the Commonwealth. Although most of the POWs held there were officers, there were also servants of various nationalities. Among the Commonwealth prisoners were several Indians, including Dr Birendra Nath Mazumdar, one of the few Indians in the British Army.[32] There was also a large group of NCOs, sent there from Annaburg, the camp near Berlin specifically set up to convert Indians to join Bose's *Legion Freies Indien*.

At the start of 1942, Indian soldiers at Annaburg had protested when they were issued with cotton underwear rather than the warm pullovers sent by the Red Cross. The Germans made them stand on parade all night, without coats or blankets in heavy snow. When their NCOs discussed what to do, the Germans opened fire, and twenty-eight POWs were wounded. The Indians were then put back in their barracks, but eleven senior NCOs were beaten, taken to the police station, flogged and then sent to Colditz.[33] These men included Dafadar Major Ganpat Ram of the 2nd Royal Lancers, who later escaped from Épinal.[34]

There was at least one other Indian officer at Colditz besides Mazumdar. In June 1942, Lieutenant Singh wrote to the Commandant from Colditz, protesting about his rate of pay.[35]

Ison Alli and the crew of the *Iceland* were taken to a different kind of camp – Marlag und Milag Nord, a complex of camps for sailors near Bremen on the North Sea. Among the 5,000 merchant seamen were over 500 Indian lascars from at least eighteen ships.[36] Merchant seamen were often destitute, their money and possessions being at the bottom of the sea, and they had little chance of getting work.[37] For the first few years, these sailors were in the main Milag, but from the middle of 1943, they were separated out into a different building in the woods: the *Inder Lager*. Relations with the main camp were not cut off, however: lessons in Hindustani were offered to English speakers, and the camp theatre benefited from donations of turban material to make wigs.[38]

The conditions at the *Inder Lager* were better than in many other camps. One Red Cross report towards the end of the war stated that the barracks were spacious and well furnished, and 'the Indian camp is probably the best situated portion of the Marlag. The prisoners do not look unhappy; no complaint has been made.'[39]

There was a theatre, which was 'furnished with taste', a mosque and a chapel for the thirty-five Catholics (mostly from Goa). In 1944, the camp saw something of a religious revival for its mostly Muslim inhabitants, with the Red Cross reporting many prisoners learning Arabic and copying out the Qur'an. There may have been mixed motives for this religious fervour, as the Red Cross also reported that the Muslims refused to work because of the time required for prayers and studying the Qur'an.[40]

The lascars at the *Inder Lager* were well aware of the Geneva Convention of 1929, as all prisoners were. This agreement had been signed by fifty-three nations including Britain, Germany and India, but not Japan or the USSR. Copies were available in Stalags, and a large poster version was displayed in the *Inder Lager*.[41] Generally speaking, the Germans stuck to the Convention as far as Commonwealth prisoners were concerned but ignored it for Jewish and other civilians in concentration camps, as well as for Russian prisoners, coming from a country that had not signed the Geneva Convention.

The International Committee of the Red Cross (ICRC) was responsible for delivering parcels, inspecting the state of health and hygiene in the camps and ensuring levels of food were stable and healthy.[42] The ICRC delegates – all Swiss men, mostly medical doctors – risked their safety in aiding the captives inside every camp in Europe, Africa and Asia. Ten of them died during the course of their work, including Johann

Jovanovitz of the Berlin office, shot by a German sentry whose signal he had not observed.[43] As well as being medically trained, they were fluent in multiple languages and able to communicate diplomatically with the prison authorities and the prisoners themselves.

In theory, each camp was visited every few months by members of a team based in Berlin. The visit included careful inspection of all the buildings, looking at menus and checking stores of food and medicines. The delegates met the guards, the camp leader, the Man of Confidence and the chaplains, and any POWs who asked to be heard.[44] In practice, this did not always work out, as one delegate complained in late 1943, 'It is really very difficult to know exactly how things are, as the Inspector has never been allowed to talk alone with the Indians, in any of the camps where he has seen them'.[45]

The reports themselves – written in French – varied widely, becoming more standardised as the war went on. There was a lot of emphasis on hygiene, food and medical conditions, but few anecdotes and no escape stories. The May 1943 report on Work Detachment 1520 near Baden-Baden, for example, reported that there were 809 Indians in residence, the canteen stocked pepper, vinegar, paprika, beer and notebooks and the men were working loading railways and levelling terrain. The overall conclusion was that this camp was mediocre and insufficient.[46] Generally, the reports were more favourable in their overall conclusions, at least until the end of the war.

A vital part of the work of the Red Cross – one that lingered in the memory of all Indian POWs – was the delivery of parcels. In the case of Indian POWs in Europe, these parcels originated with the Indian Comforts Fund (ICF) in London (see Fig. 5). Their work became a focal point for the Indian community in the UK – among their packers was Mrs Bhattacharya of 43 Green Walk in Hendon – backed up by eleven members of the Indian Pioneer Company, doing the heavy work.[47]

In 1945, one of the packing centres was hit by a V-1 flying bomb. The manager, Miss Goodfellow, recalled, 'One of our Pioneers emerged from some wreckage saying, "Two arms, two legs, all present and correct, thank God."'[48] Over the course of the war, the ICF sent a staggering total of over 1.6 million food parcels to Europe.[49] The parcels were shipped to Marseille via Lisbon, to Geneva by rail and thence by rail to the camps, a remarkable case of international co-operation, even in the darkest times. A typical Indian food parcel provided several tins containing curry powder, dhal, atta and ghee, peas, fruit, cocoa powder, milk powder, fish, syrup, cheese, sugar, chocolate, a bar of soap and a packet of sweets, and was designed to last one prisoner a week.[50]

Article 11 of the Geneva Convention states that prisoners' food should be 'equivalent in quantity and quality to that of depot or reserve troops'.[51] As it turned out, the German Command made a decision at an early stage to keep rations low as they knew the Allies would fill the gap through the Red Cross.[52] For the Muslim prisoners, the question of halal requirements was always present, and as the Germans forbade the Indians to slaughter animals themselves, many Indian Muslims went without meat for the duration of their captivity, making do with the fish in their parcels. On one occasion, when the Swiss legation visited a hospital in Italy, the British medical officer told them about a Muslim sepoy called Zug Lal, suffering from anaemia. When an Italian doctor wanted to feed the latter with meat to boost the iron in his blood, the soldier refused.[53] In contrast, the fifteen Indian Christians at Stalag XIIA at Limburg near Koblenz wanted tinned bully beef and requested they receive the standard British parcels instead of ICF-issue.[54]

In some cases, the hunger was worse at the start of captivity. Many years later, the son of mule driver Chanu Khan recalled the march to his first camp in the summer of 1940:

> During the journey, they were hungry from 6–7 days. They saw a dead donkey on the road. All of the men except my father and another man rushed to the donkey to eat it. Then they beat them with rifles to push them away from the donkey. After they reached the camps, they had nothing to eat. Some women came there in mercy with biscuits, milk and bread and gave small amounts to my father and other prisoners … they had to suffer a lot. Then after 15 days, there was contact with the Red Cross and proper food was supplied.[55]

Towards the end of the war, when food supplies in Germany were running out, these parcels were what kept the Indian prisoners from starvation. They were also vital for sustaining morale, as this letter from an unnamed Indian prisoner shows:

> By the grace of God and your good wishes, I am quite comfortable. The foundation of our joys and sorrows and life itself is dependent on the weekly parcels received from the Red Cross. Should these

amenities fail to arrive we see stars in the broad daylight. Our actions and movements are governed by this one fact. News of arrival of a fresh consignment of parcels spreads among the prisoners with the rapidity of an electric current. Prisoners walk with great nimbleness when they see the lorry with the parcels approaching and stare at it with great expectation.[56]

Some men took a practical approach to the shortage of food and grew their own. Jemadar Siddiq Ahmed (who later escaped to Spain across the Pyrenees) was working as a doctor in an Oflag, but still had time to plant lettuces, carrots and peas as well as 'a few kinds of flowers'.[57] And a lieutenant at Oflag 54 wrote in the summer of 1942:

> I am a very keen gardener now the Red Cross sent some seeds, and I look after cabbages, carrots, turnips, lettuce and radishes with loving care! If you could send some seeds I would be very pleased and could put them in next spring, if I am still in prison by then.[58]

In fact, he would have three more years to endure, to hoe and till and watch his seedlings.

As well as reporting on food supplies, the Red Cross always wrote about the extent to which prisoners' religious needs were being met. For Indian POWs, this was a more important issue than for the more secular Britishers. The Geneva Convention requires 'complete freedom in the performance of their religious duties', but this freedom was often restricted by the Germans; a cause of frequent complaint by the '*kriegies*'.[59]

In one camp, at the end of 1943, there was not enough spare accommodation to make space for a mosque and a temple, so the prisoners were forced to pray in the corridors.[60] The prayer leaders must have been ordinary soldiers with a strong religious background, as there is only one Indian 'chaplain', as such, recorded as having been taken prisoner – the Muslim *maulvi* of the 22nd Animal Transport Company.[61] The ICRC reported a common complaint from work camps, that 'priests should be exempted from work', indicating that the job of leading prayers was a considerable commitment.[62]

It seems likely that extended incarceration proved to be a spur to greater religiosity among some prisoners.[63] Just as 'there are no atheists in a foxhole', perhaps there are few atheists behind bars, and a prisoner falls back on his god. Sepoy Shah Mohd wrote home from Lamsdorf thus: 'Your brother wishes to tell you that he is stronger and healthier than ever before. He is getting on very well and is getting plenty of time to study Quran, as we have nothing to do but play and read.'[64] In this case, it seems that religious observance went together with enhanced well-being.

Other prisoners were doubtful of this. Sergeant Postman Mukandan observed in Aversa, 'The physical and mental sufferings made many of us very religious-minded. Reading of too many religious books turned some men into intolerant fanatics.'[65]

In February 1944, an extended correspondence between Germany, London and India indicated the seriousness with which religion was taken. The Muslim Man of Confidence in Stalag VC requested a *fatwa* (guidance) on four matters, including whether Muslims could perform reduced prayers as they were in prison, and requesting permission to eat tinned meat as Muslim POWs 'are losing their weight and becoming the victims of certain diseases'.[66] Six months later, the replies came from Principal Madrasatul Waizeen at Lucknow – for the Shia branch – and Grand Mufti Darool-Alum at Deoband, representing the Sunni perspective.[67] Although the two authorities disagreed on the question of reduced prayers, both forbade tinned meat, as the type of meat and the method of slaughter were unknown and therefore not to be trusted. Some Muslim prisoners put the requirements of their faith above all other considerations.

Denied access to their physical home and certain knowledge of what was outside the wire, prisoners and their families relied on letters – sheets of paper touched by loved ones, a physical connection across thousands of miles. When one army wife finally received a first letter, it was read and reread many times as 'during a war … a letter can start a heart beating or stop it altogether. I learned to value this small piece of paper.'[68]

According to the Geneva Convention, *kriegies* were allowed two letters and four postcards per month (more for officers), sent free of charge.[69] The Red Cross reported on 'voluminous mail from Indian PW in Germany, which was almost always written in unfamiliar dialects'.[70] At Marlag und Milag Nord, in 1944, the lascars wrote and despatched around three letters each per month.[71]

Given the relatively low level of literacy in India at the time, it is likely that those who could write – clerks, NCOs, educated comrades – were kept busy as scribes.[72] Article 36 of the Geneva Convention states,

'As a general rule, the correspondence of prisoners shall be written in their native language.'[73] The Germans, however, were tight on censoring mail. Lacking staff who could read Indian languages, the authorities often took the simplest route and forbade correspondence in anything but English.[74] At Limburg, there were even complaints that the Germans had destroyed letters written in Hindustani.[75] A lifeline cut.

One surprising lifeline – revealed in a voluminous file held in the Imperial War Museum in London – was the extensive correspondence between Indian POWs and retired Indian Army officers and their wives in the UK.[76] Mohamed Afzal's letter at the start of this chapter was one such, written to General Barrow in Buckinghamshire. This scheme was initiated by MI9 and organised by Mrs Mary Bell, mobilising her address book of 150 correspondents, who wrote 1,000 letters a month to around 2,000 POWs. MI9 were pleased to report that 'every Indian Prisoner of War was adopted in this way'.[77] The epistolary skills of some of the men are clear, for example in this letter to Mrs Bell from R.R. Dave of the Indian Postal Service:

Dear Mrs Eva Mary,
It affords me great pleasure in penning a few lines to your kind self. Yesterday, I happened to come across a letter penned by you to a P.O.W. and that goaded me to take indulgence of writing this letter card.

It has been eight months since I have been captured. I belong to Indian Post and Telegraph Department. I am all hale and hearty young lad of twenty and five. The present state of my being doesn't dispirit me because I live in hopes – hopes of early emancipation. Formerly I was a player and now am a passive spectator of this sanguinary war. Passive by means of prayer. I have a staunch belief in prayer. I haven't the fortune of receiving a single line from my long-separated wife who must be lamenting about me. I am anxious about her. Mrs Kafila R. Dave c/o K.N. Rawal Esq, Dungra Bhint, village and post office LUNAVADA, H.O. BARODA INDIA. Praying for your prosperity and health,

Yours faithfully,
R.R. Dave[78]

Through this system, some Indians kept in touch with retired colonels and majors for many years, and even met up after liberation.

Thousands of miles away in a POW hospital in Burma, an officer called Harbakhsh Singh wrote a poem designed to lift his spirits:

Although you are miles from the home that you love,
A strange soil beneath you, and a strange sky above;
Morning and evening, and all the day through,
Someone Is Thinking Of You!

Someone remembers, somebody cares,
Your name is whispered in somebody's prayers;
Think of the things that are lovely and true, for
Someone Is Thinking Of You!

Through danger and weariness, peril and pain,
In moments of doubting when faith seems in vain;
Keep the bright hope of FUTURE in view, for
SOMEONE IS THINKING OF YOU!![79]

This officer was doing his best to keep his own spirits up, to bolster his morale. Even without letters, he asserts, a prisoner can find solace in the thought of those who care.

Other sources of solace were needed though, for enforced idleness could mean long periods of boredom. Havildar Sardar Mohd reflected later, 'Having nothing to do day after day, and thinking all the time of our homes so far away, and with no apparent likelihood of seeing them for many months was the worst of all.'[80] In such circumstances, many turned to sport to keep a healthy mind and body, to avoid thinking of the past or the future and make the most of the present moment. At Lamsdorf, a barefooted Indian team excelled in the international hockey tournament, beating all six teams except the Australians, who managed a 1–1 draw.[81] At the 1943 sports day, Dafadar Major Mohammed Khan was proclaimed *Victor Ludorum*, having won more sports than anyone else in this enormous camp.[82] At a later sports day at the same camp, one of the 'exciting highlights' was Mehdi Khan's time of 9 minutes 43 seconds for the 2-mile race (the world record being 8 minutes and 37 seconds).[83]

On a visit to Limburg, the ICRC delegate had noted the almost complete lack of leisure facilities and pastimes for the 2,131 Indian residents and sent in a list of requests that included games, books, an accordion and a cover for the *Guru Granth Sahib*.[84] The Red Cross, the YMCA and private agencies were able to supply good amounts of equipment – a later photo of the library at Limburg shows it was well stocked. At Marlag und Milag Nord, games included the Indian favourite, Carom.[85]

Meanwhile, the officers had considerably more time on their hands. Jemadar Dost Mohd at Oflag 54 wrote home complaining, 'We have no work to do except reading English the whole day'.[86] At one Oflag, gambling by British and Indian officers in the camp casino got out of hand, to the extent that it 'endangered discipline'.[87] And at Oflag 79, an art club was in full swing, with an 'eagle-faced Sikh' its 'most striking model'.[88] At the same camp, Captain Anis set up a fund to provide scholarships for the sons of VCOs to attend universities: £2,000 was raised.[89]

One of the activities that POWs took part in to while away the time was the learning of languages. As an educated man, Havildar Shirke of the Post Office knew the value that education could bring. So, when posted to Annaburg:

> [He] ventured to advise them [sepoys] on the importance of education … Within a few weeks' time, English and Marathi classes were started by me with the help of two assistants. In the beginning the strength of the school was small, but at the end of the month, English and Marathi classes were being attended by 150 to 250 students. In June … I was sent to Leipzig Lazarette 'hospital' as an interpreter. I handed over the school administration to one of my colleagues. In spite of the limited resources of the camp I was given an exceptionally generous farewell party.[90]

Shirke saw that his mission was to help his fellow prisoners however he could.

Another language student was Lance Dafadar Bhim Singh of the Armoured Corps, who had been the Indian Man of Confidence at Neuburg in June 1943 – clearly somebody who was trusted by his compatriots.[91] Later that year, he was transferred to Lamsdorf, from where he wrote to Mrs Bell:

> Most respectfully I beg to state that I am attending the Stalag School, learning the Russian language and studying some other subjects. But I am [short of] Russian books. Because there are no Russian books in the school library. Will you please be kind enough to send the following books to me.[92]

He then listed five books for learning Russian, an interesting choice for an Indian POW. In Lamsdorf, he was close to the advancing Red Army, so he may have been planning ahead for the moment of liberation. He may also have been trying to predict what would happen after the war, aware as a Punjabi of the long track record of competition between Britain and Russia around Afghanistan. Equally, he might have been a supporter of the Communist Party, for whom the possibility of learning the language was a godsend. It may also have been a product of the availability of a good teacher. We will probably never know.

No story of German POW camps would be complete without reference to the theatre. Mohamed Afzal's letter shows how much musical and stage shows were valued. With unlimited time to rehearse, and an audience that was quite literally captive, this was a golden opportunity for future Bollywood stars. At Oflag 79, Naravane played a female character in a production of 'Bilayati Bhopal'.[93] Meanwhile, at Marlag und Milag Nord, the Bengali lascars produced two plays based on traditional folk tales – 'Vir Argon', and 'Bijar and Basunto'.[94] The Red Cross reported in July 1941 that there was an Indian orchestra and a separate Indian dance/music ensemble, which gave a performance that was 'truly a rich spectacle'.[95]

When Havildar A.P. Mukandan arrived at Stalag V-C near Strasbourg in December 1943, he recalled 'our spirits rose again. Naik Mathews of the Mahratta Light Infantry regaled us with music from his prison-made violin.'[96] Music was such an important part of maintaining morale that prisoners even made their own instruments.

For prisoners below the rank of corporal, there was much less time to give to music and the stage, for the Geneva Convention allowed the Germans to put them to work, provided there was no direct connection to the operations of the war.[97] Workers were paid in *Lagergeld* (camp money), which could be used in the canteen to buy food, stationery and even beer or wine. With so much of the German workforce conscripted into the army, the contribution of POWs to the German economy was enormous. By the middle of 1943, over 2.5 million prisoners of war of all nationalities were at work in Germany.[98]

The experiences of Indian soldiers as workers for the Reich varied enormously. Many were allocated to work on the land, which had the advantages of fresh air, freedom in the fields, more food and being treated as part of a household. Naik Roda Khan wrote in September 1941, 'The summer was pleasant here. Our men are employed on fatigue duties and they find it pleasure to go outside the camp, to have a fresh air and see the fields full of crops just like India.'[99]

A little later, the still small numbers of Indian POWs were doing a variety of jobs, including agriculture, brick-laying, painting, road-making and paper-making.[100] Six months later, a lance corporal wrote:

I am a stone polishing machine operator now which is not a bad job for a POW but I wish I was doing electrical work … I can speak a little German but I don't get on very well with Jerry. I sleep on a straw pal-liasse with two other men in what used to be a pigsty so I don't have exactly a luxurious time.[101]

The forty-eight Muslim POWs employed at the Grathel mattress fac-tory at Buehl near Baden-Baden in early 1944 seemed to be much better treated. The Red Cross report on their detachment noted:

The treatment by the guard as well as by the director of the factory, Mr Hut, is highly commendable. Both are taking a fatherly interest in all 'their young Indian boys' who appreciate this comprehensive attitude very much and expressed only one wish, that they might be left here under the present conditions.[102]

With the Allied invasion of Europe just months away, these men would soon lose their cushy billet.

Not all work conditions for Indian soldiers were so good. Some were given enticements to work in ammunition factories, contrary to the Geneva Convention. Those who refused to do so 'were starved, forced to do menial and degrading tasks, beaten and made to suffer severe pun-ishment'.[103] In May 1944, Indian POWs were given accommodation next to a machine room, leading to sleep deprivation and nervous collapse. The Swiss intervened and the detachment was closed.[104] Working for the Reich could bring income, fresh air and exercise and the opportunity to meet people outside the camp. It could also lead to serious ill-health.

★★★

The experiences of Mohamed Afzal and his fellow prisoners in Europe must all be taken within the context of mid-twentieth-century ideas on race, which varied across the Continent. The British Empire was founded

on the transatlantic trade in enslaved Africans, and the widespread but
not universal belief that white Britons were superior to all other types of
people, and especially to black or brown-skinned people. Attitudes that
in early twenty-first-century Britain are repugnant and widely rejected
were broadly accepted 100 years ago, finding their way into everyday
speech and children's books. Linked to these widespread attitudes was the
idea of the 'civilising mission', that British and French colonisers had a
right or duty to spread their culture among 'primitive natives'.[105]

With such a background to grow up in, it is hardly surprising that
the Britons who met Indian soldiers often started from a position of
assumed innate superiority. British people in the 1940s lived in a racist
environment, just as a goldfish lives in water. The goldfish exists and
breathes and drinks in water but cannot see it. So it is with racism in the
1940s: it was everywhere, a pervasive part of the fabric of society and the
background to thinking, however much an individual was anti-racist.
People were immersed, steeped, soaked in racist beliefs and attitudes.
When Captain Naravane swam in the sea at Mersa Matruh, in Egypt, a
British officer said that he wanted a portion of beach reserved for whites
– 'he disliked the smell of black "bodies" swimming in the same portion
of beach' as him.[106]

In the camps, many British prisoners were meeting men from South
Asia for the very first time. Along with the feeling of superiority there
was also a smear of patronage – Ambulanceman Cyril McCann reflected
that most Britons hadn't been abroad before, had 'probably been to
Clacton for a holiday' and therefore Indians and their religious practices became a 'bit of a butt of a joke'.[107] Racial slurs were commonplace
among some inmates. RAF Sergeant Harcus casually refers to the 'wogs'
compound' in his memoir, when telling a story of a fight between four
Scots and an Indian.[108]

Other white soldiers showed different attitudes. Harry Buckledee of
the 11th Hussars made friends with an Indian called Ranji, who 'often
came to our hut for a chat. He was an educated, exceptionally well-
mannered chap and he was really curious to know what life was like in
Britain.'[109] They met up by chance in East Anglia at the end of the war.

On one occasion at Lamsdorf, when the water supply in the Indian
compound broke down, a bucket chain was formed through a hole
cut in the wire. A British Army corporal watched as the 'Brylcreem
boys' (a nickname the Sikhs received for the time they spent on hair
care) returned with their empty buckets, to be abused by German

guards. As the corporal had served with Indian troops, he felt they were 'his boys', so he wanted to help. Picking up four empty buckets, two in each hand:

> He came to a halt a couple of feet in front of a guard and addressed him in German, the guard shook his head and yelled at the insistent corporal, the corporal yelled back and up came the rifle butt – where it hurt. The stalwart [corporal] never retreated an inch, no sir, not in front of a crowd of 'brylcreem boys'. His knees sagged a little but up came four metal buckets, two on each side of the guard's ears. There were two clunks, a loud yell from the surprised guard and a cheer from the 'brylcreem boys'.[110]

The corporal ran off before the guard could shoot. This display of solidarity demonstrates what some men would do to support their comrades, even those of another nationality.

German attitudes and behaviour towards *Kriegsgefangener* of different nationalities were complicated. The Geneva Convention recommends the separation of 'different races or nationalities'.[111] Faced with a plethora of nationalities among their prisoners, the German High Command took an easy route – the soldier's uniform should determine who goes in which camp.[112] Thus a Pole, a Jamaican and an Indian could end up together, providing they were all in khaki. Surprisingly, this pragmatic approach extended even to Jewish soldiers in the British Army. They were not forced to wear the Star of David, as civilians were, and were generally treated the same as their gentile counterparts. The Germans were worried that ill-treatment of Jewish POWs would lead to reprisals against German prisoners held in the Empire.[113]

Nazi ideology did penetrate the camps when it came to other nationalities, however. Nazi thinking had outlined a precise hierarchy of 'races', with 'Aryans' (including Indians and north Europeans) at the top, followed by other Europeans, then Slavs, Africans and Jews at the bottom. Russians were seen as *Untermenschen*, or 'subhuman', and treated particularly badly as POWs, which was often noticed by the Indians.[114] Alongside that, the Aryan idea meant that some Nazis and some Germans saw Indians as equal to Nordic Germans, and therefore racially superior to Jews, Slavs and black men.

French colonial soldiers from North and West Africa were often very poorly treated at the point of capture and later.[115] The German propaganda magazine *Signal* consistently drew black soldiers with thick lips and large eyes, and published photos of such *indigènes* with raw meat in their hands, alongside captions like this from July 1940: 'At the edge of the road prisoners of the French armies, to be counted by the thousands, a colourful mixture of people in all the colours of the earth.'[116]

Similarly, the SS committed atrocities against African-American soldiers captured towards the end of the war.[117] So although Indian POWs had suffered much in North Africa, once they reached the German Reich they were generally handled in the same way as white men from the Commonwealth.

Of course, the Nazi Party and the German army were by no means coterminous. In general, Commonwealth prisoners of war could expect better treatment from the *Wehrmacht*, the *Luftwaffe* or the *Kriegsmarine* than from the SS or the Nazi Party. Many of the men who guarded the camps were veterans of the First World War, especially as the war dragged on and the younger ones were called to the Front.[118] Their job was an odd mixture of control and care, restricting people's movement while looking after them. In general, this was a cushy job, but not one that attracted great pride in the work, nor always the best soldiers. One British prisoner expressed a widely held opinion thus: 'The guards at the camp were hardly the cream of the German army. Because the Reich needed men for the dreaded Russian Front, the high command tried to contain its prisoners with the minimum of guards, usually reservists or veterans of the Great War.'[119]

A vital part of the guards' work was to prevent escapes. Before Épinal, there had already been many Indian escape attempts. Apart from the 575 in Italy mentioned above, seventeen had reached Switzerland.[120] Two men of the 2nd Royal Lancers – Mohd Siddiq Khan and Mohd Gulsher Khan – escaped from a train in the west of France and spent a month walking across France to the Swiss frontier in the early spring of 1943. The Swiss authorities described it as a 'very arduous journey, all on foot'.[121]

For an Indian to escape successfully was much tougher than for a Briton. The language barrier, skin colour and the lack of a deep understanding of customs made them stand out. The colour of the skin becomes, as a French writer put it, 'an additional layer of barbed wire'.[122] But Indians were just as likely to try as anybody else.

Among the first Indian other ranks to reach Switzerland were a trio – Umar Singh and Dipchand from the 2nd Royal Lancers and

Harbakhash Singh, a lance naik in the RIASC. They were captured together at Tobruk, when Harbakhash was just 21, and went through many camps together until they landed at Altenburg. Harbakhash Singh said, 'We worked out our escape plan together and I escaped on the same day. I decided not to travel with them because I was wearing my turban. I got an ordinary hat from a French farmer and hence hid my turban.'[123] When asked about the motive for his escape, Harbakhash Singh gave the incontrovertible reply, 'I didn't want to be prisoner in Germany any longer'.

Once again, we see in Indian POWs a remarkable desire to hold on to religious convictions, even at great inconvenience. The *pagri*, or turban, is a sacred garment for a Sikh, marking him out in accordance with the desires of Guru Gobind Singh, who said, 'My Sikh will be recognized among millions'.[124]

The three companions spent the next fifteen months in the land of the Alps and took advantage of the conditions. A series of photographs from the mountain resort at Adelboden shows them skiing (see Fig. 4) and Harbakhash with a local girl on his lap.[125] The caption on the back of one photo records that 'He was good at knitting'. For this young man, at least, Switzerland was a place to practise some skills, get to know some Europeans and enjoy himself. He probably didn't think that he would soon be joined in this haven by hundreds of his countrymen.

Part II

Épinal

4

Frontstalag 315

A golf course is for golf, a tennis court is for tennis, a prison is for escape.[1]

France in the summer of 1944 was a country feeling the squeeze. Since the German takeover of the unoccupied zone in November 1942, the Vichy government of Maréchal Pétain had been edged out to the point where few people saw it as a government at all. The empire overseas was increasingly joining the fight against the Germans, with large numbers of North African troops among the Allies in Italy. The Resistance was growing, and in September 1943 had its first substantial victory with the liberation of Corsica. Despite German and Vichy propaganda, many French citizens were well aware of the progress of the war from the BBC, 'Every night we huddled around this radio – *Bam Bam Bam Boom*, the gong announced the Free French: *Ici Londres, les Français parlent en Français*.'[2]

At the same time the *Milice*, the German-armed Vichy militia, were flexing their muscles, cracking down on dissent. The whisper of a 'Second Front' – an Allied attack on France – was everywhere. Across the country, ordinary French people were being forced to make a choice.

That choice was especially complicated in the north-east, where Épinal is located. The Belfort Gap is a flattish, low-lying area marking the watershed between the Mediterranean and the North Sea. With the Vosges Mountains to the north and west, and the Jura to the south and east, it has long been a route for invading armies. Julius Caesar marched through from Besançon to the Rhine in 58 BCE, when he defeated Ariovistus and drove the Germanic tribes from Gaul.[3]

It was and still is a political and linguistic borderland which, in the nineteenth and twentieth centuries, changed hands several times, with the folk of Alsace–Lorraine being squeezed between two warring nations. The two regions were occupied by the Germans from 1871 to 1918, although the French successfully negotiated that Belfort – with its history of resisting sieges and its strong fortifications – be separated from Alsace, and therefore kept within France.

The region was close to the front line in the First World War and was badly scarred by the fighting, with Épinal being touched by the first German advance. Alsace and Lorraine returned to France in 1918 but were always in Hitler's sights as part of his expanded Germany. They were annexed in 1940, with cities like Metz, Strasbourg and Colmar now becoming part of Germany and large sections of the population being forcibly removed as part of a programme of Germanification. Épinal, Belfort, the Vosges and the Haute-Saône – our theatre for the drama that was to play out – all found themselves once more on the borderland, as part of the *zone interdite* – the forbidden zone intended for settlement by Germans. The Nazis felt sufficiently confident in the future of the area as part of their expanded *Heimat* that they opened their only concentration camp in France there, at Natzweiler Struthof in the Vosges, 100km east of Épinal.

Culturally speaking, this is a rich area, with a long history of farming and manufacture. The farms and forests which would serve as hiding places for the escaping Indians were also fertile countryside for enabling the French citizens to survive lean years, with mushrooms and fruit growing wild. Slightly further south in this generous land was the village of Étobon, where the hilly, wooded country starts to descend towards Belfort. This peaceful agricultural place was the home of the family of Jules Perret, blacksmith and farrier for his neighbours, who respected him highly. One of his two sons was also a prisoner of the Germans.

Jules Perret and his family will feature large in this story, thanks to his remarkable diary, kept throughout the war in an ingenious fashion. 'I squeezed little slips of paper into my purse, on which I wrote my notes, and after that I hid them in a bottle which I slipped under the slats of the stable floor, under the horseshoes. If they'd found them they would have shot me.'[4]

As well as his work with horses and iron, 59-year-old Perret had a farm, and was also an active member of the Resistance, having served in the artillery in the First World War. His diary, therefore, is always an extraordinary mix of rural, local and international, like this entry from 3 September 1943:

Things are happening everywhere. Here, attacks on the railways. Russian victories. The Americans landing in Italy. The King of

Denmark arrested. State of siege in Norway. Tito takes back several villages from the Germans. Here, Jeanne [his wife] cuts the spent blooms from the carnations. And we're harvesting hazelnuts, and distilling plums. Four barrels of 180 litres each. What riches![5]

His family would soon be dragged back into the war with a vengeance, and his neighbours would play a crucial role in helping Indians reach the Swiss frontier.

The town of Épinal itself is built on both sides of the northward-flowing River Moselle. To the east, the country climbs towards the Vosges Mountains, separating the Moselle from the Rhine. Just 75km away to the west is the village of Domrémy, the birthplace of Joan of Arc, the Frenchest of all French women. With a chateau, medieval city walls, barracks and forts built in the nineteenth century, it had the military air common to so many towns and cities of the region.

Its population during the war was around 27,000, making it the largest town in the Vosges Département. About half of the wider département is blanketed in trees – useful for concealment – so the town is known as the Wooden Capital, with the timber being widely cut and used for paper-making and other industries.

The paper made here was used in the most famous of local industries, by which the town was known throughout France – *Images d'Épinal*. These were cheap prints aimed at a mass market, produced since the eighteenth century by the Pellerin family. Forerunners of bandes dessinées, they were sold across France by pedlars taking pictures to the masses. They frequently portrayed military victories, for example the mythic 1915 story of Lieutenant Péricard who called the French dead to rise from the trenches.[6] In June 1940 the local engravers had no time to depict the four-day defence of the town and the blowing up of the Moselle bridges. The occupation that followed would last over four years.

The military presence in the town in 1940 was evident from the considerable number of barracks located there. Two of those – the barracks of Courcy and Raffiye in the western suburb of Chantraine – were to become Frontstalag 315, the temporary home of over 3,000 Indians.

The barracks had been built in 1893 and extended in 1913, as part of the line of forts that included Metz, Toul and Verdun, precautions against German invasion.[7] The barracks lay at the top of the Rue d'Olima, running up from the station, with a large parade ground to the east (see Fig. 6). To the west of the barracks was a meadow, a path lined with cherry and walnut trees and then a sharp drop down to a small lake and a stone-built powder magazine. Beyond that lay open country. The Indian prisoners must have looked out and wondered how they could cross the barbed wire, calculating the distance to the border – at least 100km – and planning a possible route. The Germans, meanwhile, calculated that the security they put in place would offset the risk of escape.

The Indian POWs were housed in four large buildings, one each for Hindus, Muslims, Sikhs and Christians, built around a central courtyard with 'good arrangements for the comfort of the soldiers', according to Mukandan.[8] The buildings were uniform in size and shape, solid brick and stone with arched windows, consisting of three storeys plus a mansard roof. As well as dormitories, there were canteens, kitchens, offices and stores – everything needed for a population of several thousand.

The barracks had been vacant from the middle of 1942, the first Indians arriving on 13 January 1944.[9] At this stage, Indian POWs were being sent from Annaburg and other camps into France, either on their way to join the Legion near Bordeaux, or to Épinal.[10] Among them were 1,200 NCOs who had refused to work for the Germans. So, these POWs were the *badmash* – the naughty boys among the Indian other ranks, and – as at Colditz – the result was not a good one for the Germans.

Unsurprisingly, security measures were tight, with a 3m-high barbed-wire fence all round and many German guards.[11] The Commandant was an elderly officer called Oberst Luhrsen, described by the Red Cross as showing 'good will and sympathetic understanding; he does his best to conduct this camp well'.[12] Mukandan remembered another German officer:

> ... a kind old captain, who was affectionately known as 'Papa-di-Epinal'. Whenever all men behaved in an unbecoming manner, he would say, 'India is a great nation, striving for freedom and the whole world is watching her struggle. It would be detrimental to her success, if her sons were to behave in an unbecoming manner in Europe, in the presence of foreigners'.[13]

It is doubtful that this officer approved of their subsequent escape.

The Red Cross visited in February 1944, took many photos in the snow (see Figs 7 and 8), and reported the camp was overcrowded and unfinished, but that Luhrsen was doing his best. There was a supply of 12 cubic metres of wood per day for heating, the men slept on wooden two-tier bunks, on palliasses with fresh straw, under two German blankets but with no pillows. There were, as yet, no shelves, lockers or furniture in the dormitories.[14] Dr de Morsier, the ICRC delegate, found the question of mail to be 'one of the most difficult to settle satisfactorily', with many POWs who had heard nothing at all from their families since capture.[15] Postman Mukandan had mixed feelings:

> As in the Italian camps, the delivery of mail was unsatisfactory. To the half dozen army Postal Service personnel in the camp it was revolting to see letters being mistreated by the camp staff. A couple of us approached the camp leader and volunteered our services without remuneration on the condition that no one else fiddled with the letters and we were not required to show favour to individuals or castes. A considered reply was promised but never received.[16]

The food situation for the prisoners was improving. At the February visit, de Morsier reported that the men were cooking for themselves, but it was hard to find enough volunteers willing to do so. They were expressing dietary preferences also, requesting rice, macaroni, and bread and butter rather than carrots or cheese. They were receiving parcels from the Indian Comforts Fund, but the 100 or so Christians and the camp doctors requested Canadian or British parcels as well, as they contained meat.[17]

A month later, when the Red Cross visited again, conditions were better, with a special kitchen hut, Muslims and Christians cooking together, and Hindus and Sikhs doing likewise. Fish and dried vegetables were being used as a substitute for meat; there was a stock of 21,000 Red Cross food parcels, which men cooked as individuals or in small groups in their rooms.[18] Mukandan wrote about further sources of supplies:

> Occasionally we were permitted to go to the market to buy additional articles of food such as onions, condiments, vinegar etc. We enjoyed these trips very much. The French shopkeepers were extremely obliging and went out of their way to meet our requirements and to give us news of the war in their broken English. Barter flourished both in and out of the camp.[19]

One can assume that they were escorted by German guards on these trips.

The Red Cross reports also give us a remarkable insight into the attitude of Colonel Luhrsen towards his charges. The ICRC delegate de Morsier had a long meeting with the Commandant and recorded some of the German's thoughts in the February report, including the following:

> Laziness, indifference and even a leaning to sabotage are manifested by the prisoners in all the work they do … The reactions of the prisoners are of the simplest and most direct kind. They behave like spoilt or badly-brought-up children … They stop up the flushes of the latrines with empty preserve tins … They needlessly and without reason break the windows … if the weather is at all cold, they prefer to urinate in the corridors rather than visit the latrines, especially at night.
>
> The bearing of the men and even of the NCOs leaves much to be desired, and any respect for superiors in rank seems to be non-existent. Military discipline means nothing to these men.
>
> Racial prejudice insists that a Muslim can receive nothing whatever from a Hindu or a Sikh and vice versa; certain castes refuse to be in subordinate position to others.[20]

Luhrsen concluded by stating that the camp leader was not fit for the job. De Morsier summarised the Commandant's claims thus, 'It is difficult to run a camp containing Indians'. In many ways, this tells us more about the guards than their charges. Luhrsen wants consistency, homogeneity, a Camp Leader who will pass on his orders and ensure they are carried out. In short, he wants European prisoners. Instead, he is faced with men who are very different from him and what he is used to, men who are awkward and disobliging, and who – as it happened – were excellent escapers.

Because of the nature of these bad boys and work-refuseniks, the camp statistics were unusual. In March 1944 there were just over 3,000 inhabitants, of whom nearly 60 per cent were NCOs. There were 1,376 Hindus (including Gurkhas), 973 Muslims, 488 Sikhs and 138 Christians.[21] There were hundreds of men from the Mahrattas, who held a festival on Shivaji Day in April, raising 7,000 francs for sick POWs.[22] There were also a handful from what was 'probably the least glamorous' part of the Indian Army – the Corps of Clerks – of whom four managed to make it to Switzerland (Havel Singh, Rati Ram, V.S. Sivon and Digambar Kirwe).[23]

Another clerical type was the Man of Confidence for most of the time of the camp's existence, Dafadar Bhagat Ram of the Armoured Corps, who seems to have been most assiduous in carrying out his duties.

There were also VCOs who had disguised themselves as NCOs, perhaps in order to get closer to a neutral border.[24] Among them was Jemadar Omparkash Bhardwaj of the RIASC, who managed to reach Switzerland.[25] As well as the combatants, there were the usual complement of followers, including nine cobblers and thirteen tailors, who worked hard to manage the deficiencies in clothing.[26] The ICRC photos from the February visit (see Fig. 8) show a variety of clothing and headgear, some of which look quite inadequate for the snowy weather. Indeed, many of the inmates in this series of photos are unsmiling, but whether this is due to the weather, the general camp conditions, or an antipathy towards this ICRC delegate, remains obscure. Perhaps they objected to being asked to stand outside to have their photo taken.

The camp had its complement of medical officers, British and Indian. Their experience was fundamentally different from that of other prisoners, as they were required to continue their job after capture. The familiar salutation of 'For you, the war is over' did not apply to doctors and other medical staff. As so-called 'protected persons', medical personnel (and chaplains) had a different status within the Geneva Convention.[27] They were allowed greater freedom to leave the camp, could be moved about more often to fill gaps in other camps, and might also be eligible for repatriation if they were deemed to be surplus to requirements.

Indian doctors elsewhere performed some extraordinary medical work. According to a letter from an officer of the Warwickshire Regiment, Dr Randlin Singh Seagat and Dr Sardar Ahmed performed an operation that a French doctor had said would be a waste of time. Private Bull had septic peritonitis and TB, but the two doctors operated anyway, and the young Englishman survived. Captain Lewthwaite wrote, 'I have met very many doctors in my time but I have never met any who were more devoted or attentive to their patients' interests and wellbeing.'[28]

The scale of medical personnel per camp had been laid down in a letter from the British government to the Swiss in 1942: for every 1,000 POWs there should be two doctors, ten orderlies, two dentists and two chaplains.[29] Quite how often this scale was met is not clear, but at Épinal they eventually managed to achieve the three medical officers proportionate to a camp of around 3,000 men.

The first of those was a Scotsman called Captain James Third of the RAMC, who had previously been medical officer at Stalag VII-B. Alongside him (in Fig. 7) was Dr Sham Chand Seal of the Indian Army Medical Corps. He was from Calcutta, and had joined the army in the summer of 1940, perhaps aware that being a doctor in the army might entail opportunities for learning and for advancement unrivalled at home. Little else is known about him, except that he showed up at Marlag und Milag Nord two months before the end of the war and that his father, G.K. Seal lived in Garden Reach in Fatehpur.[30]

Between the ICRC visits in February and March, Third and Seal were joined by Jemadar Din Mohd Khan, from Khabba Rajputan, south of Amritsar. This dedicated team was working flat out. When de Morsier visited in February, he observed that Third and Seal had examined 130 patients between them on one day. Drugs and soap were in short supply and there were only three trained nurses and no dentist.[31] By the time of the March visit, POWs were being treated by a French dentist down the hill at a rate of twenty-four per week.[32] Considerable efforts were made by these men to look after the many prisoners in their care.

Across the many camps where Indians were posted, there were always some men in the lazarette (camp hospital), working or as patients. Such situations were not always wholly bad, however, and each hospital became a community of its own. Ranjit Shirke of the 25 Field Post Office – who had taught English and Marathi at Annaburg – was attached to the lazarette at Leipzig in June 1943 as an interpreter, as he also spoke French and some German. He found himself welcomed by sick prisoners from France, Serbia and Poland, and was elected Man of Confidence. When he left there, he was responsible for 660 men from 'different parts of the globe. My notebook is full of their addresses.'[33]

In the west of France was a special unit for TB cases – a disease common to Indian soldiers in Europe.[34] This was Frontstalag 221, located in the erstwhile *École Primaire Supérieure* (school) at Rennes, housing thirty-five sick men and five health workers. Due to the nature of their illness, the most serious cases were given 12 litres of milk daily.

This little hospital was the point of origin of two successful escapees – mess servant Buland Khan and Nurse Bashir-ud-Din Ahmad, who was the Man of Confidence there.[35] Tragically, it was also the site of six deaths, all of whom are buried or commemorated in the Eastern Communal Cemetery in the city.[36]

According to detailed analysis of the Commonwealth War Graves Commission website, there are 261 Indians buried or commemorated in Europe who were probably prisoners of war.[37] This is less than 2 per cent of the 15,000 total, which compares favourably with the rate of 20 per cent for Indian POWs in Germany during the First World War, most of whom died from TB.[38]

Article 76 of the Geneva Convention states that 'belligerents shall ensure that prisoners of war who have died in captivity are honourably buried, and that the graves bear the necessary indications and are treated with respect and suitably maintained'.[39] In accordance with Indian religious practice, Muslim and Christian soldiers were usually buried, while Hindus and Sikhs were cremated. Generally speaking, the Germans honoured these provisions, even towards the end of the war, although there were at least a couple of instances when Hindu or Sikh prisoners were buried.[40]

In November 1944, a Christian chaplain at Hammelburg conducted a funeral for a Hindu called Yadaw from Cholapur, who had died of pneumonia after an operation for an abdominal ulcer. The coffin was carried by eight bearers, there was a wreath and a Union Jack flag, and the body was afterwards cremated at Nuremberg.[41] Funerals were usually photographed, and prints sent to Britain and thence India.[42] The grandson of Mir Zaman, who was buried at Rennes in January 1944, still has the photo that he was sent, creased and battered, but it is important to him and his family.[43]

Although the German government generally would not allow ashes to be put into running water 'for reasons of hygiene', in France the situation was different.[44] An ICRC report on the hospital at Rennes gave a detailed description of a Sikh cremation in 1943, clearly a ceremony that was unfamiliar to the observer:

> The body, covered in a shroud, is carried on a horse cart to the funerary area which is situated at the furthest corner from the camp's football pitch, next to a stream. The deceased's turban is decorated with flowers. For the ceremony the body is placed on a pile of wood about 50cms high. The face of the deceased is uncovered. Next they coat the shroud with several kilos of vegetable oil and they add wood on top of the body. This wood is then covered in oil, then they pile more wood on top so that the whole thing looks like a little hut about 1m50 high. On either side and on top of the heap of wood itself they

pile on faggots and they put straw on top so as to be able to light the whole thing with a flaming torch. The Sikhs gather around the fire until everything is burnt (about 2½ hours). During this time they pray and sing. The next day they return to the pyre and throw the ashes into the winds. Some of these ashes fall into the stream.[45]

At one Sikh cremation at Rennes, there was found to be a shortage of oil for the pyre. Fellow prisoners donated 12kg of butter and 25kg of fat, but the British government subsequently refused to reimburse those prisoners for the expense of the donation.[46]

The usual procedure for burying Muslims was laid out in a letter from the ICRC to the Indian Red Cross at Simla in January 1944:

> Bathing of the body, placing in the bier, pathway formed … Prayers according to the Koran … the priest leading the procession and the prayers. The coffin and the grave are placed in the exact direction of Mecca. The burial takes place to long prayers according to the Koran.[47]

In this way, hundreds of Indian POWs ended their captivity.

Some POWs were deemed so sick that the captors would rather their care was paid for by their home country, and so they were exchanged with German or Italian prisoners in a similar condition, following examination by a Mixed Medical Commission, consisting of one German and two Swiss doctors.[48] After an unsuccessful attempt via Rouen in September 1941, there were eventually four successful exchanges with the Germans, involving nearly 11,000 prisoners.[49] This was also an opportunity to return 'surplus' medical personnel and chaplains, as happened to Santi Pada Dutt in 1942, sent home from Italy via Smyrna and Port Said.[50] In October 1943, Yasin Khan of the Remount Department witnessed the departure of a repatriation party from Lamsdorf, 'Today the repatriation party is leaving the camp, everybody so seems happy [*sic*]. The military band is present at the gate and the repats are marching majestically some with one leg some with one arm.'[51]

Risaldar-Major Sis Ram of Rohtak was one of the lucky ones on a later occasion. He left from Oflag 79 in September 1944 with thirty-two comrades and told his story to a journalist in England:

At Sassnitz [on the Baltic coast] we embarked for a three-hours trip to Trelleborg [Sweden], where we had a big reception with bands playing. Many photographers appeared and much good food was available ...

There followed a comfortable journey in a Red Cross train to Gottenborg, where our party was billeted in hotels and huts. While there we were visited by the Crown Prince and Princess of Sweden who talked with me and enquired after my comfort.

Sis Ram sailed on the Swedish ship *Drottningholm* to England, 'We hope to see London before our departure for India. We have only one complaint – Indian masala seems very hot after being deprived of Indian spices for so long.'[52]

The book *Mercy Ships* is all about these exchanges. Its dedication is a fitting one:

[To] all those who, whatever their motives, kept talking to each other throughout the war and obtained the release of many tens of thousands who would otherwise have spent many more years in captivity.[53]

★★★

At Épinal in early 1944, the prospects of such reunions seemed a long way off. Prisoners were keen to while away the time, but there was very little equipment with which to do that. The Red Cross sent a long list of requests for leisure items, including football and hockey equipment and indoor games like chess and cards. There was also a list of musical instruments requested from the YMCA in Paris, ranging from a jazz drum to a harmonium and a 2½-octave Fish harmonica with eighty keys. Also requested were items for the camp theatre, including wigs, paper and 'artificial ornaments for the shows, as many as you can send'.[54]

The next Red Cross visit reported progress, with a large recreation room being used for 'concerts and theatrical performances', but only a few books. With the arrival of spring, sports facilities were being arranged – the courtyard was large enough for basketball and netball, and football and cricket fields were in the planning.[55] Indeed, a football game was in progress when the American bombers flew over on 11 May. As well as such vigorous activities, locals remember some of the prisoners being allowed down into the town for a beer.[56]

There was also time taken for religious observation. The Red Cross reported that the camp had a Hindu temple, mosque and Sikh gurdwara, each with two 'priests' in attendance. As there were no *maulvis, pandits* or *granthis* listed among the camp's inmates, these must have been ordinary soldiers with a strong faith and some skills relating to the rites of each religion. The Red Cross also noted that there was a Christian church, but without a priest, and 'These temples have been installed in large rooms the floors of which have been covered with blankets so that the Faithful can walk without danger, with bare feet'.[57] A little bit of India had been transplanted into France.

Another element of Indian culture that had been transplanted – or rather appropriated – was the swastika emblem. Prior to Nazi times, the symbol of the crooked cross could be found in many cultures around the world, including ancient Troy and among Native Americans. It was most prevalent in India, where it is still in use as a religious symbol, found with the arms facing both right and left. Indeed, the name *svastika* is of Sanskrit origin.[58] Following the theorising of the Indo-European root language and its connection to 'Aryan' people in the nineteenth century, the swastika spread within Europe, to the point that Rudyard Kipling used it on the spine of many of his books at the turn of the century. At the same time, some theorists in Europe started to construct the swastika as the 'armorial shield of the Aryan race'.[59] From there, it was a logical choice for the Nazi Party. Hitler himself wrote the following about the symbol: 'In the swastika lies the mission to fight for the victory of the Aryan race, as well as the triumph of the concept of creative labour, which always, in itself, was anti-Semitic, and always will be'.[60]

Arriving from one place where the swastika had one set of meanings, Indians found themselves confronted on multiple occasions with a *Hakenkreuz* with a whole other set. Of course, the Indian symbol and the Nazi symbol are not identical. The Nazis had reversed it, rotated it by an eighth of a turn, removed the dots that often surround the centre of the cross, and changed the colours. Thus, some POWs might not have perceived it as being the same thing. Some others may have felt insulted by the process of appropriation. One India Office file claims, 'Amongst the simple-minded Hindus there was a widespread belief that Hitler was also a Hindu, since he did not smoke, was a vegetarian and harboured the swastika.'[61]

But not all Hindus were simple-minded. A famous photograph from 1942 shows three sepoys of the 4th Division holding a swastika flag at Sidi

Omar, on the border between Egypt and Libya. The Commonwealth army was sweeping forward, and the flag had fallen into their hands. There is a similar flag (or perhaps the same one) in the museum of the Rajput Rifles in Delhi. There, it is seen simply for its military significance – 'a symbol of the enemy'.[62]

In a twist of fate unknown to most of the Indian POWs, the liberation of Épinal on 24 September was effected by the American 45th Infantry Division, who had landed at Nice a few weeks earlier. This division was from Oklahoma and, until 1939, had sported a yellow-on-red swastika as its emblem, in tribute to the Native American population of Oklahoma and its region.[63] In Europe, the symbol still carries its Nazi overtones, and is banned in Germany, but in South Asia the *svastika* never lost its religious and cultural significance.

Settled into their camp by the spring of 1944, with a stock of Red Cross parcels, a football field and theatre and no work to keep them busy, some of the Épinal inmates were pondering a possible route to Switzerland. There were certainly several with previous experience of escaping. At least one had a wire-cutter, while previous escapers and German guards from Austrian, Romanian or Polish backgrounds gave them advice on routes.[64] Between them, they had the skills, experience and the sheer guts necessary to execute an escape attempt. Gazing out of the windows, seeing the cherry trees in blossom and the weather improve, they calculated their chances. One said later, 'For a long time we had resolved to escape to Switzerland as soon as the opportunity presented itself. The bombing of the camp gave us that opportunity.'[65]

5

H-Hour

The Spruce Trees are in bloom.[1]

The opportunity was the Allied bombing on 11 May 1944 – part of the Allies' so-called Transportation Plan. The thinkers behind this plan asserted that 'concentrated, precise attack upon railway targets scientifically selected, might make all the difference to the success or failure of the long awaited invasion of France'.[2]

This invasion – D-Day – was planned for the start of June and was keenly anticipated across Europe. Churchill was not in favour of bombing French railways so intensively, but Eisenhower said the success of D-Day depended on it.[3] That was the clincher: Eisenhower was the Commander of the Supreme Headquarters Allied Expeditionary Force (SHAEF), and his word made all the difference.

So, from 3 March, the RAF and the USAAF concentrated their enormous power on this one aim. The RAF worked on 'area bombing' by night – drenching a wide area with bombs. Meanwhile, the Americans – with aircraft that were better armed and the much-lauded Norden bombsight – were charged with precision bombing in daylight. The Plan listed seventy-six 'nodal points' across France, the Low Countries and Germany, and led to the dropping of over 60,000 tons of bombs in the three months before D-Day.[4]

In common with some other Allied bombing strategies, this policy was controversial at the time and since. Why were the Allies dropping so many bombs on their allies? The controversy extended within the US Air Force itself, exhausted after months of bombing targets in Germany:

Howls of protest came from the bomber generals, who felt they had victory in the air war within their grasp; sighs of relief came from the bomber crews, who had been pressed to the limits of human endurance. Unlike Germany, France was within easy range of Allied fighters based in England, and the Luftwaffe had long since abandoned its forward bases. High-altitude bombers could still fall victim to heavy flak guns, but missions over France were far less dangerous than the deep-penetration raids over the Reich.[5]

The effect on the German war effort, however, was debatable. By the start of June, traffic on the French railways had been reduced to half, but lines were repaired quickly, and 393 German troop trains still ran in June: the Germans simply prioritised military traffic above all else.[6] Part of the debate was about the effect that civilian deaths would have on popular opinion in a country that would be crucial to the Allied advance. Would French men and women view it as 'a painful but necessary prelude to liberation from occupation and fascism' or would 'heavy loss of life among workers in France and the Low Countries ... lose the Allies goodwill'?[7] The RAF Chief of Air Staff warned of civilian losses of 80,000 or more and, in fact, 1944 saw more than 38,000 civilian deaths in France, 70 per cent of the total French deaths from air raids in the war overall, including the German bombing in 1940.[8] As in Yugoslavia and Iraq at the end of the century, the political and military decision was to liberate a population from oppressive rulers by dropping bombs on them.[9]

It also appears that this raid was requested by the French. According to Maurice Gillet, retired railway worker and member of the *Résistance-Fer* (Railway Resistance), speaking forty years later, the bombing was:

> ... part of the *Plan Vert*, which was formulated in London in 1942, and which called, broadly speaking, for the voluntary destruction of the railways carried out by the members of *Résistance-Fer*. Because of the few means of destruction at their disposal – lacking plastic explosives, weapons, ammunition and explosive devices – they had to appeal to London ... and they requested by radio and by means of personal messages, understandable only to initiates.[10]

The coded message sent to London by Jean Bonneville, the leader of *Résistance-Fer* consisted of just four words: '*Les épinettes sont fleuries*' – 'the spruce trees are in bloom', and called for the destruction of all of Épinal's railway facilities. Thus was the destruction requested; thus it came.

And so, in the early morning of 11 May, 973 heavy bombers took off in fine weather from airfields across East Anglia. Their mission was Operation 350: to fly 500 miles across France to attack railway marshalling yards in Mulhouse, Épinal, Belfort and Chaumont, and an airfield at Orléans.[11]

The official file states that the target at Épinal was 'bounded on all sides by a heavily built-up area, residential on the W, and industrial on the N and E'.[12] The B-24 Liberators that attacked Épinal knew there was housing near the target; they were prepared for 'collateral damage'. It is not clear, however, whether they knew there was a large POW camp nearby. The target file doesn't mention it, but Military Intelligence was almost certainly aware of its existence. By July that year, a document listing POW camps and circulated to RAF stations included the following entry for Épinal: 'Fort Military Building on summit of hill, NW of town in fairly large area. Surrounded by walls. Large 3 storey building.'[13]

Whether that information was available in May, and whether it was shared with the American cousins, remains unclear. In fact, neither the British nor the US government seemed very concerned about the safety of their prisoners when it came to military choices. During the period from November 1943 to the end of the war, thirty camps in Germany and occupied France were bombed or machine gunned by the Allied air forces, leading to the deaths of around 1,000 POWs.[14] This was despite the Red Cross's request at the start of the war that belligerents tell each other the locations of POW camps to avoid precisely this occurrence. For 'reasons of security', this never happened.[15]

At 15.41 on a sunny afternoon, the sixty-eight Liberator planes of the 96th Wing reached Épinal, each carrying five 1,000lb bombs, flying in from the west, escorted by Thunderbolt, Lightning and Mustang fighter planes. Their operation report states that 'opposition was slight':

> 68 B-24s dropped 336 x 1000 GP – 168 tons – between 1541 and 1542 hours from 16,000 to 19,000 feet. At least four groups of bursts fell in the target area and hits were seen on the Goods Depot, the Passenger Station, a long warehouse type building just south of the Goods Depot and wagons in the Station sidings. The storage sidings were also hit. Many buildings in the residential section on the east and west sides were hit by at least seven groups of bombs causing many fires.[16]

Fig. 10 – from the French authorities – shows the distribution of bombs that fell on Épinal. This map and the Allies' narrative report reveal that aerial bombardment in 1944 was not a precise science, and a so-called 'precision raid' like this could end up – to those on the ground – feeling like an area attack.[17] The bombers flew over the barracks at Chantraine before they reached the railway and several planes dropped their bombs too early, in what one authority called 'bad approaches' and against the aim of a 'concentrated bombing pattern'.[18] The French map, which names roads and buildings, shows that thirty bombs fell on or just outside the barracks housing 3,000 Indian prisoners and their guards. On the other missions that day, the bombing results were assessed to be 'fair to good' at Mulhouse, 'fair' at Belfort and 'good' at Épinal.[19] Of the three, Épinal was therefore deemed to be the most successful.

Viewed from an American airman's perspective, the day was not entirely 'good'. Due to a combination of 'meagre' German anti-aircraft fire at Épinal and elsewhere, some *Luftwaffe* fighter attacks and mechanical failure, the 'Mighty Eighth' lost eight bomber planes and five fighters that day, with nine crew members wounded and eighty-one missing.[20] One of the missing B-24s was the eccentrically named *Meat Around the Corner*, piloted by Lieutenant Stuart Goldsmith. On 11 May over Épinal, the pilot of the adjacent plane reported, 'Goldsmith had one engine feathered, dropped his bombs, fired green-green flares and failed to turn with the formation. Had very good fighter cover. Believed he was headed for Switzerland.'[21]

A few hours later, the plane crossed into Swiss airspace, the crew bailed out and the plane crashed into the ground at Jegenstorf, just north of Berne. Goldsmith and his crew of nine became part of the eventual total of 1,700 US aircrew who made it to safety in that neutral haven.[22] Among the crew was a ball turret gunner by the name of Staff Sergeant Robert Morin, flying his first – and last – mission over the Continent.[23] Whether the aircrew met any Indians during their time in Switzerland is unknown, but they remained there until the end of the war.

The French civilians on the ground knew nothing of the fate of Robert Morin and his colleagues 5km above their heads. The *Spinaliens* were used to seeing American bombers flying overhead to attack German targets in Stuttgart or Frankfurt, so they didn't respond to the sirens as quickly as they should have.[24] As the three waves of planes in a '*vol de canards*' formation flew overhead, five dark shapes started to emerge from the belly of each one. The town's director of passive defence reported that the first wave also machine-gunned the *Quai des bon enfants* along the west bank of the river.[25] A note from the French railways reported twenty-nine staff 'killed on duty', three missing and 109 wounded,[26] while 300 travellers took shelter in the underground passage at the station.

The initial list compiled by the authorities counted seventy-two dead. One man was visiting the jewellers' shop by the station, kept by his sister Mme Morin – the same surname as the ball turret gunner of *Meat Around the Corner*, 3 miles above. The list includes a police officer, two postmen, a retired teacher, a cook: the ordinary citizens of a large town.

There was Gregoire Zakaroff, a 55-year-old, born in Russia, and a four-month-old baby called Anne Marie Colin. In the middle of the list there appears '*Une tête d'homme*' – 'the head of a man'.[27] The final casualty list was reckoned to be 220 civilians killed with around 500 wounded.[28]

Many buildings in Épinal were destroyed or in flames. Whether the citizens of Épinal saw these bombers as 'liberators' that day is not known, but French attitudes to bombing by their former allies had changed since the early years of the war, when people generally supported the RAF and waved their handkerchiefs at the bombers.[29]

As it turned out, the railways were only interrupted for twenty-four hours, the tracks and essential services repaired and cleared by the same railwaymen who had requested the bombing.[30] The trains ran slowly, but they ran. At Épinal, the side effects of the action were far greater than the intended consequences.

Épinal was not alone in its suffering: such destructive aerial bombardment was experienced widely in Europe and beyond in the 1940s. Across Western Europe, around 700,000 civilians were killed in this 'excessive violence', described by the philosopher A.C. Grayling as a war crime.[31]

Military and civil planners had been expecting massive air raids since the end of the First World War. When war seemed inevitable in the 1930s, and the experience of Guernica proved that civilians were now targets, practical plans were made in cities and towns across the Continent. Shelters were built, sirens tested, volunteers trained and the public prepared with poster and newspaper campaigns. But Épinal had not yet been touched by this destruction, and so its air-raid protection measures were insufficient on 11 May. Bombs do not discriminate, and aircrew do not see their victims, but the civilian deaths of the Second World War outnumbered the military ones. In Épinal that day, French, Germans and Indians were all under the same bombardment from the Americans.

The fortified city of Belfort was also bombed that day. Jules Perret wrote that evening that his grandson and daughter-in-law were visiting the city:

> Aline told us what happened. They were at the doctor's office, near the station, when the bombs started to fall. Quickly, the doctor made everyone – patients and staff – go out into the courtyard and take shelter behind a woodpile. Stones, plaster, debris, falling and whistling all around. Each time a bomb fell, Philippe clasped his hands and prayed, 'Lord Jesus, make it not fall on us!' All the windows came crashing down. Four large bombs fell within 50 meters of them. Finally, here they are, safe and sound. Others are in mourning. Twenty were killed.[32]

In fact, the final death toll at Belfort was twenty-four killed and twenty-four wounded. Swiss customs official Francois Bourquenez, observing from the other side of the border, wrote, 'All the Belfortains ran for shelter as soon as the planes approached, while in Épinal it caused [more] deaths as a result of the imprudence of the inhabitants who did not expect the bombardment and did not reach the shelters. Harsh lesson!'[33]

At the camp on the hill, the orders from the German High Command on air raid precautions in Stalags were clear: there should be shelters equivalent to those of local civilians, doors should be unlocked during air raids, steel helmets and sand and water should be available to prisoners.[34] At Épinal, as no trenches or other shelters had been dug, the order was that prisoners should be locked in their barracks, in contravention of the High Command.[35] When the bombs started to fall, confusion, noise, death was all around. A.P. Mukandan described in vivid detail what happened that afternoon at Chantraine:

> 11th May was a bright sunny day. After the midday meal we were all occupied one way or another. The major attraction was a football match between the Sikhs and the Mahrattas which was being watched by hundreds of their supporters. At about 3:40pm the humming sound of the American bombers was heard without any previous warning. We did not take much notice as this was a daily happening and only came out and looked up when the sound seemed too close. We noticed clusters of bombs whistling through the air and thought that the planes were bombing the nearby German training centre. Before we

could realise what had happened, the whole camp was covered with
dust, stones, brickbats and fragments of glass and iron. Instinctively
we lay flat on the ground. The first round of bombs fell near the
crowded football ground, and the nearby barracks. There was utter
confusion and panic. Whoever would have thought that American
planes would bomb Allied prisoners! Many rushed out of the camp to
seek safety. The others, seeing the agony of their wounded comrades
strewn all over the yard, were attending to them when a second wave
of bombers appeared in the sky. We had no other choice but to run
for shelter leaving the wounded to their fate. I managed to jump into a
bomb crater which was already occupied by some other prisoners and
a German sentry. The bombs came in clusters again, a large number
of them falling in the camp. A rain of dust and stones passed over
our heads. After the planes had disappeared, I emerged safely from
the crater, jumped over several fences and hedges and made for the
woods. When the bombers made no further appearance, I returned to
the camp to check up on the welfare of my friends. The place looked
like a battlefield; mutilated and mangled bodies were strewn on the
playground, yards and barracks. There were many wounded among
them. Some buildings in the camp had completely vanished and only
bomb holes remained on their sites. Others were on fire. There was
death and destruction all around the camp.[36]

Bombs fell in the courtyard and on the buildings, on the external wall and
the barbed wire. The guardhouse was hit; the Hindu barracks received a
direct hit and was destroyed. Seventy-three severely wounded prisoners
were taken to the German hospital, and thirty-five bodies were collected
from the camp straight away – the final total would be much greater.

Photographs taken six weeks later by the Red Cross delegates give
some idea of the scale of the devastation (see Fig. 9). Rubble is piled
several metres high in the courtyard, with a deep hole in the middle
indicating a direct hit. The Red Cross delegate can stand up and still be
3m below ground level. Twisted metalwork is all around, trees have been
uprooted. You can see right through one of the buildings – in through
the front window and out through the back window – there is no glass
or structure in the window frame. The roof of one building is completely gone, just a few rafters left, like ribs after a corpse is eaten. Whole
buildings have collapsed. Meanwhile groups of POWs have returned
with wheelbarrows and a cart to clear up.

Immediately after the first wave, all was confusion. Havildar Tuka Ram Dalvi was later recommended for a gallantry medal for rescuing his comrades from the debris of burning buildings.[37] Havildar Clerk Ganpatrao Tawde of the Mahrattas carried wounded men to the camp hospital, where two of the doctors treated them. A clerk even in times of great stress, Tawde then made a detailed list of the dead Mahrattas – some of whom had been playing football a short time before – and carried it with him all the way to Switzerland.[38] Several accounts say that the guards, and even Colonel Luhrsen himself, ordered the prisoners out of the camp for their own safety, some accompanied by guards.[39] The attitude of the Germans seems to have been driven by fear. 'The Germans then gave orders for the evacuation of the camp, and told [the prisoners] they could go anywhere they liked for three days. They were told that if they did not remain near the road they would receive no food.'[40]

And so, for some of the prisoners, ears still ringing from the infernal noise and covered in dust, the realisation came that this could be an opportunity. As the food store was undamaged:

> We grabbed everything we could by way of food, blankets etc and we escaped in every direction. The German guards were firing their machine-guns at us but they didn't manage to shoot everywhere. Many of my comrades were hit by the bombs or German bullets.[41]

The bombing pressed a decision on them; it made it easier. The usual leisurely activities of an Épinal POW – eating, sleeping, chatting, praying – were no longer possible. When the bombs fell, everything sped up – it was do or die. All those years of planning and thinking were over. The door was open, the guards distracted, the friends were there to encourage, the way was clear.

The best route lay to the west. Through the wire, across the meadow, down the hill and into the little ravine called the *Ruisseau d'Olima*. Past the powder magazine at the foot of the hill and the little lake and onwards, spreading out into the forest. Much of this is still forested today; much more of it was then. They travelled in small groups, often with men of their regiment. Many of the men of the 2nd Royal Lancers stayed together – the regimental history recorded: 'Chiefly owing to RQMD Pat Ram's presence of mind casualties were mercifully small. At once everyone took to the woods and made for

Switzerland. Many had maps, money and food stored away against such a day.'[42]

Fifty-six of that regiment made it to Switzerland, where they joined messmates who had escaped previously. Jules Perret's cousin Charles recorded that on 15 May, 'Radio Londres announced that 400 people had been killed in the bombing of Épinal and that all the surviving POWs had profited from the chaos to take the key to the countryside.'[43]

The key was in their hands, the door was open.

Climb Every Mountain

Yet jail is a jail. It is not the creature comforts that matter. It is the deprivation of the freedom that crushes the human being[1]

So off they went. As the crow flies it is about 100km from Épinal to the Swiss border at Boncourt, where many of them would cross. But they were not crows and they could not fly. By road, the minimum distance is 123km, but these men were starting west before they could turn south. They did not know the country at all and were not completely sure of the direction they needed. They would have to skirt around towns and villages; hide during daytime, progress at night; make use of cover and take great care when crossing roads or open fields or moving over the skyline. S.P. MacKenzie in his book on German camps writes, 'Escapees stood little chance unless they had a disguise, a cover story, some identification papers, food and money, plus basic geographical and route information.'[2]

Most of these men had none of the above. They would be heavily reliant on their native wit and endurance and the kindness of strangers. As an India Office file puts it, 'For weeks afterward the French countryside was dotted with little parties of Indians with grins on their faces, asking French civilians the way to Switzerland.'[3]

This was not a joke, nor a country ramble, this was a desperate bid for freedom in territory that could be hostile as well as friendly, in the final year of the greatest conflict the world had seen, with the Germans desperate to hang on to power. But before they headed off southwards, two of the men had another task to do.

Naik Ghazi Khan and Havildar Ghulam Abbas were both from Jhelum, both in the artillery and both had been captured in May 1942. Their friend Fazal Hussain was from the same part of Punjab. He had been court-martialled by the Germans at Épinal on 15 April, on a charge of striking a soldier at a previous camp. He was found guilty, sentenced to be shot and was awaiting execution when the Americans intervened.[4]

The next morning, Ghazi and Ghulam were on their way to freedom when they remembered Fazal. They returned to the bombed ruin of the camp, rescued him and continued their way to the south. All three crossed the border together ten days later, on 22 May. In due course, the two friends were awarded Military Medals.[5] To interrupt their own flight to return for a friend who would otherwise have died – this was an act of true bravery.

After their initial mistake of encouraging the men out of the camp, the Germans did not sit back and let them get away. Colonel Luhrsen would have been only too aware of the order from the High Command that very month that defined a 'mass' escape as one involving more than six prisoners, and that such eventualities would lead to an investigation of the commandant in question.[6]

The manhunt after a mass escape could mobilise hundreds or thousands of troops, police and paramilitaries. An escape of sixty prisoners from Eichstätt in May 1943 apparently tied up 50,000 Germans.[7]

Certainly, the Germans expended considerable efforts in trying to catch the Épinal escapees, but the precise numbers involved are not clear. Some of the effort seems like locking the stable door after the proverbial horse has run off. The 2,000 pro-German Russians of the Vlasov Army (formed of ex-POWs themselves) who arrived at Belfort on 9 July were already too late for the majority of the Indians.[8] To make it evident that the Germans meant business, the collaborationist newspaper *L'express de l'Est* published a notice from the Germans:

IMPORTANT NOTICE
1 The National Gendarmerie and the Services for the maintenance of order are invited to arrest and direct all escaped prisoners to the [Feldgendarmerie] d'Épinal.

2 The mayors of the localities around Épinal have to bring to the attention of their administrators that it is absolutely forbidden, under pain of death, to receive these prisoners, to lodge them, to supply them and to favour in any way whatsoever their flight.[9]

The message was clear: if you help these men in any way, you will be shot.

After the initial rush of adrenaline and panic, dividing into small groups and plunging into the woods, the men looked around them and made their choices. Some among them, including postman Mukandan, didn't get far:

> As it was suspected there were unexploded bombs in the camp, we hurriedly collected some clothes, blankets and food and left again for the forest. We stayed there for the night and watched the fire raging in the camp and town, that is when we were not dozing from exhaustion. In the morning we made a bid for escape in the hope of meeting the French 'Partisans'. We had hardly gone a few miles, when trained Alsatian dogs tracked us for their German masters. We were taken back to a temporary camp and captivity.[10]

Others were more lucky. The citizens of the suburbs of Chantraine and St-Laurent helped them and showed them the way. Mostly, the men turned left and started to work their way south, parallel to the Moselle River. In the villages and hamlets to the south of Épinal – Xertigny, Fort du Roulon, Fontenoy-le-Château – the villagers got used to seeing khaki-clad strangers in small groups, asking for food and directions.

But not all went south. Forty-three were looked after at Belmont-sur-Buttant, 30km east of Épinal, taking them on a much less direct route to safety.[11] Some were helped on to a barge on the Canal de l'Est, where they had a 'slow and safe liberation cruise'.[12]

So they marched on through the hilly forests, past the 1,000 *étangs* (ponds) that the region is famous for, past the cherry trees of the Fougerolles area in bloom, past the small farms with their cows, pigs and chickens. The Gurkhas and Garhwalis were mountain men – *montagnards* – and must have felt at home bouncing up the rocky paths and through the woods.

A few miles south of Épinal they crossed the *Ligne de partage des eaux* – the watershed between the North Sea and the Mediterranean. Instead of water running towards the Netherlands and England, they were following streams and rivers that flowed towards the south – they were walking towards sunshine and olive oil, towards Marseille and the sea. Those of them from Punjab were used to rivers, growing up in the country of the five waters. They may not have noticed, they may not have cared, but perhaps subliminally they felt the sunshine beckoning them on.

Some escapers travelled by bus, according to a resident of Joncherey, near the border:

> Many refugees arrived in Delle by bus from Belfort. At times there were some almost every day. It was often dangerous for them because at all times the Germans stopped the bus … Luckily, it was a large gas-powered vehicle that had two doors, one in the front, the other in the back. As soon as we saw the Germans, we pushed the fugitives to the bottom of the bus, we discreetly opened the door and we made them get out while the gendarmes climbed up to the driver. They weren't very smart, they never saw anything but fire. It even happened with Hindus. They had fled from Épinal, had arrived as far as Belfort and they had simply got on the bus to come to Delle! With their Hindu clothes, do you realize? When we realized they were there, we hid them as best we could and brought them down to Grandvillars. We knew that the roadmender of the village was a smuggler and that he could lead them to the border by passing through.[13]

Guts were not in short supply when seeking modes of transport. Dew Bhan Singh was a sepoy in the 11th Sikhs, from Sialkot, captured at El Alamein. Having already escaped twice before arriving in France, he was ready to run when the wall came down. Amazingly, he managed to make some of the journey hidden in a German ration lorry, and crossed the frontier on 1 June.[14]

Navigation was difficult among the trees, with hills taking them up and down and streams to cross. Many stories say that they followed the high-tension power lines leading south towards Delle and the frontier.[15] One party of Mahrattas:

> … met a French farmer, who told them to get well into the forest, and led them for a couple of miles to show them long strips of khaki coloured paper about 1 foot long and two inches wide. These strips had been dropped by Allied aircraft and been placed in the forest at about 200 yard intervals to show the safest and shortest route to Switzerland.[16]

This was a joint effort to help them. One can almost sense the local people willing them along the route. Another escaper reported some advanced navigation skills in his party:

We oriented ourselves by compass and map, also by the sun ... We moved at night, during the day we slept. Our route led us mostly through high grain fields or through forest ... Despite the civilians being helpful to us, we always had to hide. We used threads to confirm to ourselves the correctness of the distances on the map.[17]

Some routes were longer than others. Naik Barkat Ali had travelled in May 1941 with the 29 Field Ambulance from Ahmednagar in India to Basra in Iraq.[18] From there, he was posted to North Africa, where he was taken prisoner in late 1942. With an unknown comrade, he walked at least 200km from Épinal. His route took him south to Belfort, where he may have noticed the Lion of Belfort below the citadel, symbol of the city's resistance to the Germans in 1871. Then south again to the industrial country round the Peugeot factory at Sochaux. After that, the country rises into limestone hills of the Franche-Comté, with the road zig-zagging after St Hippolyte, home of the red-and-white Montbéliarde cattle and the extraordinary looking Comtois horse – brown with a yellow mane, built for hauling wood in the forests.

Further and further into the farming country they went, higher and higher, until they could see Swiss farms on grassy slopes among pines across the valley to the east. It is not known whether they had a guide, or whether they travelled alone, but somewhere near Grand'Combe-des-Bois they headed downhill, descending the steep slopes to the river below, along a hunters' path, through hazel and pine and sycamore, on the Sentier de Bonaparte, named after a restaurant on the Swiss side.

This is quiet country, little visited by humans, home to deer browsing among the mountain bluet flowers, the lupins and the mint, while kites circle overhead, looking for small mammals and birds for dinner among the beech trees. Their boots crunched on the curious white snails that live by the river, which seem to get their colour from the limestone.

As they reached the bottom they found another footpath, used by fishermen and smugglers, trees dripping with dark green lichen. At this stage, the River Doubs is a small mountain river, with a force that is used for generating electricity, and a gorge known as '*Vallée de la Mort*', or Death Valley. Upstream to the right was Les Graviers, a gravelly beach; downstream, the old glass factory of Verrières des Guêpes. And 20m away – straight ahead – lay Switzerland: their goal and their dream, after seven days of walking and two years' imprisonment. Just upstream from the Bonaparte footpath, they crossed the narrow, fast-flowing river.

The unknown companion made it across safely, but Barkat Ali did not. According to an official telegram from the British Embassy in Switzerland, he was shot by a German soldier at this edge of the Reich, but a Swiss report simply says he drowned.[19] His body was pulled out of the water, carried up the steep hill to the town of La Chaux-de-Fonds and examined by Dr Ulrich.[20] From there, he was taken to the town of Vevey beside Lake Geneva and interred in the municipal cemetery, in a special section separated by a low hedge, with a large stone sword engraved in bas-relief on a cross.

This is the enclosure of the Commonwealth War Graves Commission, one of 23,000 burial sites around the world, but the only one in Switzerland.[21] Barkat Ali's headstone stands sideways, at right angles to the rest of the graves. Next to him is Jit Bahadur Limbu, a naik in the Gurkhas – his headstone has the distinctive crossed *kukris* at the top and the Sanskrit inscription, 'I bow to the Lord'. He also escaped from Épinal, reached Switzerland and died after an accident playing football in Losone.[22]

Barkat Ali's father, Hasan Ali, and his wife, Bibi – both living in Punjab – were informed about his death in due course. The young man would never return.

Someone with more luck was Havildar R.R. Dave of the Postal Service, captured at Tobruk, who had attempted to escape in September 1943 in Italy. He was in a group of five who reached a village called Champagney near Belfort:

> We had to cross a tunnel, the entrance to which was guarded by German sentries. We hid ourselves in a dilapidated house nearby so as to make the attempt at night. During the day, a routine search was made in the locality and one of the patrols came right into the house in which we were hiding. All of us were terrified almost out of our wits, but our luck held. After a cursory examination of the premises, the patrol passed on and we breathed a sigh of relief.[23]

A few days later, on 23 May, they crossed the border unaided near Abbévillers. But they were still wary:

> We could not make out whether we were in enemy occupied territory or in Switzerland. So leaving my companions hidden among the trees on a hill, I went forward to reconnoitre. Before I knew it,

I ran into a farm-house where some uniformed men were sitting. Due to the near-resemblance of their unforms, I mistook the Swiss guards as German soldiers and ran back for the woods. But they overtook me and then I came to know that they were, in fact, Swiss soldiers. Seeing my flight and pursuit by soldiers, my companions had panicked and fled in all directions. We had to do a lot of running and shouting to call them in.

Dave and his group were, in fact, near Fahy in Switzerland, where finally they started to relax:

At last we assembled in the farm-house and were given a good meal. I still remember how the little daughter of our host burst into terrified shrieks when she saw my long beard and unkempt appearance. I can't describe how happy I was to breathe the first whiff of freedom after so many horrible experiences and I can say that though my feet were swollen with fatigue my heart was swollen with jubilation.[24]

That particular day was a busy one on the frontier, with sixty-two Indians crossing over to freedom.

Siddiq Khan was another havildar who told his story well. He hailed from Montgomery in Punjab (now Sahiwal in Pakistan), where his father was a headmaster. He joined the 10th Baluch Regiment at some stage before the war and was one of 500 men of his regiment captured at the Cauldron in June 1942. His list of camps includes Capua and Udine in Italy, a 'harrowing train journey' to Spittal in Austria, where he began serious escape planning, Annaburg and Limburg, where he watched the RAF bombing the area around Frankfurt every night, and finally Épinal. Immediately after the bombing, he and his companions took shelter overnight near the camp. The next morning:

They saw an old man climbing up the bank and on approaching him for help, he took them to his house, fed them and guided them across the canal on the general direction to Switzerland – all this, despite the language barrier! On their march, they came across a peasant woman working in the field who was also friendly and took care of them. Her son ... told them to follow the overhead electric cables, which would eventually take them into Switzerland but warned to keep some distance as the line was frequently patrolled. For the first time they had a better defined direction. Over a hill overlooking the village of [Plombières-les-Bains] they met a young girl who helped them in getting across the village and again at Melisey were given shelter in the hay loft. Here [Siddiq] managed to get a small map which proved to be quite useful ...

Next day, moving towards Champagney and then to Banvillars [Siddiq] met six Indian escapees in the village churchyard. The priest was helpful and sheltered them, while it rained heavily. Here, they got introduced to a French Underground operator who briefed them on the ground situation and gave [Siddiq] a sheet of newspaper, printed only on one side as the secret pass to establish contact with the French Underground. They moved on to village Chatenois located across a canal and decided to cross the bridge at night. Nine more Indian soldiers joined the group here. At night the bridge was crossed in two's, with all precautions, but the movement was detected and challenged, which forced the entire lot to dash across and run for the nearest wood. Luckily there was no pursuit. Along the way, a river was crossed by swimming and shelter and food were provided by a peasant woman living near the bank. When [Siddiq] showed the newspaper sheet, they were advised to go to Dampiarte, where they met a female member of the Underground. She took them to Les Bois, placed them in a safe house and left for a while to make final arrangements.

After a few days the lady returned and accompanied them to Fesche L'Eglise, a village close to the Swiss frontier. They stayed in a forest and were joined by two guides next day. They were told to shed unnecessary load and briefed on how to freeze under German search lights. [Later] the party moved through the forest and waited for the night to cross the open patch adjacent to the border. After midnight, the party crossed the border in small groups, not very far from the German post and having turned towards the Swiss post was challenged by its guards. The guides explained and the party was assembled and taken to a Police station. The long journey to freedom had come to a happy end.[25]

Siddiq Khan was one of 124 Épinal escapees who crossed over on Friday, 19 May, the busiest day on the frontier. His story demonstrates how many of these men depended on the French for help. It is notable that his memory for place names and spellings is pretty accurate, so one can retrace his exact route on a map.

So, who were these French folk who helped so generously and in such numbers? With the Germans, the *Milice* and, later, the Russian

Vlasov Army combing the countryside, with the threat of death known all round, again and again the stories told are of food, shelter and guidance from the population of the land.

The escapers knew that if they were picked up they would be returned to a camp with proper beds and regular Red Cross parcels, while their helpers would be taken to the concentration camp at Natzweiler Struthof, or worse. One Épinal escaper was acutely aware of this, 'My greatest concern is that the family who saved my life may have suffered reprisals if the Germans found out that they had helped a prisoner of war'.[26] Hundreds of men, women and children were involved in the effort, and there are almost no stories of betrayal.

Jean-Marie Coulon was one who helped, and still recalled his experience in 2023. At the time he was a 12-year-old schoolboy at Raddon et Chapendu near Luxeuil:

> Our schoolmaster explained to us … that in the Vosges, a barracks where Hindu prisoners were housed was bombed and these were lost in the forests of our region because they are looking for the direction towards Switzerland.
>
> What was our discovery, one Thursday, while we were collecting dead wood, to find, hidden behind a large stone, four men dressed in khaki. They followed us and at the edge of the wood, remained sheltered. We told my great-grandfather François Xavier Constant Coulon. He gave us money and bread coupons which we took to the baker. The baker handed out two large loaves and two small ones [and] accompanied us to find the hidden men. We must, he told us, keep the secret of our meeting.
>
> The next day when school opened, the master also informed us of the secret. In the morning a patrol of soldiers accompanied by the mayor arrived at the school. The German officer interrogated us: some didn't understand what's going on and we, my cousins and I, played dumb. As he left, the mayor in turn said, 'Whoever finds or encounters Hindu soldiers must quickly report it to the guard.' This was the first time we had carried out an act of resistance.[27]

Some of the helpers were established members of the Resistance, but for many, like the young Jean-Marie, this was a new experience. Although some escapers had picked up Red Cross supplies during the first crazy minutes after the bombing, they could not have lasted long, and so the men became dependent on what the local population could provide, augmented by some foraging. They were lucky to have ended up in such a fertile part of the country, to be escaping in the late spring. One of the Mahrattas reported, 'One old French lady stopped us, and without any explanation from us, said we were escaped prisoners and she was very pleased; she gave us some excellent bread and cheese.'[28]

Later, the same group was deep in the forest:

> The going was very slow. And at about 4 o'clock in the afternoon we were stopped by an old French farmer, who was an ex-soldier of the last war. He told us to wait, went back to his home, and two hours later returned with his son and daughter, bringing eggs, bread, butter, cheese, two bottles of wine, three bottles of beer, a French–English dictionary, a cheap compass and a map.[29]

For this lucky group, there was a veritable feast that evening. Such support lifted the spirits as well as filling the bellies.

As well as nourishment, local people acted as *passeurs*. This French word can be translated as ferryman or smuggler, but neither of those seems to carry the degree of goodwill that was shown in this case. Perhaps a better word would be accompanier or companion. These were local people with deep local experience. They knew the roads and the footpaths; they knew where the cover was good and where one would need to move fast and low. In many cases – especially at the border itself – they were peacetime smugglers as well, specialising in tobacco or alcohol, but in wartime taking French Jews, Resistance fighters and others who had more to fear from the Germans. Some were in it for the money, some were patriots, and some were '*Les résistants de la dernière heure*' – the Johnny-come-latelies who turned their coats when they saw which way the war was going that summer.[30]

The scale of the assistance given was reflected in the number of medals awarded by the British and the French after the war. Emile Lepaul of Aillevillers, in the north of the Haute-Saône Département, supplied six Indians with food for four months that summer.[31] Victor Heidet lived in Valdoie, on the northern side of Belfort, with his wife Anna. Among many other resistance activities, he was one of the *passeurs* who took escapers past Belfort.[32] He may even have been one of those mentioned in the accounts above – sadly, neither side remembered the names of the other side, except in a few cases.

And even in the city – in the northern edge of Belfort itself – Louis Lamey hid seventeen Indians in his house at 17 Rue du Cardinal Mercier.[33] Lamey was subsequently murdered in Buchenwald and awarded the *Croix de Guerre* posthumously. Seventeen Indians and their families owed him a deep debt of gratitude.

Five of the Mahrattas did remember the name of their helper – at least, his first name. Among this group was Ganpatrao Tawde, the Mahratta clerk, carrying the list of names of his comrades who had died at Épinal. On 30 May, they met:

… a French Sergeant major named Maurice, who made himself responsible for a party of five Indians. He said he was a member of the *Maquis*, and had already helped 800 Allied prisoners to cross the Swiss border.

He took the Indians to his dug-out in the hills and showed them his cave, in which were a large collection of Mk II Sten guns and other automatic weapons which had been dropped in France by Allied aircraft. He made the Indians discard their battle dress and provided them with civilian garments, and after giving them a good meal, armed himself and led them on to another member of his force.

The next day the party was given three guides – two Frenchmen and one Pole, all armed with Sten guns and pistols. The whole party marched that day and the night of May 30/June 1, and at 0530 on the latter morning they reached the Doubs river, the boundary between France and Switzerland. There the three guides left the Indians, showed them the crossing, saw them across safely – and disappeared back into France to continue their good work.[34]

It is possible that the trio of guides took them to Bonaparte, where Barkat Ali had been shot, or further north. Swiss records show that Tawde and companions achieved their '*Passage de la Frontière*' on 1 June, but sadly they don't tell us exactly where they arrived. In due course, Tawde was awarded the Military Medal for his exploits.[35]

Other escapers took a more easterly route. Chavanatte is a village nearly in Alsace. One day in early June:

Mr. Emile Favé of Chavanatte was mowing his hay at the end of the Laparu pond … Seeing movement in the bushes, he was quite surprised when a turban emerged from the clutter of this back part of the pond. First of all, as it was very hot that day, he thought it was a mirage ... under the turban there was a very bearded head which advanced towards our brave peasant. Quite worried, Mr Favé let the character come closer while clinging to his whip by the small end.

Arriving next to the mower, the man began to jabber in a strange language, probably English. Finally, Father Favé, who only understood French and the patois of the country, succeeded, by dint of gestures, in understanding that he and his companions wanted to go to Switzerland and that they were very hungry. During these discussions, a dozen guys, just as ragged and looking exactly like the first, approached. By gestures, Father Favé succeeded in getting them into the strawpile: it must be said that they were about five hundred meters from the German border and that a watchtower, installed about fifteen meters high in a fir tree, overlooked the whole plain up to Suarce.

After many gestures, Mr Favé managed to show them the direction of Switzerland and above all he made them understand that they should not show themselves before dark. After that, he went back to his farm to get a good bag of food, which he left with them, being careful in case the German customs officers observed his actions. The next morning, there was nothing left in the bag hanging from a bush and the nest was empty.[36]

Like many of these chance helpers, Favé remembered this encounter for the rest of his life.

Meanwhile, the story of their mass breakout and their arrival in Switzerland was starting to be known. The *Times of India* ran a story on 25 May, and another the following week, which said there were 1,500 still hiding along the border and 230 who had already crossed (actually an underestimate).[37] Papers in Britain also picked up the story, with a report in the *Lancashire Daily Post* full of wildly exaggerated numbers.[38] The press interest did not last long, however, with D-Day just around the corner. Soon the whole world would be looking at France again, in this case, the north coast.

The Twain Shall Meet

It is difficult to always write the truth, nothing but the truth.[1]

Étobon – 80km from Épinal by the shortest walking route – was a significant place for many of the fugitives. Until now, they had mostly been unescorted. Following the pointing forefingers of the French, or a compass if they had one, they were slowly making their way southwards. After Étobon – perched between forest and plain – they were mostly escorted, guided by the men, women and children of the Resistance towards and past the fortress city, across the Belfort Gap to freedom.

Foremost among those brave civilians was the whiskered countenance of the blacksmith-farrier, Jules Perret himself, squirreling away his diary entries – some written in a patois which the Germans wouldn't understand – in a bottle hidden under the stable floor. This chapter tells the story of the many encounters in this hamlet beneath the woods, using mostly his words.

Étobon is a small village, with a population of 266 in 1936. Among the outlying farms with their wheat and maize fields, their fruit trees and their cows that produce the famous Comté cheese, the little centre contains a school, the forge where Perret worked, a *Mairie*, where the civil administration can be found, a Protestant church and its *presbytère*, or vicarage.

The strong Protestant identity of the village is significant in the sanctuary it afforded so many of the refugees. 'Resisting is in the Protestant DNA', according to a local pastor – the word '*resister*' is inscribed on the memorial in the village cemetery and recalls the story of the eighteenth-century Huguenot, Marie Durand, who spent thirty-five years in jail at Aigues-Mortes for refusing to renounce her faith.[2] One can imagine then that there was a sympathy among these tough, woody farmers for the Muslims, Hindus and Sikhs on the run. As one local writer put it,

'The instinct of these men warns them that they have nothing to dread *chez nous* and they can walk openly during daylight.'[3]

Jules Perret's diary will guide us through this chapter. He starts his narrative for Sunday, 14 May 1944 thus:

> This is a day that will go down in history. I was driving my cows this morning with [grandson] Philippe ... We were about to arrive at the bend in the road called the 'Turn of Belverne' when suddenly appeared in front of us six almost black men ... barefoot, some without jackets, all badly dressed. I said *woah* to the cows and we tried to talk to each other, and I understood that they were five Hindus and a Redskin from America, prisoners who had escaped from the Épinal camp.[4]

Jules guided the six men to a hiding place at a mill and indicated that he would bring them food and take them further that evening. 'They seemed to say "Yes", but I think they didn't quite understand.' He returned home by truck, told his son Jacques and his neighbours Mr Pernol and Tournier, and collected eggs, bacon, cheese 'and especially bread', and a pot of Sunday soup from his wife, Jeanne, and returned to the mill by bicycle with Jacques.

The fugitives were restored by the food, 'The hot soup was welcome, but only one wanted bacon, a Buddhist surely, and also the Redskin, he ate everything. And then we had to make more plans.'[5]

Jacques escorted the Indian soldiers to the woods of Montedin, while his father nipped home again to collect some clothes. He also asked Marlier – the Protestant pastor – to write a letter in English to the Indians, explaining the plan. Jules met them at Montedin Woods, delivered the clothes (two pairs of old shoes, socks, two jackets, a sweater and some old caps) and the letter:

> The Huron speaks English and several others do too. They were very happy, they got dressed and wrote me a beautiful letter where they ask that God bless our whole family and especially the lady who had made them such good soup and also the pastor who had written the letter ... I led them through the woods to Chenebier ... I gave them multiple recommendations to hide, sneak, crawl if necessary to cross the border. For me, Jules Perret, who so loved reading the books of [Fenimore] Cooper and others where we talked about the Indians,

seeing myself piloting a descendant of these Indians, a descendant of the Hurons as he said, it was funny.

Jules writes more of the 'Huron':

I will tell you that he had no eagle feather in his hair, nor moccasins with scalps. No, he had my shoes that I put on the first time to see my sons in Colmar in 1931, one of my jackets and a cap. He was a Canadian paratrooper taken prisoner in Italy. He is an extremely friendly 24-year-old man, he lived at 5 rue Rosemont in Montreal, the Hindus had all been to Tobruk. We parted with tears in our eyes all with strong demonstrations of friendship.[6]

Charles Perret – Jules' cousin – now gets involved, and gives us another version of the story:

[Jules] is delighted with this meeting, finding it astonishing and auspicious that it should be he who has this fantastic adventure. What really pleases him is to have discovered amongst these travellers an authentic American Indian – a Huron with red skin. Being a passionate reader of Fenimore Cooper, he thinks that he is living through an adventure story and decides on the spot to get the Indians to follow him, and lead them safely to the goal that they seek: the Swiss frontier.[7]

As a keen reader of James Fenimore Cooper's 1826 novel *Last of the Mohicans*, Jules was clearly delighted that one of the refugees was a First Nation Canadian. After the war, he wrote to the *Mairie* of Montreal, in an effort to find the man. Charles Renaud, the head of the Secretariat, wrote a very polite letter back, assuring Jules that the search was continuing and that 'as soon as we have news on this subject, we will hasten to let you know'.[8] There was no further communication from Montreal. There was no record of a Canadian soldier in Épinal, nor of any that crossed the Swiss border that summer. The mystery of the Huron remains.

The next day is Monday, 15 May, and Jules reports five more Indians:

How funny to find ourselves with these 10 men, these foreigners arriving from Asia. They are happy, confident to find some help. They believe they are saved.

Ah! Not yet! There are these shaggy beards, hair in buns under the turbans, there is especially a need to adapt their uniforms. For the first 5, I gave them all civilian clothes. I even gave one of them my black coat, that good Vincennes greatcoat, but I've run out of clothes now.

After dark, Jules and his family escorted the escapers in pairs to the pastor's house, through the orchards and gardens, keeping out of view. They arrived safely to be greeted by Mr and Mrs Marlier:

In this room there was a beautiful spectacle. We put them on ten camping mattresses and made a fire for them. They all stripped to their shirts as soon as they arrived and Madame Marlier washed their feet. She dressed the wounded one well and we left them to sleep.[9]

And so the *presbytère* – the parsonage – run by M. and Mme Marlier, in the heart of this quiet village, became a hospital, a dormitory and a safe haven for countless prisoners on the run.

The next morning – Tuesday, 16th – Jules returned to the parsonage:

At daybreak I went very gently to light a fire for them. They were all still asleep, except the fat sergeant who was near the stove and Jeanne started to make them a pot and tea when Tournier came to say that there were 6 new ones at Jeangeorge.[10]

At this stage Jules took a photo of them on the steps of the presbytery, opposite the *Mairie* – the only known photograph of any of the men between Épinal and Switzerland (Fig. 11). In his journal, he annotated the picture and gives a commentary on many of the men. The four men on the right in the front row are the first that he met, together with the one with the wounded foot, who did not join the photo. Third from the left is a naik, whom Perret identifies as a sergeant, in his shirt-tails with bare legs. Next to him is a tall man who gave his gold identity bracelet to Suzette, and to whom Jules showed a photo of a *sadhu* in his possession, whom he resembled. The last one in that row is 'a very handsome man too, very stout, very strong'. In the middle of the terrace is what Perret calls an officer – possibly a VCO – who had carried a rolled umbrella with him all the way from Épinal. 'I said to him [in jest] "Oh! *Tchinberlène*". He gave me a nice smile and said,

"Yes" – we know that the great English statesman Chamberlain almost always carried an umbrella.'[11]

At three o'clock, a woman from the next village arrived with another seven men, and Jules jokes that 'the yard is full'. Later they ate:

A good pot of *houzard* [soup] and all these men will set off an hour before nightfall. They are moved beyond what can be expressed by seeing the welcome we have given them. They don't know how to express their gratitude. We only ask them not to tell anyone that we have hosted them. This they swear.[12]

That evening, Jules put a ladder up to the barn, and the Indians descended:

What goodbyes, what handshakes. How many wishes. Jacques, Marcel and Robert took them down to the Etang des Chats and led them through the valley... I watched this Indian file which snaked along the hedges then crossed the meadows and entered the cover. If a German had been facing me, he would have seen everything, just like me ... You must be careful. They will arrive by the old wood road, at the Forge de Chagey bridge where they have an appointment with FFI from Chagey who will take them to Brevilliers tomorrow evening.[13]

Before they left, one member of this first group wanted to give the family a present. Jules' grandson Philippe Perret recalled that his aunt Suzette received a gold bracelet, with 'Melvin Nichols 38054308' on the obverse, 'Love Lorene' on the reverse.[14] This may be the identity tag of the Canadian. Philippe still has that bracelet in his house at the forge, and he also recalled that one of the escapers was knitting socks the whole time he was there – an unusual occupation for a man in rural France at that time.

Charles Perret takes up the story, relating how when passing behind a neighbour's house:

I hear a noise in the kitchen and approach for a look. Four Indians are sitting there, in the middle of a meal. One has a head wound ...

The tableau which they presented, seated in the middle of an assembly of the curious behind them is rather strange. The divine vengeance which fell on Babel also fell on this peaceful place where two groups of humans try to explain in two different languages, without success.

We take them to Culchaud [his house] by the back route and there they are in our remote house. As if it was the Eve of Ascension Day, Marguerite [Charles' wife] has prepared a tart that she places on the table; she quickly heats up some soup and some vegetables. Our guests start by eating the tart, then the vegetables, then the soup. Their broad smiles tell us that they are perfectly restored. I take them to join another group hidden since the morning in a straw pile near Thure woods where two *maquisards* of Etobon – Jules Tournier and Marcel Nardin – have to take them and guide them through the woods to Chagey ... From Chagey, a truck will take them without fatigue (but not without risk) to the Swiss frontier.[15]

Later, Charles led the expanded group off 'in the direction of the promised land':

Before leaving they thank us. One of them fumbles in his pocket to give a present to mother – 'Mummy!' This word has the same significance in all languages. The mother wants to prevent this gesture by the Indian, but he announces 'tea'. Marguerite weakened and accepted this gift because she has long adored tea and has been deprived of it for a long time. Each one, in his turn, wants to demonstrate his gratitude. But that's enough, they must leave. There is one other word that the escapers know '*La Suisse*'. I pronounce this evocative word, the four men follow suit, loaded with their bundles. On crossing the threshold they turn again to *la maman* who wishes them good luck and kisses them.[16]

They moved off, through the tall grass and into the pine trees – a long column snaking its way to freedom.

Later that day, a young man called Henri Croissant brought a new escapee – a French speaker – to Jules' house. Jules took him to the pastor's house:

He is a sergeant major named Abdul Manan, he is a teacher, he has one brother who is a captain, another lieutenant. He gave me his address, he lives on the border of Afghanistan. This morning I went to bring him lunch. I made him a fire and gave him everything he needed to shave, wash and even do laundry.[17]

It is probable that this man was one of the men from the 22nd Animal Transport Company of the RIASC, taken prisoner in this very neighbourhood in June 1940. There is one Abdul Manan in the Swiss archives, a native of Abbottabad on the North-West Frontier.[18] This would explain his fluency in French, having spent most of 1940 in France, and substantial periods since then.

While Abdul Manan slept Jules learned that the Germans had been searching the next village on his proposed route, so he decided to take Abdul Manan by a different route:

> I disguised him with an old jacket and a hat and we each took a scythe, we would have passed in the middle of 1,000 Boches who would have suspected nothing. I left him on the edge of the scrub, promising him that I would come back to see him again before he left. When I got back I found Charles [Perret] who came to tell me that he had four new ones at his place. After some discussion it is decided that he would lead them to Abdul. I showed him exactly where he would find [Abdul Manan] and a little before dark when I returned with a thermos of hot tea, I found the 6 men ...
>
> How happy he was to see me again and especially to drink hot tea. It was Suzette who wanted me to bring the tea!
>
> Of the other four, I must speak. Oh! These figures! They look Chinese or Tibetan: three young people and an old sergeant. This sergeant has a fierce air, almost ferocious.
>
> In the afternoon ... I learned that the big convoy the other day was driven by the Chagey Syndicate truck to the border.[19]

This Chagey syndicate *camionette* was a small pick-up truck with two seats in front and a flatbed, belonging to the Co-op. It was driven by a young man called 'Legrand', who had been adopted in the village as an orphan.[20] That evening, Jules heard of a group of thirty Indians passing through the district. The numbers were rising. Nearly a week after the bombing, more and more escapees had managed the 80 or so kilometres from their camp.

The next day was Ascension Day – Whitsun in the English calendar. Jules' daughter Suzette met thirty more escapers on the road to Chagey:

> ... all loaded with bulky kit. We don't understand why. Several days after the bombardment of Épinal these men can still flee, taking

everything they want. It looks like all their guards have been killed and they looted the camp. Suzette and René saw a passing German car on the road. They [the Indians] were crossing the village in broad daylight, it's crazy.

Towards Belfort there passed a huge convoy [of Indians]. The local Resistance escorted them in arms. If the Germans had seen it would have been bad.[21]

It sounds almost as if the sheer volume of escapers all across the countryside had outstripped the German capacity to track them and catch them.

Friday 19th – eight days since the bombing and eighteen more exhausted escapers were awaiting escort southwards. There was a close shave when three Germans arrived, demanding help cooking their eggs. One of Jules' neighbours took them to his house while the Indians kept quiet in the next room.

Perret was clearly charmed by his Indian guests. Even as large numbers pass through the village, he attempted to learn their names, where they came from and their stories. He saw them as individuals, not as a mass of people, and often called them 'my' Indians, with a slight air of patronage. Jules and his neighbours were clearly concerned for the individual human soul:

> It's good to hear them talking to each other, they have such a sweet language. Sounds like chirping birds. These are said to be from Nepal, there are many from Delhi. Those of Bombay are much blacker. They are picky about food, some eat bacon, others beef, others do not want meat.

More arrived over the next couple of days. Saturday 20th was a very busy day, starting with nine newcomers:

> This time we opened up the apartments and brought them straw in the upstairs room. There is one of those from yesterday who has not left, he is ill. This morning Mr Pernol brought him a good coffee with Kirsch in it but because of the alcohol he didn't want it. It would have done him good though. I went to bring him tea later with Suzette …
>
> I give him tea, aspirin which he sucks like a candy and I distribute the rest of our apples to them. If you had seen these people … With

both hands they took mine. Sunday's Redskin had a similar expression of friendship and said to me 'tank you, Dad'. He wasn't much more tanned than the rest of us, but he had bigger cheekbones. He was a very handsome man. There was also a very handsome Hindu, a tall one with a nice moustache.

Noon – Another 9 new ones. That makes 18 for tonight!!!

5pm – Another 5, that's 23. Suzette goes back to them with tea, milk, sandwiches. Oh! What a sight these 23 tanned, exhausted men, lying in this small room trying to recover before resuming tonight's stage.

6pm – Another 6 new ones, that's 29.

7:30 – I am now writing this at the top of Tabac field where I have been sent to watch the road.[22]

The next day was a Sunday, Mothering Sunday in France and other countries. Jules and his family and neighbours went to church as usual:

We come out of worship to celebrate Mother's Day. Yes, mothers of all countries, honour to you who have given so many children …

Jacques was proud to lead these men, these poor men who, exaggerating the danger, believed their safety, their very life, depended on the fidelity of their guide. He loved them all, he talked to them, he helped them. Ah! He's like me, he's my son. Twice Jacques saw workers in the woods. A gesture and all these men were hidden without a breath, without a word. As soon as the intruders left, the convoy resumed its rapid and silent march.

The next day, there was news of a German crackdown and of Indian POWs becoming increasingly assertive. Perret reported Germans firing on escapees at Champagney, 10km north of Étobon. One escaper was injured. Perret also reported that it was becoming more difficult to cross the border, with parties limited to a maximum of five people.

On Tuesday, 23 May, Jules' children, Suzette and Jacques, fed seventeen in the woods in the morning, and their neighbour Marcel did the honours in the evening. Perret says, 'It makes us happy to see them eat when they are hungry. How can men be allowed to suffer from hunger? Even to hungry Germans I would still give.'

Jules Perret set off with a new group to Chagey:

One of these men, a small, very [dark-skinned] native of Bombay only wanted to walk towards me. There was one almost white who looked like [neighbour] Mr Radef, he had blue eyes. Another young man named Cham-Dram speaks good French. He asked me if the English were paying us to do this for them. I surprised him by telling him no and that we were all risking our lives helping them.

Over the next few days, towards the end of May, there was a new twist to the tale. As well as the groups leaving Étobon every evening, guided by the villagers, Jules also started to encounter Indians coming from the south. These were men who got close to the border and found it impossible to cross. In some cases, their comrades had been shot and killed near the border. Jules wondered what to do with these men. With his cousin Charles, they worked to enlarge the *baccus* (shelters in the woods):

On Pentecost Monday we come back to the same place with Jacques Perret and Edgar Quintin. We bring tools: billhooks, saw, axe – to help our protegés repair and enlarge their home. Edgar cuts long grass … which they use to make beds. The closest stream gives them drinking water, and every day we bring them food furnished by the locals in turn. One of the Indians comes with us to the designated place in the middle of the village where the soup tureen is deposited.[23]

Hiding in this wood – the Bois du Chérimont – was relatively easy. Indeed, some prisoners stayed there for nearly six months, supplied by the villagers. Even in 2023, this is thick, deep, beech wood with few roads. The forest is surrounded by villages with open farmland and Protestant churches with their distinctive ceramic-tiled roofs. Étobon lies to the east, Belverne to the south, Frédéric-Fontaine and Clairegoutte to the west and Ronchamp to the north, with its chapel of pilgrimage, destroyed during the liberation campaign in September 1944 and rebuilt by Le Corbusier after the war.

This is the last bit of wooded country, for beyond Belverne, the land drops to the Route Nationale 19, from Belfort to Vesoul and on to Paris. Indeed, a Roman road runs through the forest, perhaps a relic from Caesar's conquering army. There were coal mines at Clairegoutte (its name means 'clear drop') and woodworkers all around, making use of the abundant raw materials. The beech trees and pines grow close together and approaching vehicles can be heard a long way away, so this was a perfect place for concealment.

'*Les Hindous*' constructed *baccus* – at their simplest, a hollow in the ground covered with branches, some of which are still visible today. With deer and boar grazing wild, with soup coming from the villagers, this was a haven from the craziness all around. Like the villagers, the escapees who sheltered here 'saw the forest as their ally against the malice of the times'.[24]

One of those who still remembers the guests, and helped with their supply, is Madame Lise Large, née Bonhotal.[25] Born in 1927, she still inhabits the same house on Rue des Combes in Chenebier, the last house in the village before the woods. Her father ran a garage in Héricourt, which was requisitioned by the Germans. She was a teenager when the Indians came, and described them as 'good men, discreet'. Every evening, they would descend into the village for something to eat, going to a different house each night – 'everyone around here joined in', she said.

In Clairegoutte, a young man would load up his bike with leftover food, cycle into the forest and leave a parcel at a specified place, returning later to pick up the empties. One day, he went up and found the food from the previous day still there, so he realised that these men had crossed the line and reached safety. The precise number of soldiers who were sheltered and fed in these woods will never be known, but many estimates put it at around 200.[26]

Most of the early escapees chose to move on, however, to seek the promised land of the border. As May turned to June, the numbers reaching Étobon dwindled. But soon there would be a change of pace, a new atmosphere in the woods and villages. On 5 June – the eve of D-Day – Suzette Perret was approached by a scruffy man in the field, who turned out to be a Russian. Her father, Jules, explained how these French peasants managed to communicate with their multilingual visitors, 'You are going to think: "How do they manage to understand each other?" Yes! It's curious but I have always been able to come to good conclusions with all the foreigners. Either by writing, or by making signs, gestures, drawings.'[27]

Tuesday, 6 June was the long-awaited day, and Jules records in great detail what he had heard on the BBC and from his fellow resistance workers:

9 am – This is the Anglo-Franco-American landing!!! This day, eagerly awaited by some and anxiously awaited by others, has arrived. It was on the northern coasts that the big blow took place.

Evening 11 o'clock – it's incredible, it's wonderful, it's miraculous. The radio has just given us details.

Rommel, who had inspected the entire coastline, had declared Europe impregnable. The English have just ended their program with these words: 'Courage' this time that's it. See you tomorrow.[28]

As June rolled on, Jules wrote more and more about the activities of the Resistance, as the French did what they could to disrupt German communications. By this stage, there were fewer Indians around, and those that are mentioned were mostly hunkered down, sheltering in the woods and awaiting their delivery – the arrival of the Allies.

The Germans arrested civilians and shot some of them for aiding fugitives – this was a dangerous business. Some Indians gave up on Switzerland and were trying for Spain instead. On 14 June, cousin Charles Perret writes:

We see Indians every day. They seem to be fixed in our forests, which creates an upsurge of danger for the neighbouring villages. This morning a famished fugitive came into our house, and benefited from our lunch ... they accept the simplest food, potatoes, milk, fruits. If in doubt, they prefer to die of hunger.[29]

The Muslim holy month of Ramadan fell in this period, starting on 21 August. Whether or not the men in the forest observed the fast is open to question. Travellers are usually exempted from fasting during the holy month. They all liked to smoke however:

Almost all of them are great smokers and suffer from lack of tobacco. For this reason they make frequent visits to [my house] because they know that I don't smoke. They ask timidly 'Mummy, Cigarettes?' but the stock is quickly exhausted ... If they only have a little tobacco, the group forms a circle and the pipe passes from hand to hand. In this case the pipe or the cigarette doesn't touch the mouth of the smoker who takes care to form a tube for the smoke with his closed hand.[30]

Charles Perret continued with his assessment of the wood-dwellers:

> They are not strong for work ... their faces bear no resemblance to
> the hard features of soldiers of the master race. All are imbued with a
> great softness of character and their gestures are precise and effemin-
> ate. We have to accept them as they are and rescue them since they are
> unhappy human beings in danger.[31]

The summer continued. The Allies broke out from the Normandy
bridgehead and another landing in the south of France brought new
hope in mid-August. By the middle of September, Jules knew that liberation was not far away. On 20 September, he encountered some new
fugitives in the woods:

> We had to go around under the bushes. Jacques was a bit ahead of
> me. Suddenly I hear him cry out in surprise: 'Oh ... come quickly
> daddy, look who this is.' The underside of the stone was arranged as
> a dwelling and there was our friends the Hindus. There was Radef
> with the blue eyes, the old grey sergeant, the moustached Turk-faced
> man and others. What a surprise for us and what joy for them ...
> They are not fat, we gave them all our provisions, even cigarettes that
> the Germans had given me all those days, we showed them the apple
> tree of the mill and we left each other very tender because probably
> forever this time.[32]

At this stage, the hope in the village was still that they would be liberated
soon and the dark years of occupation would be over. It was not to be,
however, for even darker days lay ahead.

8

Barbed Wire and Borderstones

Frontiers are invented by men, not by nature.[1]

After they left Étobon came the hardest section for many of our escapees: reaching and crossing the actual border. For some, this proved too hard. Many were recaptured. On 27 May, Jules Perret recorded:

> This morning, making hay … with Suzette, we saw three Hindus, but they refused any help. By gestures, they communicated that they were coming back from the Swiss frontier and that their comrades had been killed. Twelve had already returned to Jeangeorges. They can't get through to Switzerland any more.[2]

There is a sense of bitterness there. The routes were getting more and more difficult as the Germans clamped down. A battalion of the Vlasov Army of Russians was searching the forest: it was to be a bloody autumn.

Some took the decision simply to lay up in the woods (or occasionally in a house) and let it all pass by. A Swiss newspaper reported on 25 May that there were 1,700 hiding in the forests near Belfort, although that figure could only have been based on estimates.[3] One who made it to Switzerland said later that he wouldn't have gone to Switzerland if he had known the English had landed in France.[4]

D-Day came just twenty-six days after the bombing, and there was a growing sense that liberation was just around the corner. Two sappers with eight camps under their belts – Farid Mohd and Mubarak Ali – took refuge in a village north of Belfort (sadly unnamed) and got caught in the no man's land between the advancing French and American forces and the retreating Germans. Farid Mohd was wounded in the chest but survived.[5]

Naik Shivdeo Singh of the RIASC came from a village called Gunnah, near Lyallpur (now Faisalabad in Pakistan). He had been the assistant to the head of camp at Épinal – clearly a man accustomed to leading.[6] According to a report in *Fauji Akhbar*, he didn't manage to escape on 11 May, but succeeded shortly afterwards while being moved to another camp. While on the march:

> ... noticing that there was no guard within several yards of him, he slipped out of the column and dashed into a villager's house. Here he found an asylum. Later, the French handed him over to the Maquis, who took him to a secluded clearing in some woods where Shivdeo Singh was amazed to find over 70 other escaped Indian soldiers. By popular vote, Shivdeo Singh ... was elected to command the party ... Under his leadership and after many narrow escapes from German patrols the Indians eventually contacted the American forces invading the South of France.[7]

Once again, the lack of detail in this report is frustrating, but this leader managed to survive and to bring another seventy men with him to safety.

Some were less fortunate. Artilleryman Havildar Daya Ram was from the village of Achina in Haryana. One of the first to reach Étobon, he was ill with tuberculosis. He stayed hidden in the woods for nearly five months, but eventually succumbed to his illness and died on 15 October, aged just 23.[8] He died at the house of Emile Bonhotal, and although he was a Hindu, his body was buried in secret, as the villagers were worried about smoke from a cremation being spotted by the Germans.[9] His body was exhumed after liberation, and surprisingly, it was not cremated then but reburied in the cemetery of the church at Chenebier.

After Étobon, many of the escapers took well-trodden routes to get them through the plains around Belfort, where cover was thinner and German soldiers thicker. Most of them were escorted by *passeurs* of one or another network. From Chagey – 8km south-east of Étobon – many were taken on the next stage by an 18-year-old girl called Charlotte Biediger (see Fig. 13). As a teacher at the primary school, she spoke English. She had joined the Resistance in 1943, working as a nurse, smuggling weapons and escorting escapers towards the border. Accompanied by a 15-year-old boy called Maurice Courtallain, she took groups of Indians to Brévillers, a distance of about 7km, and handed them on to their next escorts.

Distances that can be driven in minutes these days would have taken hours in such conditions. With all the caution that was needed, taking time to explain the route in English after every stop, keeping silent on the march and listening out for vehicles, this could have taken all night. Charlotte and Maurice then had to return to Chagey.[10]

At Florimont, there were two more young women risking their lives to help the fugitives. At an isolated farmhouse called *Le Coin du Bois* (Woody Corner) lived Joseph Yoder and his wife, with their four daughters and one son. While the mother was Catholic, Joseph came from a Mennonite family. Although Mennonites were traditionally pacifists, Joseph was a decorated veteran who had fought with the artillery at the Battle of Verdun in the First World War, when over half a million French and German soldiers became casualties in a battle that lasted ten months.

Despite having a farm to run, Joseph and his family were not prepared to sit back and do nothing during the occupation. So, Denise – aged 19 – and her 16-year-old sister, Marie-Louise, committed to becoming 'fighters of the shadows'.[11] Their father was busy with the farm and their brother was just 13, so the teenage girls stepped forward. Over the course of a few weeks that summer, Marie-Louise and Denise conducted an extraordinary total of sixty-seven Indian escapees, feeding them and accommodating them in the barn opposite the farmhouse, next to a spreading chestnut tree. Food was scarce, but the children 'were allowed a few bars of chocolate per month, which wasn't great, and they exchanged bars of chocolate for potatoes to feed the people who passed by, to take a break and to leave at night'.[12]

We know they escorted exactly sixty-seven because of a certificate issued by Georges Frézard, *Maire* of Grandvillars and erstwhile Resistance leader, still treasured by the Yoder family. It is most probable that these sixty-seven were spread over a period of weeks rather than being all together, and the family kept a tally – to the younger brother, it seemed as if the Indians were there permanently.

The two girls took them on to the next staging post at the farm of St André, a distance of 7 or 8km. They were very much aware of the need to take a slightly different route each time, to avoid creating deep tracks in the fields that would be visible to the Germans.

Later, shortly before liberation, a smartly dressed man came to the farm and asked them, 'Did you help?' Marie – a truthful young lady, proud of her actions – said yes, but her father quickly jumped in and said no. He suspected the stranger of being a collaborator, and indeed they saw the man soon after in a German military vehicle. Later still, the two young women refused a medal. As well as the sixty-seven Indians, numerous Allied aircrew and locals on the run, Marie-Louise also guided to the frontier a young man called Albert Marchand, who had been slaughtering animals illegally. He came back after the liberation and in June 1947, reader, she married him.[13]

The next village was Faverois, and then the farm of St André. This spacious farm was owned by the Dieny family, just 800m from the border. As such, it was a target for German patrols and customs officers, who would sometimes hide in the forest nearby and watch the farm. The son of the farm – Jean Dieny – was 19, a member of the *Jeunesse Agricole Catholique*, and therefore in contact with many young people in the region and with the local Resistance groups. One large group of at least fifty Indians was taken to the frontier, but then lost their way on the Swiss side and returned to St André in the early morning. Denise Dieny was 12 years old and saw them in front of the barn in broad daylight.[14]

> Enough to give cold sweats to the whole Dieny family! Even 70 years after these facts, Madame Dieny-Bidaux still has shivers when she thinks of the return of these Hindus. After feeding them, they were hidden in piles of hay for the day, and it was then necessary to reorganize the passage for the next night and, this time, to hand them over to the Swiss border guards. These Hindus did not know a word of French and it was very difficult to explain to them that the Swiss soldiers were not Germans, despite the similarities in their clothing.[15]

The second time, they were successful. For a long time after the war, the family would tell and retell the story of how the Hindus went twice to the frontier.[16]

The main route from the farm to the border was along a forest track to the aptly named Porte de France. The path runs for about 2,000m through walnut, maple and pine forest, very peaceful in the summer of 2023; very different seventy-nine years earlier. At the end of the narrow track, the dark woods with their wild mushrooms and water lilies open into sunny parkland with a mansion beyond, like a vision of liberty seen in a dream. The Porte itself still stands: a metal gate separating France from Switzerland; occupation from freedom.

Built for the wealthy Burrus family, who owned the mansion as a gate to enter France, during the war years it became a portal to freedom.

The gate was locked, and the two keys were held by *passeurs*: Monsieur Dieny at St André, and Charles Mougin in Faverois. One of these keys would be needed for the fugitives to cross over. Once unlocked, the gate opened into the wide gardens of Charles Burrus' mansion, now an old people's home – the terminus of one *passage*.[17] If one could dodge the German patrols, unlock the gate, realise that the Swiss patrols were truly neutral and not the enemy, one could reach the Promised Land.

The classic British and American escape stories end here. The heroes have crossed into Switzerland, and all is well. *La Grande Illusion, The Colditz Story* and even *Hannibal Brooks* climax with a Swiss border crossing. The crucial difference was on one side they were shootable, on the other side, safe.[18] Any border – this border – can be a potent image in the imagination: Steve McQueen trapped in reels of barbed wire, Jean Gabin and Marcel Dalio trudging through the snow. In reality, the border was the end of an important chapter rather than the end of the book.

The borders of neutral Switzerland are not simple – they wiggle and zig-zag. In the south-west, Geneva protrudes into France like a proboscis. In the south, Ticino reaches down towards the Mediterranean. In the north, the little German town of Büsingen am Hochrhein is entirely surrounded by Swiss territory, and the Swiss city of Schaffhausen could easily be mistaken for German territory. Indeed, on 1 April 1944, the Americans did precisely that, dropping 60 tons of bombs on the neutrals, killing forty civilians.[19] On the north-west side, the Swiss area known as Ajoie or Porrentruy is like a pimple, an extrusion of Swiss land into French land. This was a lucky twist of geography for the Épinal escapers and all the others who sought refuge from Nazi persecution in France – wiggly borders are much harder to police and much easier to cross.

Another remarkable fact about the Swiss borders is that they don't represent a linguistic frontier. The Swiss of the Ajoie speak the French language, with pretty much the same accent as the French of the Franche-Comté and Belfort. Families moved back and forth. There is a fluidity here, a sense of cultural connection. The smugglers knew the customs officers on both sides and knew when the best time was to cross. The Germans had been in residence as customs officers and border guards at Delle since 20 June 1940, but according to a young man living on the Swiss side, 'the German customs officers guarding the border weren't very fierce. For the most part, they were fairly old people who only wanted one thing, to go home.'[20]

For much of the war, there was almost nothing physical in the fields or forests that demonstrated you were at the frontier. Indeed, it was possible to not realise that you had crossed. One young Swiss man observed a group of Indians who had entered his country but took fright when they saw some Swiss soldiers in uniform. They turned and ran, unfortunately straight into the arms of some German soldiers instead.[21]

When Dr Mazumdar and his two comrades crossed in the summer of 1943, they were guided by a *passeur*, who said, 'Here's the frontier, you step over it, there's Switzerland.'[22]

The frontier itself was not always difficult once you were there – the issue was getting that far. In some places, there were older, traditional markers: *les bornes de la frontière*. These are boundary stones of varied designs that run all round the borders of Switzerland. On the French side, some date back to Napoleonic times. They stand about a metre high, carved from stone, with the Fleur de Lys on one side, and the Ours de Berne on the other. They are numbered to show how far along the border you are and also bear a date. There is one at the Porte de France dated 1932.

From the end of 1943, the Germans started to put barbed wire along the frontier. The River Doubs and its steep gorge served as an extra barrier further south. There were watch towers and surveillance points on both sides, and frequent patrols, often with dogs to sniff out refugees. As 1944 rolled on, the frontier was increasingly militarised; increasingly a place of bullets and death. But it was still passable, with luck and with help. A photograph of a German soldier shows a single fence of five strands of barbed wire coming up to chest height (see Fig. 14). This is an obstacle that is crossable.

Another route taken by *passeurs* is a little further west, on the other side of the border town of Delle, known as the *passage du Transformateur*. Before the war this was a site for the exchange of contraband goods. Tobacco from Switzerland was swapped for cigarette papers from France – 'It was better to be a smuggler of tobacco than of people'.[23]

A path on the outskirts of town runs down to the farm of the Monnot family, living just 100m inside France. They were known for welcoming refugees and sending them on. When the Germans realised, they took over half the house and used it for surveillance of the border, requiring much greater precautions by the smugglers. A field of maize separates this farm from another farm that looks just the same, that of the Steckmanns. But while the Monnots and their maize were in France, the Steckmanns and their walnut tree were in Switzerland. No barbed wire ran here until 1943, one simply knew.

There were also complications on the Swiss side. Where the old road crosses from Delle is a customs office. Right next to it is a curious feature known locally as the *Queue au loup* or 'wolf's tail', where a bit of Switzerland, the width of a football pitch, sticks out into France for a few hundred metres. If you didn't know the country, you could walk from France into Switzerland and back out again very quickly. A young man in Delle recalled seeing a group of thirty or more 'dirty, filthy, armed with clubs' crossing a stream very close to the *Queue au loup*, 'I stopped, they asked me "Switzerland? Switzerland?". I showed them the direction to follow. They left barefoot, in rags and rode through the fields. At the time I didn't realize who they were.'[24]

Elsewhere, the border is more obvious. There's a sharp, right-angled bend in the frontier east of Delle, near the so-called Enchanted Forest. On Mont Renaud hill there is perched Point 509, a watch tower among the beech trees with a good vantage all round. From here, the Swiss frontier guards could observe the smugglers and refugees and pick them up if they needed to.

The first person to welcome any of these sepoys to the promised land was a Swiss customs officer called François Bourquenez, a 'peaceful gardener from Boncourt', who had previously worked for local tobacco industrialist Léon Burrus.[25] Taken into the frontier force in 1939, he was also used as an intelligence agent by the Swiss Brigade de Couverture Fédérale, gathering information on what was happening in France. On the night of 15 May – just four days after the Liberators had visited their camp – Indar Singh and Bhura Ram crossed the border from Delle to Boncourt. Both men were NCOs from near Rohtak, west of Delhi, and both were Hindus.[26] Bourquenez interviewed his two guests, gleaning as much information as he could about German troops, French morale and Allied bombing. He then wrote a lengthy report, and escorted Singh and Ram to the local police at 08.45 on Tuesday, 16th – the same day that Jules Perret photographed his guests on the steps of Étobon parsonage. Little did Bourquenez or his superiors guess quite how many would follow Indar Singh and Bhura Ram, or how many interviews the quiet gardener would conduct. In fact, there were to be exactly 500 of them in all.

The last stage of the journey was often the most difficult. Many men waited patiently in the woods, hoping for the right conditions. On the night of 20 May, there was a heavy storm, and many of them took advantage of the noise and the darkness to cross over.[27] One group of Mahrattas had what their officer described as 'an exciting time' as they approached the border:

> They had been badly split up; one group ran into a German post and was fired at; the dogs were let loose, and the men hid in the crops. They had four horrible hours lying on the ground and fearing recapture at any moment. Luckily, all went well and they continued to walk on. After an hour or so they stopped to brew some tea. A farmer came up and advised them to go another 1,000 yards, as, he said, that was Swiss soil. The party ran on and crossed the border safely – but two minutes later a German motor cycle patrol appeared, just too late to do any harm![28]

Weary, footsore, hungry, but at the same time relieved, elated and victorious, they stepped on to Swiss soil. For the first time in years, they were free. Long familiar with the Red Cross flag – red on white – they now saw its white on red reverse on the Swiss flag and felt the comfort of familiarity.

Paul Frelechoux, a 20-year-old resident of Boncourt, recalled them arriving in groups of two or three, mostly at night. Because they were unsure of which country they were in, and because Swiss and German uniforms were similar, they would lie down when they saw a soldier and try to identify them from their buttons. The Swiss had the distinctive cross on their buttons, recognisable as the Red Cross.[29]

Sometimes, they arrived in larger numbers. Elisabeth Pretre of Boncourt described it as 'some evenings, whole columns crossed the village'.[30]

Generally, they encountered a civilian first, who then passed them on to the authorities. Often it was farmers who would welcome them, give them something to eat, and call the police. One local resident had a habit of telephoning the relevant embassy in Berne.[31] This was a friendly, family business that must have felt quite strange to the new arrivals.

As well as François Bourquenez, there were many officials there to record, count and interview them. Indeed, after a few days, the Swiss authorities drafted in extra help, including two British officers from the Indian Army who could speak Urdu.[32] At the end of May, the *Times of India* reported after a party of Gurkhas had crossed, 'They spoke an unknown language and knew only a few English words. Frequent repetition of the word "Gurkha", their brown complexion and turban-like head cloths established their identity.'[33]

Luckily the wife of one of the customs men could speak English.[34] A Swiss report written soon after said:

> The Indians were severely fatigued when they crossed the border; during their 8-day escape their provisions had been scant; on the other hand, they were free of vermin and well dressed; only their footwear had suffered badly … Then, separated according to religion, they were transported off to the various quarantine camps.[35]

The transport was by rail, and the station staff at Boncourt got very used to seeing Indian men in uniform waiting for trains. They were photographed repeatedly by and with locals (see Fig. 15) for, as one 18-year-old said, 'Hindus with turbans, in Boncourt it was not common'.[36] The relief is visible in their faces, many of which are radiant with smiles. Mostly, they are still in uniform, some with walking sticks or bundles, others looking more ragged.

One extraordinary photo taken shows a group of around thirty at Boncourt Station, all lined up with one row sitting, one row standing behind, with some Swiss civilians and officials. There are not so many smiles evident here, perhaps they objected to being lined up in such a military way after their freedom while on the run. Some of them look quite old, some look haggard and drawn. They carry few possessions and sport a variety of headgear, including berets, woolly hats and turbans.

By the end of May, 454 had crossed, there were forty-two more in June and four more in July and August. On 7 June, six Muslims of the Baluch Regiment and the Frontier Force crossed over. They may not have realised before their arrival, but the day before had been D-Day – the Swiss would have been quick to tell them. The war was moving towards the end, and people across Western Europe knew it.

9

Resistance

Indian soldiers are taking part in the liberation of France.[1]

As the summer of 1944 advanced, the situation across France became more confused. Allegiances shifted, troops of multiple nations came and went in large numbers, hope was on the rise. And the shifts were sometimes rapid. In the overall *longue durée* of French history, the summer of 1940 and the summer of 1944 act like bookends surrounding the Vichy regime and occupation, with liberty and self-determination outside the brackets. The summer of 1944 is also a time of pride, in retrospect, when France regained its self-respect through the activities of ordinary people like the farmer's daughters, Denise and Marie-Louise Yoder, and the Naidet family, whom we shall meet in this chapter. This was the time of the rise of the Resistance, celebrated, mythologised and commemorated almost from the moment of liberation.

There had been individuals and networks of the Resistance since the beginning of the occupation, of course, growing as the war went on and increasing with the German take-over of the south of France in the autumn of 1942. The Resistance was not a single entity, some showed loyalty to the Communist Party; some were supporters of De Gaulle and the Free French. After the invasion of Normandy, they were increasingly regularised and known as the *Forces Françaises de l'Intérieur*, or FFI. Many had been members of the armed forces during the First World War (like Jules Perret) or at the start of this war, like Francois Michel De Champeaux, who had worked with the Indian troops in France in 1940, and then joined the FFI in September 1944, becoming the chief liaison officer with the American XV Corps advancing up through Lorraine, Alsace and into Germany.[2]

In rural areas, the Resistance were generally known as the *Maquis* – the word means scrubland. In country places like Étobon, with the threat of men being taken to Germany for manual labour, the RAF dropping arms and equipment and the increasing fragility of the German occupation and its Vichy supporters, the numbers enrolled in the *Maquis* rose dramatically in 1944. Throughout the year, across the nation 140,000 *Maquisards* were armed by the RAF and 24,000 were killed in battle.[3] As well as pitched battles, sabotage continued and increased – the Peugeot factory at Sochaux near Belfort was destroyed by its own workers in November 1943.[4]

Not all the *Maquisards* were local peasants. Addi Bâ Mamadou had come from Guinea in West Africa, joined the French Army in 1939, was imprisoned by the Germans but escaped and joined the *Maquis* in the Vosges. He was captured by the Germans and shot on 18 December in 1943, but his contribution is well remembered in France.[5]

The contributions of Indian POWs, however, are less well remembered, and even disputed. The *Times of India* ran a story in August 1944 that spoke of Épinal escapees fighting with the *Maquis*, acting as snipers and guerrillas, 'Indian soldiers are taking part in the liberation of France. When the full story of their exploits is told, it will prove to be one of the most remarkable chapters in the history of the Indian Army.'[6]

On the other hand, a local French historian specialising in the period wrote, 'It is worth pointing out that these escapees categorically refused to take up arms again against the Germans.'[7]

Where lies the truth? The British Establishment was keen to make much of Indians taking up arms. The French were keen to minimise or even erase it. In both cases, they had a strong motivation for that stance.

Partly, this can be explained by tracking the movements of 950 Regiment of the German army – Bose's *Legion Freies Indien* or *Azad Hind Fauj*, recruited in the Stalags.[8] In the summer of 1944, they were in south-west France, near Bordeaux, part of the Atlantic Wall designed to keep the Allies out. After the Allied landings, the Germans were forced to withdraw from the south and centre of the country, and 950 Regiment went with them. During that withdrawal, several atrocities were committed and several Indians were shot out of hand by the FFI in Poitiers.[9]

Their retreat took them though the Belfort Gap and the Vosges, and into the area around Colmar, where they stayed for several weeks.[10] This left a strong impression in some parts of France, an impression that has almost completely overridden any memory of the escapees' involvement against the Germans. Additionally, some Indians – as, indeed, some French themselves – switched sides twice. One member of 950 Regiment helped an escaping American officer and was shot by the Germans.[11]

There are, however, a few references in French sources to Indian involvement. One source reports an Indian who joined the FFI of Montbéliard.[12] This could be the same unnamed 'old sergeant' referred to in admiring terms by Jules Perret on 17 May, 'This sergeant looked fierce, almost ferocious. The story of this Hindu does not end there. He did not want to go to Switzerland. He wanted to stay with the [Resistance] of Montbéliard … he was always after his rifle, polishing it. He was a tough fighter.'[13]

A week later, Perret wrote, 'The Germans are reacting. They fired on the Hindus at Ban. One wounded … They say that, near Vesoul, a group of Hindus who were being attacked rushed a German patrol, destroyed it and took the guns from the dead soldiers.'[14]

Some Indians were prepared to join the struggle for the liberation of France, perhaps having been welcomed by French civilians, or perhaps on general anti-German principles. A telegram from the British Embassy in Berne to the Foreign Office in London on 10 June reported thirty Indians and four or five air force evaders who joined the *Maquis* to the west of Belfort, tasked with cutting the road from Belfort to Besançon and clearing the Swiss frontier when the moment arrived.[15]

Another story from the Allied side is that of Nadir Khan. He was a havildar major in the Sikh Regiment, captured at Benghazi. During his imprisonment he 'gave the authorities considerable trouble' and so was sent to the punishment camp at Graudenz. In due course, he ended up at Épinal, having stolen a map and compass along the way. After the bombing, he joined the FFI for a period of five months and was 'employed as one of a band of silent Killers. His job was to stalk and kill any German at any time and he maintains that he actually got eleven.'[16]

He didn't escape into Switzerland but stayed with the FFI until the Americans arrived in September. The only source for this information is the medal recommendation in the National Archives in the UK, which would have had to be supported by an officer and approved by the chain of command. The note of doubt in the word 'maintains' is interesting. Nevertheless, the point of this medal is – as with most awards – to encourage the others. At a time when public opinion in India was moving against British rule, it appears that HQ was keen to keep the army on board as much as humanly possible, and gallantry awards were a key part of that.

One of those who took on a supporting role in the *Maquis* was a lascar called Moti Rahman, one of fifty-one sailors captured when the German cruiser *Atlantis* captured the *Kemmendine* in July 1940, en route to Rangoon.[17] Rahman was from Chittagong, one of the oldest ports in India, and was employed as a donkeyman, operating the steam-powered winch used to load and unload cargo. He was taken on to the *Atlantis*, then transferred to a transport ship which was then sunk by a British submarine in the Atlantic. After a few hours in the water, he was again picked up by the Germans and transported the long way to Europe, spending several years seeing 'the inside of so many German prison camps that he cannot remember them all'.[18] Having spent time at Marlag und Milag Nord, he was transferred to Épinal. After the bombing of the camp, according to a report in *Fauji Akhbar* (not a strictly neutral source):

> After wandering for days in the woods, Moti joined the Maquis, and he cooked for a detachment of that force until the Allied invasion of South France.
>
> Then he was taken to an American Army invasion unit which had made contact with the Maquis, and that was the end of his troubles.[19]

Fateh Singh from Rohtak took a more active role. He was one of the many POWs from the 2nd Royal Lancers who escaped successfully from Épinal, having already escaped from a prison in Hanover and been recaptured. According to *Fauji Akhbar*:

> Falling in with the Maquis he was an active member of this famous body of guerrillas; among his exploits with the Maquis was an attack on German barracks and posts coinciding with the invasion of Southern France.
>
> Fateh Singh and his French comrades were later joined by a party of Canadian paratroops. One of Fateh Singh's prized trophies is a map of Mulhouse area issued to him when with the Maquis.[20]

He later crossed the border near Réclère.[21]

Although these stories may have been exaggerated for propaganda effect, there must have been some truth in them. There are simply too many to have been all falsified.

Some of the other *Maquis* stories involve a romantic element as well. The most intriguing – and perhaps the most frustrating – is that of Jai

Lall from Rohtak. Lance Naik Jai Lall was one of the many POWs from the Royal Indian Army Service Corps – the RIASC. They represented around 12 per cent of the men in German POW camps, and sixty of the 500 who made it to Switzerland were from the RIASC.

Like any army in the Second World War, the Indian Army had a long tail – a minority of men were in the front line, with the bulk being support troops. The job of the RIASC was supply and transport – getting the equipment, the ammunition, the petrol to where it was needed. They were truck drivers, bakers, clerks, depot workers, and they also included the 22nd Animal Transport Company. Many had been taken prisoner at Tobruk when the whole garrison fell into enemy hands.

Jai Lall had been taken soon after that, at El Alamein in June 1942 – he was a Grade 3 Driver with the Transport Company of the 18th Brigade and had already been posted with Paiforce in Iraq or Persia. He was a young man, around 20 years of age, with a prominent mole next to his nose and piercing blue eyes. He was also a man of ambition.

Having been in the usual run of camps, including Avezzano and Limburg, Jai Lall escaped from Épinal on 11 May.[22] Unusually, it looks as if he travelled alone, and headed slightly west from many of his comrades, for he ended up at the little village of Bouligney, about 40km south of Épinal, on the edge of the forested area. According to a rather fanciful article published in *Fauji Akhbar* the following year, written by a journalist and based on Jai Lall's own account, he was discovered in a most romantic fashion – rather like 'Sleeping Beauty' – by a 16-year-old French girl called Denise Naidet:

She had found him, one fine morning, in their barn, sleeping the sleep of the innocent. With great effort she stifled a cry. She knew his presence in the barn was a great danger to herself, her parents, her brothers and sisters, in fact the whole village … The Germans had been combing the whole district. Many had been arrested: but a few were still unaccounted for. The Germans announced rewards for their arrest and threatened reprisals against those who offered them asylum.

Her first impulse was to give him away. A stranger of God knows what far-flung land. Probably an Asiatic. Yes he must be an Asiatic. Of all the Asiatic races only Indians were fighting for the Allied cause. Yes he must be an Indian. These Indians are a brave people. They fought for the liberty of France in the last Great War. Father has often told many stories about their heroic deeds. Fie on me to have thought of betraying him. No, no, it is impossible. I must protect him from his enemies, the enemies of France.

She approached gently and woke him up. He got up with a start and saw a beautiful maiden beckoning him to keep quiet.

'I know you are one of those who ran away from the Epinal camp [the] day before yesterday. The Germans have been searching around the whole of the district. Many of your companions have been recaptured. But a few are still at large. Your life is in great danger. But I'll protect you.'

'But I don't know anything about the Epinal camp.'

There he lied. Since the day of his arrest at El Alamein in 1942 he had been planning his escape; but all his efforts had, so far, proved fruitless. The Allied air raid on this camp was, therefore, a God-send and in the confusion that followed Jai Lal [*sic*], along with many of his fellow prisoners, made good his escape. For two days he remained in the woods, keeping himself away from all habitations and human beings. Hunger, fatigue and his good luck at last drove him to this barn, where he lay exhausted, in deep slumber, until the young … beautiful French maiden woke him up.

'Then who are you and what brings you here?'

'I am a captain in the Army. I have been dropped by a parachute to organize resistance against the Germans.' He lied again; but not without reason. During his hiding in the woods he had had enough time to formulate his plans which he now wished to put in practice.

'Are you an Indian?'

'Yes, I am an Indian. I belong to the province of the Punjab in Northern India.'

'What is your name?'

'Jai Lal. And yours.'

'Denise. You sit here quietly. I'll be coming in a moment.'

Denise went to her home, called her parents, her three brothers and a sister. She related the whole story to them and sought their advice. They were unanimous in giving Jai Lal protection and help. For three days Jai Lal hid there, while Nazi search parties combed the surrounding countryside in vain. When darkness fell Denise took him food. His only clothes were his battledress. The kindly French people gave him an old jacket and trousers and a pair of boots.[23]

The bones of this story are confirmed by the Naidet family, and many of the details match up. Denise's nephew, Jean-Noël, still lives on the

Rue des Cores, next door to his grandfather's house with its fruit trees bearing cherries and Mirabelle plums, overlooking the main road. Paul and Georgette Naidet did indeed have five children – three boys, called Pierre, Serge and Jean, the oldest sister, Yvette, and the young one, the 'beautiful maiden' called Ginette, but known as Denise.[24] They still remember the '*Hindou*' who lived with them that Indian summer, and Jean-Noël's mother recalls him going off on a bicycle with Denise.

The flowery detail of the story is only found in the accounts that came from our hero, Jai Lall himself. Which poses the historian a question: we already know that he is lying – he's told us that he pretended to be a captain – so how can we trust his word on other details? We can only present what we've found, show the mismatch and leave it up to the reader to believe what you will.

Soon after his arrival in the village, according to our hero's account in *Fauji Akhbar*, the story moved from flight to fight:

After a few days the hue and cry died down. Jai Lal suggested to Denise's two elder brothers that they should join him in the fight against the Germans. They agreed and gave him two rifles, a pistol, and ammunition, so the group came into being.

Their first action, at the end of May, 1944, was the destruction of a military goods train by mining a bridge. In June they held up three German trucks, taking six prisoners and capturing two rifles, two submachine guns and two vehicles.

Following this success, ten local Frenchmen joined Jai Lal's company. By the end of the month the band totalled 30. They held up another small German convoy, taking arms and ammunition.

The resistance group lived in the woods. Food was supplied by the villagers, and money obtained from the captives. The group wore a form of battledress made secretly by the village tailor. All wore the badge of the French Forces of the Interior on their left breast.

At the end of June a French captain took over command of the group, now 50 strong. Two months later they scored their biggest victory over a strong German transport column on the road to Mayencourt, not far from St. Loup, capturing a lieutenant, five other ranks, and a quantity of equipment.

On another occasion Jai Lal was personally responsible for the capture of a German officer, complete with motor-cycle.[25]

This all sounds rather exciting. What an adventure! Unfortunately, the French records and the local memories do not bear out this version. There was a Resistance group in Bouligney, for sure. Pierre Naidet – the oldest son – was a strapping young lad of 21. Like his father and his brother, he was a stonemason, which entailed 'walking through the village with 50 kg of cement on your shoulder'.[26] Knowing of their strength and skills, the Germans wanted them to work on building fortifications in Normandy, but the brothers had other ideas. Every time the Germans came to pick them up, the brothers slipped over the wall and took refuge in the forest.[27]

Pierre lived to be 97 and died in 2020, and the regional newspaper published an article about his memories of the Resistance in 2011, 'We were 7 or 8 at the start, with not many weapons, a few hunting rifles. Gradually, we found ourselves around thirty, the weapons arrived with the prisoners.'[28]

He recalled sabotage, liaison missions, dynamite and attacking a German convoy: the same events that Jai Lall recounted. But no mention of an Indian in their company, let alone at their head. Their greatest success was 'when we unhooked the carriages of the train at Bains, pushed them 10 meters and they sped towards the station at Aillevillers: we heard when they tumbled over at the station! How we laughed!'

The journalist asked Pierre if he felt no fear. 'Fear of what? We didn't think of that! Living hidden, in the woods, changing location, saying nothing, facing enemy columns, risking one's life, seeing one's brothers in arms perish before one's eyes … the daily life of the FFI.'

What can we make of this? Jai Lall was there in that village. He lived with the family for months, he joined in the *Maquis* activities with Pierre and Serge, that much is certain. It seems highly unlikely that they would allow a man who spoke little French to lead them, and no corroboration of that has yet emerged. But the British saw fit to award him the Indian Order of Merit, second only to the Victoria Cross in precedence.

Liberation came to the village on Saturday, 16 September, at the hands of the 3rd US Infantry Division. Rolland Naidet – Denise's cousin – was aged 10 at the time. The next day, Rolland's uncle René was not prepared to wait for the Americans and went off hunting Germans. He was captured, his eyes and teeth were put out, and he was shot – his memorial is in the town square at St Loup. Rolland recalled seeing a jeep arrive on the previous day and the American soldiers in it saluted the '*noir*' in the village, whom we assume was Jai Lall.[29] If that was truly

Jai Lall, the fact that they saluted him would indicate that they believed him to be an officer. The story that Jai Lall told was different:

> An armoured column rattled up the road. Jai Lal ran out to meet them
> – only to be met with a burst of fire. They were American troops who
> had failed to recognise him as an ally.
>
> Later, British paratroops arrived, and Jai Lal, armed this time with
> a white flag, contacted them, and explained who he was. Soon after
> he reported to British Army Headquarters in Paris.[30]

So, what happened next? According to what Jai Lall later told British officers when he was in England, on 12 August – five weeks before the date of liberation – he had married Denise in the Catholic church at Bouligney.[31] The *Fauji Akhbar* report said, 'The marriage was a hurried affair. No church bells rang. No guests invited. It was a unique marriage in many respects. A Punjabi youth wedding a French belle. The spirit of adventure, a feeling of common danger and Patriotism had drawn them nearer.'[32]

A few weeks after that, they were both near Paris, staying with a M. Auguste Miouris. The report from the Indian Army liaison officer says, 'There has been question of validity of marriage.'[33] To add to the mystery, there is no record of the marriage in the village records, although nephew Jean-Noël thought that they had flirted and cousin Rolland thought that they had been married, and even that there was a baby. This story is hard to unravel.

★★★

In a similar way, Havildar Major Vishram Rao Shinde of the Mahrattas had a busy time after his escape. He led twenty of the prisoners out of the camp after the bombing, under fire from the guards. He and four of his comrades joined the local FFI near Roulier de Xertigny, where he fell ill and was cared for by a local girl called Francoise Bazin. Of course, he fell in love.[34] When he was better, he joined in the FFI activity and eventually the Americans reached him in the autumn. He was also awarded the Military Medal.[35]

These were not the only Indian POWs with a romantic entanglement in Europe. The Garhwals still tell stories of two men from their regiment who escaped from a German POW camp during the First World War, married and had children and never returned to India. This seemed to be more difficult in the 1940s. Sepoy Bindra deserted from the Legion in July 1944 and joined the *Maquis*. Later, he took up with a French woman, who had a child by him, and Bindra was allowed to return to France temporarily under escort, to 'give the child a name'.[36]

It's easy to think that European women would have had nothing in common with Indian men, that the language and cultural barriers were impassable and such relationships were doomed. Paidal Khan's story shows how hard people were prepared to try. He was taken prisoner in North Africa in 1942, and after various camps, landed at one near Dresden, possibly Stalag IV-E at Altenburg. The Baluch regiment history continues:

> In August 1944, while attempting to escape he was shot in the knee and admitted in a hospital. Here he was nursed and cared by [*sic*] a German girl, named Rosa who persuaded the doctor not to amputate his leg. The soldier could only murmur his gratitude to the girl, which she with the aid of a dictionary tried to answer. On recovery, Paidal Khan went back to his camp, taking [with him] the memory of the girl and her tender caring. When the Russians came he was set free and allowed to move into the city, pending repatriation to the British Zone. He sought out the girl and offered his protection and when called by the Russians, requested permission to take his girlfriend with him, which was granted.
>
> In Berlin, Paidal Khan sought out the highest Urdu speaking officer, told his story and got permission to go to Konigsberg [*sic*], the girl's hometown. On 29 October 1945, he was married at the Registry Office and on return to Berlin, it was solemnized under the Islamic Law. Their honeymoon was brief, since Paidal Khan was soon despatched to India via England and his wife was interned in a Displaced Persons Camp. They maintained a steady flow of letters in Roman Urdu, while the [regiment] made efforts to reunite them.[37]

The regimental history does not tell us whether these efforts paid off.

Another German story with a less positive outcome came from Wittenberg, Martin Luther's town, and concerns a prisoner on a work detail:

> Indian POW Shaktee Singh was digging a ditch in June 1944 when he noticed that a woman was watching him from a nearby house. She smiled when he looked at her. He saw her again on the following days.

In an unguarded moment, he threw some chocolate and soap through a window of her apartment. Then, he visited her and they kissed and hugged. A few days later, they had sex. It is unclear whether a guard noticed him or whether a neighbour denounced them, but the affair was discovered. The court martial in Leipzig sentenced Singh to three years in prison on December 22, 1944. He denied everything, but she confessed, and, as usual, her confession was used as evidence against him.[38]

Again, it is unclear what happened next, but we can hope that he was freed a few months later and got home in due course.[39]

In one case, there is clear data from both the French and the British sides about the presence of a soldier of the Indian Army in the *Maquis*. But this was not an Indian soldier, rather he was a Gurkha. Harkabahadur Rai was a havildar in the 2nd Battalion of the 7th Gurkha Rifles, captured at Tobruk with so many of his comrades (see Fig. 16). He went through the usual succession of camps in Italy and Germany and ended up at Épinal in 1944. He wasn't part of the mass escape on 11 May, but escaped a little later with another Gurkha havildar.

After various adventures, he ended up with the *Maquis* of Lomont, a large camp near Saint-Hippolyte, south of Belfort. The *Maquis* here were under the command of an American, Captain Ernest Floege – known as Paul – who had been born in Chicago of German parents. Despite his 45 years, his SOE file says he was 'remarkably fit' but 'very much an egoist'.[40] He had been parachuted in by the RAF in early May to help organise the local *Maquis*. They had men, they increasingly had arms, they had a structure of sorts, but they needed somebody like Floege to bring them together. This is precisely what he proceeded to do.

Floege's mixed band of French peasants and workers was joined by one man from far-off Nepal, whom nobody quite knew how to place. As Harkabahadur himself said, 'All the Frenchmen I met always took me for a man from Indo-China, and I usually had to show them on a map where Nepal was.'[41]

After various routine *Maquis* activities throughout the summer, and with the Allies advancing across France, Floege's forces had built up to the point that he felt ready to try something bigger. On 22 August, he took his men to the high ground of Lomont. The Germans attacked immediately up the mountainside. Floege asked for volunteers to hold them off, and Harkabahadur put himself and his Bren gun forward.

He wrote, 'I had the job of holding a road block and shot about 12 magazines full into advancing Germans. My party also knocked out a German tank. The Germans had set fire to a village and a lot of civilians were killed.'[42]

Floege's account is somewhat different, however. He wrote that the '*Hindou*' with the only machine gun 'seemed paralysed with fear', so another soldier took the weapon.[43] Again, we will never know what happened in the heat of that battle. The Gurkha havildar had put himself forward, in the line of fire, and perhaps he found the action too much at that precise moment. He was not fighting for his homeland, so perhaps his motivation was less than that of Sergeant Thibault, who took the gun.

Eventually, the Germans were pushed back with heavy losses. Floege's men took more and more of the mountainous borderlands, including a frontier crossing, until the Allies arrived on 9 September.[44] Harkabahadur went back to England, and on 6 October – after several press interviews – he was on a boat back to India.[45] In due course, he was awarded the Military Medal.[46]

Others joined the FFI elsewhere in France. There were several in the Bordeaux region who had deserted from the Legion.[47] One such was Signaller Benjamin Nambi, a Christian in the Signal Corps. In the spring of 1945, a British officer of the Indian Army was in the Médoc area, when:

> … he was astonished to see a Hindu soldier in French FFI uniform loading a lorry with some French soldiers. He spoke good English and gave Lt Friend the following details.
>
> He is … Signalman Benjamin Nambi, who was taken prisoner by the Germans in Tobruk. Later he was sent to France as a worker dressed in German uniform. In 1943 he ran away and joined the Maquis of Lesparres. This latter part was confirmed by the local inhabitants.
>
> He stated that he most emphatically wished to return to the British forces and eventually to India where he has a wife and children.[48]

It looks as if even some of those who had been part of the German army were sufficiently trusted by the French to be put in uniform. Their loyalties had been stretched, even to breaking point, their motivations can only be guessed at.

Fig. 1: A group of Indian POWs at Altenburg, June 1941. (V-P-HIST-03103-15, ICRC)

Fig. 2: Sikhs at prayer at Altenburg, June 1941. (V-P-HIST-03518-05, ICRC)

Fig. 3: Tug of war at Limburg, 1944. (V-P-HIST-E-00531, ICRC)

Fig. 4: Harbakhash Singh skiing at Adelboden. (Photo: Klopfenstein, Adelboden)

Fig. 5: Staff of the Indian Comforts Fund outside India House. (Papers of Leo Amery, AMEL 10/38, Churchill Archives Centre)

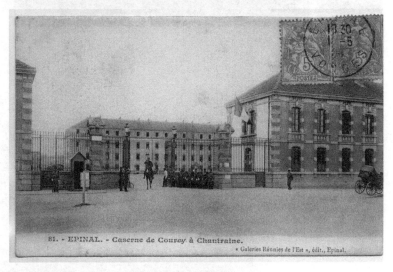

Fig. 6: Gateway to the barracks at Épinal, the central part of the POW camp. Popular postcard from before the Great War. The gateway and the buildings in the foreground still stand, surrounded by a housing estate.

81. – ÉPINAL. – Caserne de Courcy à Chantraine.

« Galeries Réunies de l'Est », édit., Épinal.

Fig. 7: Some of the medical staff at Épinal. Dr Third is probably extreme left, with Dr Seal next to him. (V-P-HIST-03441-25A, ICRC)

Fig. 8: Snow at Épinal, February 1944. (V-P-HIST-03439-22, ICRC)

Fig. 9: Clearing the rubble, 26 June 1944. (V-P-HIST-03436-02A, ICRC)

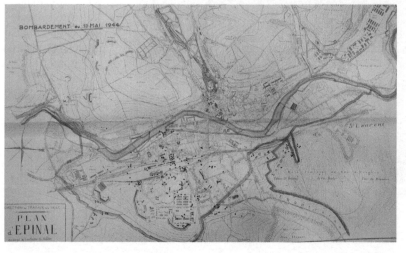

Fig. 10: Map of the 'Bombardement du 11 Mai 1944' from the local authorities. (Archives Départementales des Vosges, 16 W 17)

Fig. 11: Tuesday, 16 May 1944 – thirteen escapers on the steps of the *presbytère* at Étobon. (Jules Perret, Photo Presbytère Évadés, 1944, Société d'Émulation de Montbéliard, Fonds Jean-Marc Debard)

Fig. 12: Jules Perret. (*L'illustré* magazine)

Fig. 13: Charlotte Biediger in traditional Alsacienne costume in 1937, which was forbidden during the occupation. (Private collection)

Fig. 14: German at the Swiss frontier, near Delle. (Private collection)

Fig. 15: New arrivals in Boncourt, May 1944. (Private Collection)

Hav. Harkabir Rai, 7th Gurkha Rifles, who escaped three times from German P. O. W. camps.

Fig. 16: Harkabir Rai. (*Fauji Akhbar*, The United Service Institution of India)

Fig. 17: After the delousing process in Olten, a naik (possibly a Rajput) collects his clean clothes. (Swiss Federal Archives; J1.257#1997/157#25★)

Fig. 18: 12 April 1945, the liberation of Oflag 79 by Gordon Horner, *For You the War Is Over*. (London: Falcon Press, 1948)

Fig. 19: Gurkha ex-POWs at a funfair in London, summer 1945. (*Fauji Akhbar*, The United Service Institution of India)

Fig. 20: Arrivals at Lahore Station. (*Fauji Akhbar*, 25 September 1945, The United Service Institution of India)

Fig. 21: Épinal Cemetery. (Ghee Bowman, 2023)

Fig. 22: 20 May 1949, dignitaries leaving the *Mairie* after the *Croix de Guerre* ceremony at Étobon. (*L'illustré* magazine)

Fig. 23: Suresh and Samsher holding a portrait of their father, Jai Lall. (Ghee Bowman)

Fig. 24: Some of the Épinal escapers, February 1945. (*Fauji Akhbar*, The United Service Institution of India)

ESCAPED FROM NAZIS

Indian soldiers who have spent long periods in German P.O.W. camps recently reached home after their escape from Nazis.

RIGHT: Some of the P.O.Ws, from L to R: Sepoy Mohd. Zarait, Hav. Ganpatrao Rawde, W/O R.R. Dave, Jem. O. P. Bhardwaj, Hav.-Major Amir Zaman.

Major J. E. Little-Jones, 5th M. L. I., officer-in-charge of the repatriated prisoners, with Jem. Ram Pratab Singh.

L to R: Hav. Bhopal Singh Rauntigal, Royal Garhwal Rifles; V. S. Sivour, I.A.C.C. and Sowar Harbans Singh Sandhu, P.W.O. Cavalry.

Sowar Daryao Singh, 2nd Royal Lancers.

Sowar Fateh Singh, 2nd Royal Lancers.

Hav.-Major Shripatrao Gaikawad.

Willkommen, Bienvenue, Benvenuti

Post tenebras lux [after darkness, light].[1]

Meanwhile, the Épinal escapers had arrived in their Promised Land: the Helvetican Confederation, Switzerland. This is an old country at the core of Europe, where three major languages meet, a land that defies concepts of nation state and nationalism. Major watersheds are found there, rivers that flow towards the Mediterranean, the North Sea and the Black Sea. And just like a watershed, when you cross a ridge you are in a new language zone. In Fribourg, they speak French on one riverbank, German on the other.

There is always water around in Switzerland: lakes, snow, streams and rivers. There are always mountains too, in the background of any conversation: jagged teeth, like canines, with snow imperfectly painted along their tips.

For the new arrivals from Épinal, crossing its North-West Frontier, it might have felt familiar – especially for those from Punjab, Kashmir or Nepal. Perhaps they felt an affinity with this mountainous place with its mix of languages and cows all around. Like India, agriculture is crucial in this country of small farms and large barns, cowbells and vineyards and stacks of firewood. Their stay lasted just one summer, from May to September, but we can imagine that it lingered in their imaginations for years afterwards.

Broadly speaking, the Swiss people were spared the turmoil of the war that raged all around, across every frontier. The Indian Ambassador there in the 1950s wrote, 'My one thought travelling up and down the country was that this is what all Europe might have been, if the European had not destroyed himself in two World Wars.'[2]

From November 1942 onwards, the Swiss people inhabited an island of neutrality surrounded by the Axis occupation. Of course, they had sympathies for this side or the other, partly driven by their linguistic roots. But simply because the majority spoke German does not mean they were pro-Nazi before or during the war, indeed there were many anti-Nazi Germans and Austrians. The President of the ICRC during the war – Max Huber – wrote in 1948:

> Switzerland – and we mean thereby the solid and overwhelming majority of the Swiss people – holds fast to the irrevocable political axiom of its neutrality. It will do so as long as this is humanly possible, with no thought of yielding to any momentary consideration of political expediency of any kind.[3]

This 'irrevocable political axiom' of neutrality has a long history, going back to the sixteenth century, with the last invasion of the country during the Napoleonic era. This does not mean, however, that Swiss people were not ready for war if necessary. There is a long tradition of Swiss mercenaries serving abroad, in the famous Vatican Swiss Guards and the guards for the French monarch, commemorated in the *Loewen Denkmal* (Lion Monument) in Luzern. Like the Gurkhas of Nepal, they have stayed out of wars as a country, but gained military experience and been paid for it as individuals.

The Swiss are also accustomed to hosting large numbers of soldiers seeking refuge. The prime example of this before the Second World War occurred in February 1871, during the Franco-Prussian War. A French army led by General Charles-Denis Bourbaki was defeated by the Germans and surrounded. They requested asylum for the whole army of 87,000 soldiers and 12,000 horses, and were admitted across the Jura Mountains, the majority at Les Verrières. The French were distributed around the country and stayed for only a few weeks, departing in the middle of March, leaving 1,701 of their number behind in cemeteries.[4] In a country with a population of just over 2.5 million, this represented an influx of one extra person for every thirty inhabitants, all young, all male, many hungry and wounded. They were each allocated 280g of meat and 680g of bread, and paid 25c per day.[5]

This experiment in hosting was to become a significant moment in Swiss history, and a turning point in the development of the Red Cross. For the Swiss, it was immortalised by the artist Edouard Castres, who was present at Les Verrières as a volunteer medic.[6] He led a team that painted the 'Bourbaki Panorama', now housed in a special building in

Luzern. This is a circular painting, viewed from the inside, that depicts a wintry scene with French troops of the 66th Battalion crossing the border and being disarmed by Swiss troops. The Swiss Army are in control, the mighty French are in crisis, in need of aid.

A caption at the panorama describes the intervention as 'an impressive demonstration of the strength of solidarity in times of crisis'.[7] This work of art has become a symbol for the Swiss nation, a memorial of their generosity to strangers, a stake in the ground that declares 'we can do this again'.

Interestingly, the 1871 French army included troops from North Africa – *Tirailleurs Algérien de Marche*, known as 'Turcos' and the *Infanterie Légère d'Afrique*, known as 'Zephyrs'.[8] For many Swiss, this was the first time they had met people from outside Europe, mostly Muslims. The official government report recorded:

> The Turcos and other natives of Africa, for whom the satisfaction of material instincts is the first condition of happiness, were, to the great astonishment of all the country people, the first to be cheered up, despite the cold and their costume, which did not support it. After one or two days, those among them who were not ill were as happy as finches, while the Frenchman remained for a long time still under the weight of the misfortunes of his country and the disasters of the army.[9]

Such exoticisation may have lingered into the twentieth century and influenced the 1940s encounters of Swiss civilians with soldiers from outside Europe. The Indian soldiers of 1944 were not the first from South Asia either. An official report on the Indians from Épinal, written as context for a Swiss readership said, 'What is certain is that black people came to Switzerland during the First World War; it seems that among these refugees there were also Anamites [*sic*] from Indochina, then Sikhs and Gurkhas from India.'[10]

Central to modern Swiss identity, therefore, are the twin ideas of the Red Cross and armed neutrality. The Geneva Convention was made in Switzerland, by an individual sovereign nation tiptoeing its way through the alliances and the differences. The principle of reciprocity was key – the ICRC had no sanctions for those who broke the Geneva Convention.[11]

The counterpart to the ICRC under Max Huber was the Swiss military led by General Henri Guisan. Military service was compulsory before the war, shooting clubs were universally popular and rifles were kept at home.[12] On 25 June 1940, five days after the Germans had taken over duties at the border post at Delle, Guisan called all the officers of the Swiss Army to Rütli, the site of the 1307 oath that created the Swiss Confederation.[13] At a time of real worry about a German invasion from the north, Guisan outlined his strategy, to put the bulk of the army in the national redoubt in the southern mountains, with only a screen of troops on the border and mobile forces to slow down the advance.[14] This neutrality was not a weakness, but was rather a muscular neutrality, one that was prepared to fight hard if invaded, in defence of their democracy and their independence.[15]

The Swiss record during the war is not spotless, however. The government granted credits to the German Reich and allowed arms exports and gold exchange to and from Italy and Germany.[16] As the war went on, Jews in flight from the Nazis found it increasingly hard to enter the country and all but impossible after August 1942 – around 20,000 civilian refugees were rejected at the border.[17] In October 1942, the ICRC, with full knowledge of what the Nazis were doing in concentration camps, met to discuss whether or not to launch a public appeal on behalf of Jews in Europe. They decided against the motion as they thought it would compromise their work with POWs. This decision has 'haunted it ever since'.[18]

Indians, however, were welcome. As they crossed over into the green pastures, the men from Épinal looked around them, smelled the air and started to take stock of this new land. This was a richer land than the one they had left, not occupied or bombed by an enemy, with smiles on the faces of the people instead of fear. Like other Europeans, the people were pale and dressed in plain colours. Women worked in factories – 'in India, [white] women don't even gather tennis balls, here they make munitions'.[19] There was only one place of worship, 'They are all Christians of one kind or another. They do not quarrel about their religions as we do ... They do not really bother very much about religion.'[20] Above all, they ruled themselves. There was no foreign power running the country.

Even if there are few sources that reflect this culture shock from the Indian side, the Swiss authorities were very capable of observing their new guests and making judgements on them. The Swiss military wrote a report in mid-June, intended to provide information to colleagues in future camps. From a twenty-first-century viewpoint, it reads like an old-fashioned orientalist text, revealing Swiss prejudices and experiences.[21] Like an amateur anthropologist, the author divides the escapees into Muslims, Hindus and Gurkhas, and Sikhs. Hindus have a 'considerable' knowledge of languages and their marching discipline is 'amazing'. Gurkhas are 'small, of Mongolian overtones; they have slanted eyes like the Chinese'. Hindus will fit in if you don't spoil them heavily at first. Muslims 'love their tea hot and sweet'. The discourse is reminiscent of the Indian Army recruitment handbooks, designed to categorise, classify and manage.[22]

A lot of typewriter ribbon was expended on the question of food, slaughtering and dietary preferences. Hindus 'are big eaters, one gets the impression that they would eat more if you could give more'. The report reflects on their preferred musical instruments (piano, harmonium and violin) and their love of the radio for music and the news in English. Hygiene is another key topic:

> The Indians are extremely clean. They wash their entire body once almost every day. They often bathe in cold water before sunrise. The Sikhs are the only ones who tie their hair up fully in a turban, but all, especially the Mohammedans, take great pains in their hair care.

With this focus, one wonders how often the Swiss soldiers washed, or whether they had got used to the strong smell of French and American military internees. The writer talks about games and pastimes, religious practices, smoking and drinking alcohol. 'The Mohammedans don't drink alcohol, nor the Hindus beer; the Sikhs don't smoke, the Mohammedans do a lot, the Hindus also have no smoking ban.'

The sense of frustration by the Swiss writer is palpable – why can't they be like us? And yet in some ways they are. 'Yet they are much less oriental than it is believed; along with their own card games, they play bridge and chess, also football and handball. They're familiar with the electric razor as well!'

The highest praise is reserved for the Sikhs, who are 'big, brisk men, distinguished by a soldierly attitude, which is far superior to that of the two other main tribes'. All together, these soldiers are exotic, strange, 'other', but in some cases, noble. The report concludes, 'As a broad generality, the following should be noted: the Indian wants to be treated as a human being.'

This last sentence implies a tendency among the guards to treat these men as something other than human. Even in the peaceful neutral country at the heart of Europe, the racism of the time had penetrated.

Of course, the Indians were not the only contingent of foreign troops in Switzerland at that time. Far from it, in fact. In June of 1940, 43,000 French and Polish soldiers entered from the west, very much as the Bourbaki army had done seventy years before, only this time they had tanks as well as horses.[23] The French were repatriated at the start of 1941, but the Poles stayed for the duration.[24] In autumn 1943, after the Italian capitulation, 23,000 Italians came across, followed by around 7,000 escaped prisoners of various nationalities, although no Indians reached Switzerland that way.[25]

The Swiss Army found itself building 300 new camps and looking after tens of thousands of internees, escapees and evaders. The distinction between the three categories was a legal one but could have serious implications. Internees were armed combatants like the Poles in 1940 and the 1,700 US aircrew, and were not allowed to leave until the end of the war.[26] Escapees were men like our Indians, and evaders were those who had never been captured.[27] Escapees and evaders were free to move around within the neutral territory and could also leave the country.[28] As far as the Swiss Army was concerned, an escaper from the Reich was free to go, and would be one less mouth to feed.[29] By the end of the war the Swiss had accommodated a total of 105,000 military internees, escapers and evaders of thirty-eight nationalities, including Russians, Yugoslavs and 7,500 Germans.[30] By the time the Indians crossed the North-West Frontier, there were several thousand Commonwealth soldiers in the country, including around 4,000 other ranks, most of whom had crossed the Italian border.[31]

The Britishers were organised into companies, distributed in camps around the country – perhaps the best-known being at Adelboden, in the Alps, where the USAAF fliers were placed, and where a British church was found.[32] This was a popular location to learn to ski, as Harbakhash Singh had done. The British escaper community even had its own newspaper called *Marking Time*.[33] Starting as a cheaply produced and duplicated publication, it went on to become a high-quality newspaper with adverts, cartoons and photos, costing 20c. Articles included football reports and notices on POWs' weddings to local girls, but they only managed three articles and one photo on the Indians, despite their large numbers after Épinal.

When the new arrivals had settled down, they found that they were not the only people from South Asia in the country. There were a few civilians, including a medical student called Madhukar Musale, who was attached to the British Consulate at Geneva.[34] There were also seventeen other soldiers, who had all escaped from camps in France or Germany. As well as Captain Mazumdar, there were three jemadars, twelve other ranks and one cook, Abdul Matlab of the Gurkhas.[35] They had been accommodated in hotels in Montreux and received subsistence of 600 francs for VCOs and 300 francs for the others, on top of their pay. The embassy worried about the expense and relocated them to Adelboden, where they were put in catered billets and the subsistence was stopped.[36]

Skiing proved a popular pursuit with many. Jemadar Lakhi Ram of the 2nd Royal Lancers had escaped with Captain Mazumdar and Daryao Singh from Frontstalag 153 at Chartres in France. They had taken six weeks to cross France, and entered Switzerland near Morteau on the Doubs River, nearly a year before Barkat Ali was shot there.[37] After Lakhi Ram's return to India, *Fauji Akhbar* reported that he had enjoyed his stay in the alpine country:

> It was in the friendly atmosphere of his new home that the jemadar embarked on a new career, learning English so well that he now acts as interpreter for his friends.
>
> He also took lessons in skiing with such proficiency that he was awarded a first-class certificate by the Basle Ski Club.[38]

Not everything was quite so positive for these earlier escapers, however. Two other Jemadars from the 2nd Royal Lancers – Hari Raj Singh and Ram Partap Singh – had been the first Indians to enter Switzerland, on 17 March 1943, having escaped from a train taking them from Oflag IX-A/Z, south of Kassel, in central Germany. After being debriefed by Cartwright, they were put in a hotel in Montreux 'under unofficial care of retired officer with long Indian experience', Lieutenant Colonel G. McPherson.

There is a strong feeling that the Military Attaché, the War Office and the India Office were suspicious of them – a later telegram from Berne said that McPherson was 'keeping an eye on key escapers. He believes them 100% loyal but will continue to observe.'[39]

The mistrust clearly relates to the reports of Bose's activities in camps in Germany, his recruitment for the *Azad Hind Fauj*, and a feeling that perhaps these were false escapes fabricated by the Germans with the intention that these two men might become spies. It seems mealy-mouthed to have rewarded these men's amazing achievements in crossing hundreds of miles in strange territory by questioning their loyalty.

By the summer of 1944, the British had realised that all the escapes were genuine, and there was no such suspicion of the men from Épinal. The grand total of Indians who crossed into Switzerland between 15 May and the end of August was exactly 500.[40] According to MI9, 4,916 Commonwealth escapers and evaders reached that haven, so more than 10 per cent of those were Indian.[41]

The appendix gives a complete list of all the Indians who made it to Switzerland, including the seventeen already there and the three who arrived in 1945. It is of interest to note that the 500 included 228 NCOs – a very large percentage – as well as one jemadar and one warrant officer, who had been in Épinal disguised as NCOs. Those two – Omparkash Bhardwaj of RIASC and V.S. Sivon of the Corps of Clerks – could have been living a comparatively easy life in Oflag 79 with so many other VCOs and warrant officers but preferred to join their juniors at Épinal in the hope of being able to get away.

As well as the 258 privates, there were also twenty followers – men not actually enlisted in the army, who were there to provide essential services. These are the men 'who never are in the limelight and who rarely get honours and awards', specifically ten cooks, five barbers, three water carriers – the Gunga Dins of the army – a groom and a sweeper.[42] Truly, the Épinal escapers were from all levels of the army.

They also came from right across India. As well as from every part of Punjab, their hometowns were Jaipur and Jodhpur, Lunavada and Vizagapatam, Bombay, Assam and Darjeeling. There were also fifty-one Gurkhas, who were not from India at all, but from Nepal. The largest groups were from the Indian Armoured Corps, with fifty-six from the 2nd Royal Lancers alone, and fifty-seven from the RIASC, including nine from the 22nd Animal Transport Company, who had been in German hands the longest.

Thus, we can see that it was not only the front-line infantry and cavalrymen who had the necessary levels of fitness and gumption to make that long walk. As well as the Baluchs, Mahrattas and Garhwalis, there were seven from the 1212 Pioneer Company – men whose job was digging and carrying and constructing – indicating a strong sense of community in that particular group.

Four sepoys and a naik from a Field Hygiene Section of the Medical Corps entered Switzerland together on 19 May, a clear example of men who had stuck together and kept each other going. There were four from the Indian Army Corps of Clerks and two from the Postal Service – administrative workers whose job was to sit behind a desk with a type-writer and carbon paper, but who could hike over 100km when needed.

And there were eight from the Remount Department, Muslim mule handlers from Kashmir, Jhelum, Rajasthan and Sargodha, caught up in the fiasco in Greece in the spring of 1941, who had now spent over three years in Europe. Soldiers who are not seen as traditionally heroic or glamorous or worthy of being photographed, but soldiers from across India who could screw their courage to the sticking place and walk for days on end on slim rations, hiding from their pursuers by day, with the threat of recapture always in their minds. No mean feat for any soldier.

Once they had arrived in Switzerland and eaten a large meal, they had to undergo various administrative and medical processes. The prefect of the district of Porrentruy had developed his skills in dealing with such an influx during the summer of 1940, when they were overwhelmed with French military and civil refugees.[43] A local newspaper recorded that some Sikhs:

> ... refuse at first to get rid of their turban, it is a precept of their religion. Their leader ends up convincing them, it is a hygiene measure required by the Swiss authorities. We then realize that, under the wide strip of fabric, most of them are covered with lice and vermin. They are immediately quarantined to avoid any risk of transmission to the population.[44]

A Swiss documentary film shows a delousing process (for other soldiers) that starts with spraying the men, who then strip and shower, while their uniforms are loaded into a bulk steamer for fumigation.[45] A Swiss photographer was also there to record the same process at the Disteli garage in Olten (see Fig. 17). The British Captain Edward Mumford of the Gurkhas enjoyed this process, which he had experienced on the Italian border earlier in the year. He said he had had 'glorious hot water showers and baths' and then they were given Swiss Army dungarees to wear until their clothes were ready.[46] An Indian version of events also reveals some of the medical needs, 'A medical examination revealed a few people with foot problems and many showed signs of fatigue. After the personal details were recorded, we had to undergo a body search. After 2 days we moved to Olten, and then to Luterbach and Schönenwerd.'[47]

So, they started to settle into their new home. With so many men, it was no longer practical for the Swiss to keep them in hotels, and so they found themselves once more in camps, as they had been in North Africa, Italy, Germany and France. Their first destination was four camps in Solothurn, a German-speaking area between Basel and Berne. They were – as usual – separated by religion and language, with the Muslims going to Biberist and Luterbach, the Hindus and Gurkhas in Schönenwerd, and the Sikhs in Egerkingen.[48]

Thankfully, there was rather more freedom and relaxation here than in German Stalags, as the photographs from the Sikh camp in Egerkingen show. After the influx of escaped POWs into the country from Italy in the autumn of 1943, Swiss Colonel Probst had prepared detailed instructions on the 'regime' that should be followed.[49]

Other ranks should stay near the camp but could request travel with a white permit (for short duration) or a blue permit for longer trips. There was a roll call every evening, and escapees were required to work. They were allowed to display a flag or emblem inside but not outside their barracks and could hold 'public manifestations' (celebrations or demonstrations) under certain conditions and with notice. Beer and wine were available in the camps, but the abuse of alcohol was punishable.[50]

Marriage to a local woman was permitted if the home government would permit it. No Indian took up this last offer, but several British escapees did.

Altogether, this was a decidedly more relaxed regime than they had been used to, and a step in the direction of real freedom. They were still subject to military discipline, however. There was a *Straflager* (punishment camp) at Wauwilermoos, and at least one sepoy – Mahmud Khan of the 22nd Company – spent some time there for theft.[51] As for the provision for getting them to work, the Swiss had the same difficulty as the Germans had, as reported by the same anonymous officer:

Some individuals wish to work, others less so. The Sikhs for instance express the desire to work in agriculture or to be able to work in the factories. Of the Jats it's said that they are regarded as the best farmers in India. On average, then, they should be used for field work. The view of a camp commandant is as follows: 'You can use them for sawing and splitting wood as well, but it's a bit awkward. You have to arouse ambition in the Indians, this will give satisfactory results.'[52]

There are good accounts of the camps in Solothurn, especially the Sikh camp at Egerkingen.[53] Sleeping accommodation was found in two large dining halls of the Halbmond and Hammer restaurants, with straw to sleep on. Their guards were from the 'local army' – men who had either completed their compulsory military service or not yet started. They were put into old military uniforms, marked with armbands and armed with a rifle. Their job was to guard the camp entrances and to try to keep the local population at a distance.[54]

The Indians' food was prepared in the kitchen of the local fire department, but the Swiss 'simple military fare' was not to their taste, so they also cooked for themselves in the open air. With the prohibition on contact with the locals, life in the camp was relaxed, but somewhat monotonous:

> The internees spent their time in the surrounding courtyard playing cards or games on the chessboard. In the afternoon, a march was ordered. In groups they went under guard in the direction of Santel or in the Egerkingen suburb. As it was summer and autumn, the fruits were ripe on trees and in gardens. It was thus impossible to prevent the internees taking the chance on the tempting gifts of nature. Their guards probably turned a blind eye.[55]

A local teenager told his teacher what he saw at the Muslim camp:

> They are very pious and early risers. Just imagine, every morning, as early as 4 o'clock, they begin to pray. For days in the morning I heard a strange, loud murmur from the Hammersaal, which always lasts until around six o'clock. [One of the guards] has said that they do their feet, wash their hands and head before every prayer. Then they turn against the sunrise and bow several times on their knees. Always touching the ground with his head. Then, alternately, they would get up again and hold their hands upwards, like the pastor at Mass.[56]

There was a type of fascination with these strange 'exotic' men. Coincidentally, this same part of the country had seen non-European internees in 1871. Some of the 'Zephyrs' and 'Turcos' of the Bourbaki army had been placed at a nearby village called Aarwangen, where the pastor had remarked on the curiosity of the locals, 'Young and old want to see particularly the Mohammedans with their own eyes'.[57]

That same curiosity was evident in 1944. The young women found them 'young, handsome, and exotic'.[58] Local girl Heidi Swierczynska said, 'When we knew they were coming, we ran to the Dünnernbrücke and watched them. How old were we there? 16, 18. They were very handsome men, with their long black hair. Some women [just wanted] to grab one.[59]

Another source says:

The Sikhs were young, racy men. Because of the artful process of winding their turbans they were an attraction for the population. So again and again men, women, children stood around the camps where there was no guard in between, and tried stealthily to make contact over the one-meter high fence.

Of course, their parents didn't think that was good. Federal authorities also wanted to protect local women from 'international relations'. This view was also held in the municipal council, and because the 'young girls are mostly minors, the guardianship authority should be involved', it said. However, nothing ever happened.[60]

When they moved on, their going was generally regretted:

The local soldiers who were present at the time confirm that at the end of the service it was determined with satisfaction that the internment had been completed without incident. Only once was there an incident: at an evening roll call, one was missing. But when he was back in the morning, the calm returned. The guards had to go to punishment for their negligence. That was the end of the case. A member of the local armed forces living in the immediate vicinity was allowed to go home for milking in the morning and evening. But he also had to sleep dutifully in the straw, for which he brought his pillow from home.[61]

For many in Egerkingen, it was their first contact with any foreigners, let alone men from Asia. Local teacher Othmar Bieber wrote, 'Through the contact with the refugees and internees we had the opportunity to correct some prejudices and to strengthen mutual respect.'[62] Here, the war had provided an educational opportunity.

By the middle of June, the decision was taken to move them further south. This was probably for two reasons. First, there was a hope that the climate in the south would suit them better.[63] Added to that was the renewed threat of war on the border following D-Day.

As the summer went on, all 200 camps in the north-west were emptied of internees and filled instead with Swiss military.[64] Before they left, the Swiss commandants made some final assessments. One wrote of their guests' linguistic abilities, something that any Swiss would be likely to notice:

The Indian distinguishes himself by great intelligence. The claim of one individual that he had learnt the French language in 2 months cannot be proved. The fact is that most have some notion either of German or French, or of Italian, depending on the time they have spent in the relevant countries. In Biberist, out of 146 camp inmates, approx. 50–60 from one camp commando attended a scheduled German lesson.[65]

That represents about a third of the population of that camp – quite a decent proportion. Another commandant gives his summary, 'Generally ... I would like to say that I am very surprised by the decency, order and discipline of these Indian soldiers.'[66]

Leaving some friends and admirers behind, the 500 men moved south, through the mountains towards the sun.

Indian Summer

The sleeping birds of the night, with the advent of dawn had left their dark abodes and fluttering their wings exuberantly were soaring high up into the endless blue sky. Our hearts too rejoice in the new-found freedom.[1]

At Épinal, things had moved on after the 11 May bombing. The US Air Force returned on 23 May, at 10.40 in the morning, to bomb again. This time, however, the people were prepared and went down into the shelters. Only six civilians were killed, and the bombs were more accurate this time, causing greater destruction to the area around the station.[2] Maurice Gillet was part of the Resistance, aged just 18, and remembered:

> In addition to the entire train station and area surrounding it, Saint-Maurice Hospital, the school on rue Victor-Hugo, Notre-Dame Church, the prison on rue Christophe-Denis (which housed many resistance fighters awaiting departure to death camps), and the orphanage on rue Thiers, which was opposite the former German consulate, were all destroyed by explosive and incendiary bombs.[3]

Jacques Grasser was born in Épinal after the war and said that 'we lived in ruins'.[4] His mother's house had been by the railway station, and she never talked about the war – the memory was too raw, too bloody to recall. One of the symbols of the bombing was that archetypal French hero, Joan of Arc. Her statue in Épinal remained undamaged, but 'seemed to look with infinite sadness at the holocaust of the train station'.[5]

A few days after that, Maréchal Pétain himself came to visit the town. As part of a Vichy propaganda offensive, just a week before D-Day,

Pétain went to Nancy, Épinal and Dijon to view the damage and address the people.[6] The Vichy government viewed the widespread bombing of France by the Allies as a chance to turn public opinion against the Allies and bolster their rapidly waning popularity.

Indeed, the public turned out in large numbers to see the maréchal and to cheer him at the 1918 war memorial in the Place Foch.[7] Pétain had been the hero of the First World War, and many people still viewed him as having saved France in 1940. A Vichy cartoon of the time depicted Donald Duck and Mickey Mouse dropping bombs on France, and a camera crew were there on 27 May to capture the ruins, speeches and cheering crowds.[8] This was a chance for the Vichy regime to attack – once again – the 'perfidious former ally'.[9] Two years later, the same crowds would return to the same place to cheer the new president, de Gaulle.[10]

Meanwhile, at the bombed-out barracks, the Indians and the Germans were taking stock. Man of Confidence Bhagat Ram wrote an impassioned letter to the Red Cross a week after the first bombing, reporting that of the 3,128 in the camp on the day, there were thirty-five dead, 1,923 who had been found and taken to other camps, and 833 still missing; 400 were still at Épinal, living in the ruins.[11] According to a Swiss newspaper, the second raid hit the camp infirmary, and some of those who had been hospitalised after 11 May were killed.[12]

On 22 June – two weeks after D-Day and with all of France in turmoil – the ICRC delegates Morsier and Schirmer visited both Nancy and Épinal. At Nancy, they found the camp overcrowded, with 893 Indians from Épinal still there, as well as thousands of French colonial prisoners and hundreds of black South Africans.[13]

Many of the Indians had already been sent back to Épinal, which was now in a state of clearing (see Fig. 9). Épinal now had over 2,200 POWs again, and Dr Din Mohammed Khan was hard at work in the hospital, requesting a book on radiography be sent out – clearly there were many X-rays to interpret.[14]

The drama of escapes was not over for these men, however. Many had had their appetite whetted by the numbers who had got away in May, never to be seen again. They had maybe received postcards from Switzerland or heard via gossip in the town. They had been – in modern-usage terms – radicalised. Thus, on 15 July there was another escape attempt, involving fifteen men who cut through the barbed wire and got into the woods to the west. Bhagat Ram reported, 'After a considerable time the alarm was given and the German [soldiers] went in pursuit of the fled aways. Three men were recaptured in the woods and were brought back in the Camp after being thrashed.'[15]

Another search party then found six of the escapees. They put their hands up in surrender, but the Germans shot and killed four of them. The two survivors and the four bodies were brought back to the camp, and the whole camp was called together to view the corpses. Dr Seal made a detailed medical report which said that all four were shot in the chest or thorax and died because of a bullet penetrating their vital organs.[16] Additionally, Bhagat Ram reported, the burials were not carried out in accordance with Article 76 of the Geneva Convention.

It seemed as if, in the general upheaval following two air raids, D-Day and the largest prison escape in German military history, the guards had become jumpy and inclined to take matters into their own hands. With their hands up and offering no resistance, shooting these four men was a crime against the Geneva Convention and against German orders.

The four who were killed were Suchet Singh, Laksham Khote, Ghulam Ahmed and Naubat Shah. Two are buried at Épinal, but the other two graves – for some unknown reason – are at Durnbach, in the south of Germany.[17] All four are listed as 'Mentioned in Despatches' on the Commonwealth War Graves records, normal British practice for prisoners who were shot while trying to escape.[18] Although there was an investigation after the war by the Special Investigations Bureau, they were unable to identify the specific guards involved and no prosecution resulted.[19] Among so many German war crimes, this one was impossible to prove.

At least one man who escaped that day made it to Switzerland, however. Shripatrao Gaikwad was a company havildar major in the Mahrattas and hailed from the village of Chafal, in present-day Maharashtra, in the shadow of the Western Ghats. He told his story to an officer of the Mahrattas after he returned to India.

Having escaped on 11 May, Gaikwad was recaptured 20 miles from Épinal and eventually brought back. Hearing that they were to be relocated to Germany, and determined to get away, he made some plans:

He found a large disused water drain which led out of the camp, but there were thin iron bars at the entrance. Taking a few more into his confidence they acquired a few tools and in thirteen days cut the bars.

Then it was decided to let the others know the way of escape – and over 700 of them wanted to make the attempt. All wanted to be the first, and, of course, the plans broke down.[20]

The eagerness to escape was widespread in the camp. Later, according to Gaikwad's report, he 'slipped out unobserved' on 15 July:

[And] walked as fast as he could. He came to a farm, was directed to follow the power line, and for four days lived on berries and food given him by farmers. Only on one occasion was money demanded. He had been walking for eight days, and had climbed a thickly wooded mountain when he came across a house and an old woman standing outside. He begged for food, which was refused, but on showing her ten francs she gave him a loaf of bread and some cheese. This accept-ance of money made him suspicious, but she seemed to be friendly and showed him the route.

A little way further on he saw two Gurkhas with some civil-ians, and getting nearer he identified them and was soon embracing them. They told him there were fifty other prisoners hiding in the mountain, including two Mahrattas. They also explained why the woman had accepted money for food. She was feeding all fifty of them, and they had insisted on paying her in cash. Next day the lone Mahratta escapee found his two Mahratta friends, but they and the whole party had decided to wait there until the Allied forces had reached them.

Gaikwad decided, therefore, to keep going on his own, and reached Swiss territory near Porrentruy on 25 July, one of the very last from Épinal to make it there.[21]

Another late escaper was Alex Amarasingh, a Sinhalese Catholic from Ceylon who had joined the RIASC as a clerk after ending up in Bombay with no money. He worked as interpreter in the hospital at Épinal, and knew all the medical personnel well. After 11 May, he hid with M. Francine – the local Épinal dentist – but gave himself up and was given the sad task of making lists of the dead. On 28 August, he escaped successfully through the sewers with four comrades and hid again with the dentist until the Americans arrived in September.[22]

Men like Amarasingh feared what the Germans might do as the war continued: fears that were well founded. At the start of September, with the Allies advancing rapidly, the Germans evacuated Épinal and marched about 2,000 Indian prisoners eastwards towards Saint-Dié-des-Vosges.[23] After about 30km, they entered the thick forest near Bois-de-Champ – the name means 'woody fields'. The prisoners saw their chance, and more and more of them simply stepped off the path into the undergrowth and waited till the column had passed. By the end of the day, 217 had dodged the Germans and assembled near a farm called Pimpierre, a summit in the woods connected to the valley by some very windy paths. This was perfect territory for hiding, so they built themselves *baccus*, like those near Étobon, and organised a camp. Their leader was 'the strongest of them, a boxer, as well as an adjutant who returned to Bois-de-Champ in 1945 to thank the villagers for their generosity'.

The local population rose magnificently to the occasion. M. and Mme Charnotet at Pimpierre Farm, with their six children, possessed a bread oven. So, they brought flour from a local mill and baked bread daily with the help of the baker. Marius Baly, a local farmer, brought them 40 litres of milk every day. The farmers even managed to provide meat on the hoof – several calves, which were slaughtered by the escaped prisoners.

Although the language barrier was quite large, some of the Indians spoke German and some French, so they were able to communicate their practical needs and start to build friendships. These country people were fascinated by the turbans and the ritual ablutions and prayers of the 217 Muslims, Sikhs and Hindus. There were some scares though:

> One morning, the Germans arrested M. Baly while he was transporting his forty litres of milk and he managed to 'put them to sleep' by making them believe that he was supplying the children in the area. Another time, in search of the local baker, the occupiers entered Charnotet's [Farm] and stumbled into sacks without suspecting that they were full of flour. 'They were wearing glasses made of bark' the Charnotet sons joked.

By the middle of October, the Americans were very close and artillery fire could be heard. So, the local *Maquisards* showed the Indians a hidden path through the forest westwards toward the Moselle. Soon after that, they reached the US Army and were free again. Those

217 Indians had escaped, and the brave villagers remembered the story long after the war.

After a fierce battle, Épinal itself was finally liberated on 24 September by the US 45th Infantry Division, which had previously had the swastika as its emblem. Some 5,225 American soldiers are buried in a special cemetery just outside the town. Maurice Gillet remembered the day well:

> When I heard the bells of our venerable Saint-Maurice basilica ringing out to announce the liberation of Épinal, and, after the *Te Deum* of thanksgiving for the victory of the allied forces, we heard the American, Russian, English and French national anthems, I understood that the many sacrifices which had been demanded for this liberation had not been in vain and that, thanks to these, our world would know a better life, in peaceful coexistence with all our neighbours and our ex-adversaries.[24]

The barracks on the hill were once again needed, becoming a camp for Recovered Allied Military Personnel, run by the Americans.[25] In April 1945, two Indian officers who were trying to locate missing Indian POWs found 179 Indians once again at Épinal, including some who had already done time there.

★★★

Back in Switzerland, the 500 escapers had relocated. Having previously crossed the *Röstigraben* (the Trench of the Fried Potatoes), between French and German speaking areas, they now traversed the *Polentagraben* (the Trench of the Cornmeal), which separated the German and Italian-speaking cantons. Coming through the mountains, they were now in the Ticino, where the rivers and lakes flowed south to the Mediterranean, where people spoke Italian, drank red wine and ate pasta. The 1925 Locarno Peace Treaty that decided the territorial boundaries of central Europe had been negotiated here beneath the palm trees by the lake. This was another haven for the battle-scarred veterans from Épinal.

They were not the only foreign soldiers in the area. After September 1943, this had been the crossing point for over 30,000 POWs, Italian soldiers and civilians, and many of them were still in the vicinity.[26] There were, in fact, around 150 camps for internees interspersed among the 160,000 population.[27] These included Poles, Ukrainians and *Tirailleurs Sénégalaises* from West Africa.[28]

Our escapers arrived here by train in the middle of June. The Muslims and Christians travelled first, to a camp on the Piano di Magadino, below the village of Gudo, near Bellinzona. From there, they could stroll in the hills above, where the vines on the summer slopes were loaded with black grapes, chestnuts and cherries ripened between the mountain streams, lizards skittered away from their feet and banana plants and palm trees grew and sweet, juicy figs ripened. It must have felt quite familiar to many of them.

These first arrivals were followed a few days later by a larger group of Sikhs, Hindus and Gurkhas, who went a few miles down the valley to Losone, a suburb of Locarno.[29] In due course, the Losone camp was expanded, and the Muslims and Christians relocated there. A local paper reported the arrival of the first group of Muslims:

> Losone definitely has an international reputation. Poles, New Zealanders, South Africans have enjoyed the serene quiet of the flirtatious village. Now it's the turn of the Indians. A first group of tall young men – reddish skin and raven hair – escaped from German concentration camps in France, arrived here a few days ago. And a small group, it is said, of the vanguard, which precedes a larger one, which will arrive shortly.[30]

A few days later, the *Giornale del Popolo* of Lugano reported, 'Another caravan of Indians, in their curious costumes, crossed the city to go to their destination camp near the City. The passage has raised a lively curiosity in our population.'[31] Once again, the soldiers would find themselves exoticised by the local journalists.

The camp at Losone was to be their home for about three months, and a comfortable one at that. Now a barracks for the Swiss Army, it lies at the foot of a hill on the way to Adiga, close to the River Maggia. Opposite the barracks was a fifteenth-century chapel, the *Oratorio della Madonna della Purità di Arbigo*, popular with Polish and Ukrainian Catholics who were interned here. The commandant was Major Salvisberg, assisted by Lieutenant Leber.[32]

Although the internees weren't allowed near the frontier or in the mountains, it was described as a 'very nice tight little camp'.[33] There was a football field, swimming, a cinema, a YMCA canteen, language courses, newspapers and radios tuned to the BBC and Delhi.[34] The Indians were not required to work, received a food parcel weekly in addition to their rations from the Swiss, and were paid 2.50 Swiss francs per day.[35]

You can see their eagerness in a photo from *Marking Time* – the white officers in their berets sit behind the desk checking the paperwork, while Indian soldiers behind look on, eagle-eyed. These conditions meant they were materially better off than they had been for many years, considering also that their Indian pay was still being paid to their allotted family at home. In July, they all received telegrams from their families, delivered by the ICRC, with reply prepaid.[36] Across India there must have been multiple sighs of relief as the good news got through that summer.

At Losone camp there was a change in organisation, one that would be a step towards their reintegration into the army in due course. For the first time since becoming prisoners – in some cases, four years before – they would be commanded by British officers again.

As well as five VCOs – the three who had arrived before Épinal plus the two from Épinal itself – the camp was run by a collection of Indian officers, all with experience in India. The senior British officer was Lieutenant Colonel Lavender of the 16 Punjabs, who must have been pleased to be reunited with seven men of the 4th Battalion of his regiment, including Battalion Havildar Major Amir Zaman.

One of the officers was Captain Mumford of the 3rd Gurkha Rifles, who related that the officers were sufficiently well paid to be able to live 'frugally' in the Hotel Reber, one of the big hotels in Locarno, and were provided with bicycles for their 4km commute across town and up the hill.[37] Captain Mazumdar was also posted to Losone as the Medical Officer.

The news of their dramatic escapes had spread, at least within the army. On 10 August, they received a message of congratulation from the very top – Field Marshal Claude Auchinleck, the commander-in-chief, wrote of their 'splendid escape … You showed high courage, endurance and initiative, and have further enhanced the already great reputation of the Indian Army. Well done.'[38]

They had achieved an amazing feat, but one that would soon be forgotten.

Not everybody thought the British officers were doing a good job. Dr Mazumdar had a very low opinion of Lavender and Mumford, who he thought were old-fashioned and entrenched in the 'Indian Army attitude'.[39] Mazumdar had a Swiss girlfriend, which many British disapproved of, and one evening he refused to go to see the colonel when they were having dinner together. One day, at the Hotel Reber, Lavender was talking about Indian independence and Mazumdar was not impressed with his old-fashioned attitude:

> I disagreed with everything he said ... I said colonel, the difference between you and me is this: I have lived in your country for nearly fifteen years, and I speak your language. You have lived in my country for 24 years or 30 years and you can't speak even a word of the language, so it's no good discussing, we shall never agree.[40]

As a result of that clash, Mazumdar believed that Lavender was looking for a chance to discredit him. In due course, Mazumdar was accused of stealing an ophthalmic instrument and put under house arrest. The case followed him all the way to London after liberation. Mazumdar's bitterness would linger for the rest of his life.

Although there are no accounts of Losone from any Indian soldier other than Mazumdar, there are some interesting details among the reports by the Red Cross. The first visit to the camp was on 4 July, when it had only been open to Indians for a short while. Niederer, the inspector, was impressed with the 'impeccable' order in the camp and remarked that the men give the impression 'of being very happy'.[41] 'For the most part,' he wrote, 'the Indians are great eaters of rice.' A later inspection of the kitchens caused some surprise to the Ticino quartermaster, who found that cooking pots had been used for ritual ablutions, that the men had a habit of praying on tables and concluded that 'cleanliness and order must be described as terrible'.[42]

In September, shortly before they left, the camp was visited by a delegate called Müller, who made a very detailed report.[43] The visit was during Ramadan, which Müller does not report on. He did remark on the music playing in the camp, however, which 'puts them in a dreamy state and they never tire of listening to these monotonous tunes'. This may have been a recitation of the Qur'an or other religious music. He notes that the Muslims 'had a great need to open their heart to someone', which suggests he was taken into the confidence of some men, as does the phrase 'these men spoke openly and without fear'. He found that the Sikhs saw themselves as the camp elite, invited him to a banquet that evening, and asked for permission to play football in Bellinzona. Among the Hindus, he found very poor dental condition, and a VCO who he described as 'a very cultured man, loved and respected by his troops'. Sadly for the historian, he does not name this VCO.

Over time, the curiosity of some of the locals blossomed into friendship. Clementina Glatz Ambrosini met some of the men at the river and took their photograph, showing a level of friendship had developed. She remembered their football matches at the camp.[44]

In one case, the friendship caused some considerable trouble for one of the men. Anu Pun was company quartermaster havildar in the 8th Gurkha Rifles, captured probably at Mersa Matruh in June 1942, in that last great advance of Rommel's before he was stopped at Alamein. He was aged 29, an experienced senior NCO from Shillong in Assam.[45] Pun developed a strong friendship with three children of a family known only as 'C', especially the 19-year-old eldest.[46] One afternoon, the children crossed the Melezza River and went to the camp to meet their friend, maybe to watch a football match or share something to eat. A storm broke out and the river became impassable. The three children spent the night in the camp, hosted by Anu Pun. The next morning was when the trouble started.

Swiss authorities were 'always suspicious' that any relationship between a local and a foreign soldier would become a sexual one.[47] So Lieutenant Fischer of the local army called in the children and Pun for questioning:

> The youngest initially confirmed that she had been subjected to sexual harassment; then later she retracted, saying that she had answered affirmatively to the insinuations of the Swiss commander because she had felt threatened: 'I was afraid because he told me he would put me in prison to sleep on the stones'. As for the children's mother, she declared that she knew Anu Pun 'a serious young man' personally and claimed that she was immediately reassured by the news that the children would spend the night at the Indian camp.[48]

Nothing of a sexual nature was proved against Pun, but he was given a disciplinary sentence for having left the camp several times without permission and for having a friendship with the civilian population. This experienced NCO had helped out his friends in need but was seen by Swiss officialdom as being in the wrong.

Sometimes, the Swiss could handle matters in a more sensitive manner. Early in their stay, a Swiss officer called Picot sent a 'Not Official' note asking the British officers in Losone to explain to the Indians:

> Swiss people, especially in this district have funny habits compared with their owns [sic]. For instance if they like people to go to their homes. They don't like them to do so unless they have been asked to come in. They are rather shy and a bit long to make friends with newcomers. But once they know people they become very hospitable and are very faithful to their friends.
>
> This is one of the many local habits of this weird Western Country. Just a little patience and everything will be O.K.[49]

It looks as if some of the Indians had been entering houses without invitation and some Swiss residents had complained. Picot had a wonderful way of expressing the need for caution by taking the blame entirely on the 'weird Western Country'. Perhaps he became a diplomat later.

As the summer continued, the progress of the Allies in Europe was followed with great attention by all in Losone. After the initial excitement of D-Day, the advance was stalled in Normandy for a few weeks. Things started moving again when Patton's 3rd Army broke out towards Brittany, followed by Operation Dragoon on 15 August. The US 7th Army – half of which was composed of French troops (including many *indigènes* from North and West Africa) – landed around St Tropez in the south of France. They were welcomed everywhere, the Resistance rose up and they quickly took the ports of Marseille and Toulon.

This 'August rush' was a rare example of quick Allied advances reminiscent of Guderian's blitzkrieg in 1940.[50] Large areas of south, central and western France were liberated very quickly, and the 7th Army motored north towards Switzerland and Épinal at high speed.

As early as 27 August, a jeep full of war correspondents 'gate-crashed' across the border into Geneva and splashed their story across the *News Chronicle* and other papers.[51] The game was up for Pétain. The Germans removed him from government, and he withdrew to Belfort. De Gaulle was now clearly the man of the moment in France. Hitler decided to empty the south-west of France and withdrew his troops to the north-east, so the FFI were able to liberate large areas in the east and attack border posts.[52]

Although the rapid advance stalled again in mid-September – Delle was not liberated until 19 November, Belfort on 20th – this indicated a change of circumstances for the many escaped Commonwealth POWs in Swiss camps and hotels. As Mumford put it, the Swiss government effectively said to the British, 'We have a common frontier, your chaps can now go'.[53]

And so, as the Indian summer drew to a close, the sepoys and their British officers packed their cuckoo clocks and precision watches and fell in facing the train.[54] They were allocated a single special train to carry all 500 of them. There was a second-class wagon for the officers, nine third-class wagons for the men, each containing around fifty men, and a goods wagon at the back for all their kit. They said goodbye to their friends at Losone and marched down to Locarno station, where 'a large crowd had come to the station, especially women, for whom the detachment from these new exotic friends seems to have been some-what bitter, since we have seen tears shining in several eyes'.[55]

The train departed precisely at 20.53 on the evening of Thursday, 28 September.[56] The route described a huge arc from right to left. As the crow flies, the distance is only around 300km, but some of Europe's tallest mountains lie between, so they followed the valleys. The first was the valley of the Fiume Ticino, which took them to the Gotthard Tunnel. Emerging into the lighter darkness at Göschenen, they proceeded north past the Urnersee, where the cliffs rise straight out of the lake, past the fields of motionless brown and white cows, past the farms bearing the family names written on the side. Onwards in the dark night, speeding through stations in the German-speaking towns of Arth, Wohlen and Olten, where they had stayed in June. And then on again through Berne to Lausanne, arriving at Geneva at 05.20 as the sun rose over the lake.

The motto of the city of Geneva is *Post tenebras lux* (after the darkness, light) and their journey had reflected that process, from the darkness of Hitler's Reich to the freedom and peace of the Swiss Confederation. At Geneva, they changed trains and boarded a French train. Twenty minutes later, they were back in France, newly liberated itself.

There were mixed feelings about their departure in Losone. The *Corriere Del Ticino* newspaper seemed to be pleased that they had left.[57] But the *Eco di Locarno* took a different tone, 'We wish those departing that, once peace has finally returned to the world, they can happily return to their mysterious India towards which their nostalgic memories certainly vanish.'[58]

Major Salvisberg, who had been responsible for their safe care for several months, was critical of the 'tendentious nature' of some of the press reports.[59] He concluded that the Indians 'proved to be militarily disciplined and left a good impression in every respect, including their attitude' and 'clothing and equipment as well as replacement supplies for these English military interns are exemplary in every respect'.[60]

The tears in the eyes of the women at Locarno station at 9 o'clock in the evening of 28 September indicate a level of intimacy had developed. Perhaps Anu Pun's friends from the 'C' family were there to wave a handkerchief.

And on they went. Their new train took them through Eaux Vives to the frontier, following another great European river, the Rhône. Everywhere in the large country they saw the devastation of war, contrasting strongly with the undamaged land they had just left.

At Marseille, they left the train and entered another camp. Some of the British officers struck lucky here. Mumford and three others were flown back from Marseille to England.[61] The Indians went by ship to Pozzuoli, near Naples, arriving on 8 October and proceeding by another special train to Taranto, on the instep of the Italian boot.[62] Here, they were processed once more, 'bathed, disinfested, medically examined, clothed, paid, interrogated etc'. Their friends in Europe were anxious about their progress:

> In Egerkingen, the news later spread that the ship, which was to bring the internees back to their homeland, had run into a mine and sunk with all passengers. However, letters came to Switzerland from Punjab in India, in which the returned soldiers thanked the authorities and the population for the admission.[63]

After a short stay in Taranto, they sailed again, to Port Said in Egypt, and then to the Indian reinforcement camps at Mina, in the shadow of the pyramids, where they arrived on 28 October.[64] From here, they boarded their final ship on 5 November, arriving at Bombay on 17th.[65]

They then went to a camp at Kalyan, where they were all interrogated by CSDIC, keen to test their loyalty and to gather information on those who had joined the 950 Regiment.[66] *Fauji Akhbar* sent a photographer and ran a full-page spread of photos of smiling men who had been eating decent spicy food and chapattis again (see Fig. 24).

Finally, after returning to their regimental centres around the country, they were allowed home to their families. In some cases, they had been away for five years. Never had home smelled sweeter.

Stuck in Europe

You don't know how heavenly it seems to be able to look so far over unfenced fields and have our own Indian nurses watching over us instead of Gestapo guards.[1]

While the Épinal escapees were on their slow route home, there were still thousands of Indians left in camps across Europe. Some more managed to escape, especially where the front line was advancing quickly, and a short wait would see the Allied reconnaissance units arriving.

For those stuck in camps, the final winter of the war was to be a tough one. With Russians advancing from the east, British, Americans and French from the west, the Reich was shrinking. There was chaos and confusion among the Germans, and prisoners' hopes of liberation were mixed with anxiety over possible desperate measures by Nazis with their backs to the shrinking wall. Food supplies were running low, there was thick snow and low temperatures, and the bombing of Germany intensified. Everyone knew that the 'Thousand Year Reich' was finished, but it took a long time to die.

Increasing numbers of POWs were being killed and wounded in Allied air raids. Thirty-eight died at an *Arbeitskommando* near Auschwitz when they refused to go into the air-raid shelters because they wanted to 'watch the show'.[2] Jagir Singh was killed at his workplace by a direct hit on 25 August.[3] An RAF raid at Brunswick the previous day caused forty casualties among the prisoners, including three deaths.[4] Among the deaths was Risaldar Major Malik Ahmed Khan Tiwana of the Central India Horse, described as 'a great favourite with all ranks'.[5]

Conditions in some camps deteriorated to a dangerous level. When ICRC delegate Kleiner visited Stalag XIID at Trier in February (home of 455 Indians), he reported that some prisoners were sleeping on the ground, the sanitary facilities were 'virtually non-existent' and concluded that 'there isn't a camp, properly speaking'.[6] The men were huddled together, enduring, holding on, knowing victory was coming but not knowing when or what might happen in the interim. And yet some were managing to keep their spirits up, like this sepoy writing from Stalag V-A:

> By the grace of God I am safe and sound here and I have nothing to worry about. I am receiving your letters regularly and this helps me to pass these days of separation with a quiet mind. The war will be finished very soon now and then I'll be with you all once more.[7]

Many POWs, including many Indians, were subjected to a further exercise in suffering by being forced to march many miles into the interior. The German High Command had a policy that all camps should be emptied when they were 'in imminent danger of being overrun'.[8] There was some thought that POWs might make good bargaining chips or still be useful as workers, even into 1945.

An interpreter at Stalag Luft III asked a German where they were headed. The guard replied, 'I honestly don't know.'[9] And so thousands of prisoners of all nationalities packed their few possessions and joined one of several 'death marches' from the east and west.

After his brief escape from Épinal, Mukandan the postman and his comrades had been moved on:

> As all the roads were congested with the retreating German soldiers, we were led along country paths and lanes. We had no breakfast that day and by the time we had done 5 miles from our camp, we were all tired and exhausted. As we could barely carry ourselves, we had to throw away our precious stores of clothes, cooking utensils and even blankets to ease the burden. The sun was blazing now and we soon exhausted our water bottles.

They halted for the night and slept in the open. The next day it rained, so the Germans moved them into a French 'mansion':

> As no rations had been issued to us, we were permitted to loot the food in the house. Next day we resumed our March. No rations were given. Luckily, there were plenty of apple trees, with half ripe fruit on both sides of our route. As the sentries would not allow us to

stand and pluck the fruit, those of us who went in front hit the apples with long sticks as we passed, while the others behind us picked and distributed them. Again there was no water. As the Germans had no food to give, they permitted the colonial soldiers to catch the cows and horses belonging to the French civilians. Early in the morning we marched again. By now our feet were blistered and swollen and all marching was an agony. The halts were fewer and the sentries kicked and hit with rifle butts, those who lagged behind, tired and weary.

That night, a German sergeant stole and shot four cows for the column of prisoners, who:

> … non-beef eaters excluded, rushed towards the carcass like a flock of vultures and within an hour only bare bones could be seen on the spot. Those who did not eat beef were given a few potatoes, also looted from the local gardens. There was no bread and the meat was eaten raw or half cooked. The water we drank was filthy. No wonder many of us suffered from dysentery.
>
> The next day's march broke even the sturdy among us. The soles of our boots had completely worn out and those who had blistered feet had covered them with wads of cloth and were walking with the support of sticks. Some even threw away their trusty greatcoats. The sentries shot a couple of prisoners who refused to move. Whatever the military necessity, this was sheer murder. Some others, too tired mentally and physically, seemed prepared to welcome such an end. But the fellow feeling persisted and we encouraged the weak to carry on just a little longer …

Later, they were taken by train deeper into the Reich:

> In each waggon at least two or three persons were suffering from dysentery. In spite of hitting and howling from inside, the guards refused to open the doors. The resulting torture of the sufferers and their companions is hard to describe without nauseating the reader. This ordeal lasted for five miserable days and nights till we detrained at Moosburg on the evening of the 30th. On a wayside halt, one prisoner had tried to pluck an apple. Without any warning, a shot rang out and hit his hand with an accompanying shout 'this is Deutschland, not France'.[10]

Such treatment was typical of that experienced on long marches during the last months of the war. By the spring of 1945, it was estimated that around a quarter of Allied POWs were on the move.[11] Many groups left Lamsdorf in Poland just after Christmas, and conditions became very bad indeed on these later marches. To add insult to injury, some marches were even fired upon by Allied aircraft searching the country, strafing anything that moved.[12]

As the end got ever closer, German guards often became more humane, sharing food with the POWs, even asking prisoners to sign papers saying they had been 'helpful to POWs'.[13] Major Hitchcock of the 22nd Animal Transport Company of the RIASC was on a march from Spangenberg at the start of April. 'Our guards, by now old and disillusioned last line troops, were almost as anxious to be overrun as we were, and we had little difficulty in "going slow".'[14]

A few days later, they met some American troops and 'Our guard piled arms and filed into a cow shed'.[15] For them, the war was finally over.

Meanwhile, Mukandan spent the winter at Stalag VII-A at Moosburg in Bavaria, which was:

... a huge camp which held prisoners of almost every Allied nationality. The Stalag was badly crowded, a large number of men had to sleep on the floor packed like sardines, and the washing and sanitary arrangements were similarly choked ...

Winter started early with rain. The first snowfall occurred on 9th November. Cooking of food with scanty firewood and ice-soaked green twigs became a heart-breaking job even with the help of the locally invented blower which produced the effect of a bellows. Due to lack of sufficient warm clothes and the sodden condition of the ground on which we slept many of us became more and more weak and sickly. Our limbs ached even by the exertion required to go and answer the roll call. On account of severe cold, the daily walking exercises were neglected. Even in daytime [the] majority of the prisoners remained tucked in their blankets. They hardly talked and yet one could read from their faces, the thoughts of anger, sorrow, resignation and hope ... With the advent of spring, the camp became lively once again and the continued success of the allied arms brought fresh hope to the prisoners.[16]

There is a strong sense from Mukandan's writing of determined resilience: here is a group of friends who are sticking together and helping each other all the way to the end.

Some POWs were heading in another direction – towards the Russians. Sapper Natarajan was from North Arcot in Tamil Nadu.[17] He had been in Épinal but was sent to a punishment camp at Graudenz in Poland, and then to Thorun. When that camp was evacuated in January 1945 and the march westwards started, Natarajan slipped away with some British comrades, hid in a Polish house and waited for the Russians to arrive. They then took a most unusual route home, via Odessa in Crimea, before being shipped to England. At Odessa, 'the men are entertained to concerts and music in the camp, which resembles a small town'.[18] There was a British office at the port, with an officer of the Indian Army stationed there, and a British Red Cross detachment dispensing Cadbury's chocolate, newspapers, underwear and cigarettes.[19] The first thirteen Indians from these eastern camps – including Sapper Natarajan – embarked on 7 March and reached home via Egypt.[20]

For some POWs, the last few weeks of the war were feverish. At Milag, on the North Sea coast, the men knew the Allies would be arriving soon. The final visit of the ICRC was by Mr de Cocatrix on 14 March 1945, and he reported on a polarisation of activity, 'Religious life is intense. The theatre is used as a mosque. At every hour of the day, faithful facing the East read the Koran and pray.' While at the same time:

> A certain number of prisoners were in the 'games room'; Roulette and other games of chance are played there all day; tobacco and cigarettes serve as stakes; they also play with money. All this happens in a deafening noise, not without multiple gesticulations.[21]

In fact, the lascars in the *Inder Lager* were fortunate – Marlag und Milag Nord was liberated by the Scots Guards on 28 April 1945.[22]

The actual moment that a camp was liberated was long remembered by the POWs. In Moosburg, in Bavaria, Mukandan still had his diary:

> 29th of April, a day memorable in the lives of all prisoners of Stalag VII-A, dawned with a slight mist hanging in the air. From midnight there had been a complete cessation of fighting. Was it just the calm before the storm? The atmosphere was tense and the danger great. Hurriedly we finished our breakfast and stood out in groups watching

the horizon. At 9:00am there was a sudden burst of small arms fire half a mile west of our camp. The firing continued for a few minutes with full force during which some anti-tank guns also joined in. We were greatly encouraged by the appearance of an American observation plane which kept hovering over our camp. Suddenly some bullets whizzed over us and we lay down on the ground. After 15 minutes the fight moved south towards the town. At 11:30 AM the fighting ceased and a couple of tanks of the 68th (American) division smashed through the main gate of our camp. An American officer came out of the first tank and hoisted the stars and stripes on the main flag staff of the camp. On seeing this all nationalities in the camp hoisted their national flags over their respective barracks. (Alas! We Indians had then no flag of our own.) This was freedom at last. Cheers echoed from one end of the camp to the other. Thus I regained freedom two years and 10 months after my capture at Matruh.[23]

This is the last portion of Mukandan's diary reproduced in the history of the Postal Service. He may have been one of the large group of released Indian POWs – perhaps as many as 1,000 – paraded in Germany before US General Allen. The general 'expressed amazement at their wonderful smartness and bearing' after such a long time inside.[24]

'What next?' was the question on everyone's lips. For most Commonwealth prisoners, the voyage home would entail a diversion to Britain.

First, of course, more processing. All released POWs were issued with a booklet on repatriation, with a special section for the Indian Army, opening with 'You are now starting your journey to your homes in India'. This was designed to reassure, explaining that they would be taken to camps in England, with Indian rations and butchers sent from India, advances of pay would be made and they would be issued with campaign medals. When they got back to India they would have three months of special war leave, but the booklet was keen to make the point that the Empire was 'still at war with Japan and general demobilization will not be possible until the end of hostilities'. The spectre of further action in Asia was raised.[25]

The next stage of their journey was to a camp in France or Belgium, where an Indian Army liaison officer would personally explain the process.[26] For the first time in years, the men were able to feel pampered. There is one Indian account of this process from *Fauji Akhbar*, written by

Jemadar Diwan Chand Bhaskar. 'We all were brought down to Brussels in Belgium by air. Here we had a great reception and we were offered so many things viz. sweets, cakes, cigarettes, all sorts of clothing and shaving kit etc., that we couldn't carry all these with us.'[27]

They were then taken to an airfield to join Operation Exodus: RAF and USAAF planes that had delivered supplies were filled up with POWs. They were turning round at great speed – sixteen bombers per hour at Brussels – and by the end of May, a staggering 354,488 POWs had been airlifted to the UK.[28] Again, the press were there to accompany them and interview them. Macdonald Hastings of *Picture Post* spotted some Indians, 'Many of the Indians were broken-hearted because they had lost their turbans – but an Allied officer of the Military Government turned them loose in a German cotton mill and they had all decked themselves out in the most wonderful coloured materials'.[29]

Hastings and the photographer, Magee, flew back with the released prisoners, over the white cliffs of Dover, and noted that 'they didn't cheer. They hugged their knees and laughed and laughed till one or two of them cried.' On arrival at airfields in England, some needed to go straight to hospital, but most of them were taken to their new camps, where a British officer reported 'they react well to a little light banter'.[30]

One blue-blooded English officer landed at an airfield near Aylesbury and wrote, 'I shall never forget that golden moment when I stepped out of the plane and stood in the long grass, drinking in the joys of an English spring day'.[31]

For the Indians, it would be several weeks and several thousand miles before they could experience that same feeling of coming home. Of course, not all of them followed the same route or travelled at the same time. Some of the Épinal escapees had to stay in Switzerland a while longer. Fifteen of them were still in hospital – fourteen privates and one havildar – at least seven of them with TB.[32] By November, they were in a sanatorium at Leysin, in the mountains above Lac Leman. They were eating well – sardines, tuna, eggs, mutton, rabbit and poultry – and one at least was feeling ready to study. Risal Singh from Rohtak told the ICRC delegate that he wanted to study French and German languages, physiology and hygiene. He had looked around him and wanted to know more.

Captain Mazumdar was with them for a while, although he said that the few remaining British officers kept him at arm's length, as they knew he was under threat of court martial for the allegation of stealing.[33]

Jai Bahadur Chattri, a sepoy in the Medical Corps, wrote to Mrs Bell in January, saying that most of the men were now cured and that he was looking forward to seeing his family after 'four long years since I left my home in Nepal'.[34] All these sick men went home in due course via England.[35]

As 1945 continued, a few ex-prisoners were still in odd places around Germany and elsewhere. Men who had been separated from their comrades by the Germans, or who had been in small work detachments or in hospital were not always sure what they should do and didn't have enough English to make themselves understood.

Some took advantage of their new-found freedom to explore a little. By the end of June, the Indian Army liaison officers who had been crossing Europe by car, picking up individual soldiers, could report that they had completed 'the main task of recovery and evacuation of Indian Army ex POW'.[36] Three Indians were found in hospital in the Russian zone in August in a state that a doctor described as 'wasted but just living'.[37] They all died, far from home and family. Signalman Shree Krishana Dave wrote to his father from the same hospital in June:

My dear father
Again a few lines hoping you are well and enjoying. I am quite all right here. Now I am in Ruski hands. When Ruski sends us to English then I may come soon. If God wishes then we shall meet very soon.

Do not have any sort of worry about me. I understand yours and my dear mother's loneliness but God wishes so.

Rest is everything all right here. Convey my best regards to dear mother. My [pranams] to both Jija Ji and sisters. With best wishes and hearty cheers from

Your son
Sgd
S.K. Dave [38]

Despite his brave face, Signalman Dave died soon afterwards, and would not see his mother or father or sisters again.

In southern and western France in late 1944, the picture was a complex one for the British, trying to separate POWs who had switched sides from those who hadn't. Two officers from the Indian Army spent many days, many miles and many reams of paper travelling to

Bordeaux, Poitiers and all around, interviewing Indian ex-POWs and ex-legionaries. They included Legionary Kirpal Singh of the Bombay Sappers & Miners. He had been imprisoned by the FFI, who cut his hair and beard by force – he was later shot and injured by a drunken French guard at Poitiers. In contrast was Dafadar Shah Muhammad from the Remount Department, who had escaped from a prison in Bordeaux in May 1944 and fought with the FFI for three months.[39]

Among those who had gone home via Marseille were the Épinal escapees who had been sheltered by French civilians in the north-east and liberated during the autumn of 1944. One such was Mahal Singh, who had been looked after by Emile Bonhotal in Chenebier. He wrote two letters to the family, whom he addressed as 'mummy and daddy'. The first came from Marseille, on the day they sailed, the second was from Italy two weeks later. Mahal wished 'Best complements to all. I request to God for your long life and as the same for Mamman. Very much love to babies.'[40] Like so many of his compatriots, Mahal Singh owed his liberty to the kindness of the strangers of north-east France.

Some other ex-prisoners stayed in Europe much longer, for reasons that have vanished in the smoke of history. In September 1946 – sixteen months after the end of hostilities – Dhondu Rawat of the Mahrattas and Partap Singh of the Hospital Corps were found by the Indian Military Mission in the French-occupied zone of south-western Germany and flown to the UK.[41] Even more remarkably, two more were discovered in Austria in January 1947 – Harbans Singh of the 11th Sikhs and Sant Singh of the RIASC.[42] Whether these men had been seriously ill, had fallen in love or were simply happy in their new homes will probably never be known.

One who had definitely fallen in love was Jai Lall of Madina, in Rohtak, who had joined the FFI in Bouligney. In September 1944, he had been near Paris with his new wife, Denise. Paris was an obvious magnet for ex-POWs who were wandering around trying to keep out of the way.[43] A few weeks later, he was in Poitiers, having been picked up by an officer tasked with collecting the Indians in western France. Jai Lall took off in an American jeep without permission and crashed the vehicle into a telephone pole. The officer did not believe his story that another vehicle had run into him.[44] This story fits the picture that we already have of a young soldier who was always up for an adventure, not always respectful of authority, and quite capable of stretching the truth. A few days later, they went to Rennes, and then England, where

Jai Lall remained until the end of April.[45] I doubt he spent his months in England sitting quietly, writing letters.

★★★

In north-eastern France – in Étobon in particular – the agony of the wait for liberation was prolonged. Although the French regular army had linked up with Harkabahadur Rai and Floege's *Maquisards* on 8 September, it would be still two more months before Jules Perret was able to greet those men and women on his front doorstep. Much would happen in between.

After the dramatic advances in August and early September, the Allied thrust weakened in the autumn, as the supply of manpower and equipment slowed, and the German defence stiffened. In Étobon and the surrounding villages and woodlands – where many Indians still sheltered in their *baccus* – the Resistance was increasingly more active. On 19 August, with the Vichy government evacuated to Belfort, Jules Perret was busy again in his forge, 'I've changed from a blacksmith to an armourer. Lots of rifles … to be repaired. Another distribution of ammunition.'[46]

The *Maquisards* moved from preparation to action with ambushes, 'gunfire everywhere' and plenty of German prisoners taken. Perret willed the Allies to hurry up, 'Come quickly, American friends, before things get bad!'[47]

And then on 13 September, things did get bad. A German motor patrol entered the village. The *Maquis* attack and all the Germans are killed; their lieutenant died in a field of potatoes. They buried the officer the next day 'in a dip in the ground, in Charles Suzette's field, near my poplars'.[48]

By 25 September, the front line was even closer and local men were taken away by the Germans to dig trenches in the rain. Perret prepared for the coming battle:

I buried a crock of lard in grandmother's basement, our money and five jars of roasted meat in ours, and Suzette's trousseau, put in crates, in grandmother's storeroom; and here and there a demijohn of schnapps, 50 liters of Tunisian wine, my writings.[49]

Two days later – 27 September – saw the events that are remembered in Étobon and Chenebier every year. Early in the morning, Russian

Cossacks working for the Germans collected all the men of the village of Étobon in the school hall. Sixty-seven men gathered, including the mayor and the pastor, but not Jules Perret. Thinking they were going to Héricourt to dig trenches, the men were marched 3km to the church at Chenebier, and twenty-seven were taken away to Belfort. A Cossack that Perret described as 'a real runt, Sicilian', counted out ten men, lined them up against the church wall and shot them with his sub-machine gun, an SS guard helping with his rifle.[50] Then ten more, another ten, and a final nine. Thirty-nine young men of Étobon were murdered that day, including Jules Perret's son, Jacques, and seven others with the same surname. The people of Chenebier were made to dig a mass grave and throw the bodies in.[51]

But still the occupation dragged on, and the village was not liberated until seven weeks later on Saturday, 18 November:

> Things happened quickly. At 10 o'clock … I hear shouting. 'Here they are! Here they are!' Oh, you who have never experienced a moment like that, you can't understand! I rush outside, I see two tanks in front of the house, surrounded by a cheering crowd. They weep for joy. They embrace the soldiers. They cover the tanks with chrysanthemums, they toss fruit to them, they hand them bottles. Long live America!
>
> They're wearing strange headgear. We ask, crowding around them, 'Who are you?' They respond, 'We're French, like you. We're the resistance from the [south of France]'. New transports of joy, tears, too: 'You came two months too late!' 'Why?' 'They massacred 40 men, all our youth!' We see their faces harden, their fists clench.
>
> After the tanks, the infantry. Among them, armed and helmeted, five women, very dignified, one whose husband and son had been shot …
>
> I wanted to have the church bells rung, but an officer said it would be safer to wait until the boches were out of cannon range. Now we can get started. A little before noon, how our beautiful bells rang![52]

For the women and children and the old men of Étobon, the clear-up could begin. Ordering coffins, visiting graves and digging up the supplies that had been buried. Life started again. On 7 December the massacred thirty-nine were exhumed, and Perret wrote, 'Tomorrow I'll ask the families to send sheets and pillows for the last sleep of our children'. Over the next few days, the families identified the bodies and on Saturday the 9th they were buried properly in the town cemetery outside Étobon.[53]

★★★

The camps in the eastern counties of England became home to many thousands of Indian POWs in their long journey home, including many of the previous residents of Épinal. A minority went direct to India from Marseille, much to the irritation of British commanders wanting a single system. Generally speaking, the men were well looked after in England, with good food and medical attention, and many opportunities to fill their time. They were unhappy about their financial situation, however, being paid just 15 shillings in cash per month, plus forty cigarettes a week, which was not enough for most men.[54] Compared to the Britishers around them, they were not well off at all. There were some incidents of conflict and racism during their time in England, as well as some stories of integration and warm welcome. For most of them, this would be their first and only experience of the UK.

The camps were established in East Anglia, the same place where the USAAF bombers had taken off from on 11 May. They were staffed by around 2,000 men from the Indian Army, including butchers for halal and *Jhatka* meat, Hindu, Sikh and Muslim chaplains and a Post Office.[55] The HQ was at Shadwell Court in Thetford, and the camps were spread over a wide area, with Gurkhas at a camp near Newmarket, Punjabis at Sugar Hill, lascars at Didlington, and Madrasis at Camp 50, near Bury St Edmunds.[56]

The camp at Cranwich was for those who had been picked up in German uniform. They were questioned by one of the sixty-two interrogators of the CSDIC – the Combined Services Detailed Interrogation Centre.[57] They were then classified white, grey or black, official shorthand for 'faithful', 'questionable' and 'traitor'.

During the autumn and winter of 1944, the numbers of POWs remained very low. Sugar Hill Camp reported its first real POW by name – Kanshi Ram of the 10 Baluchs, who arrived on 12 September.[58] The staff of the camps kept themselves busy with training and entertainment and helped the local farmers digging potatoes and sugar beet.[59] Over the winter – the 'coldest winter in England for 50 years' – they kept warm and active with snowball fights and a competition for the best snowman.[60] The numbers of POWs started to pick up in 1945. A report in May makes sober reading:

> POWs were mostly in a very bad state of health on arrival, many had lost all sense of proportion and had forgotten what discipline was. They had to be [handled] with firmness combined with tact. They took about two weeks to settle down and showed a great improvement on receiving new clothing and equipment. Many were sanctioned special diet after medical inspection.[61]

Another report describes them as 'on the whole quiet, retiring, uncommunicative and completely bewildered on first arrival'.[62] There is a deep sense of shock and trauma here. Liberated, fed and clothed they had been, but they had not recovered.

Many of the men needed the extra care provided in a hospital. Accordingly, the 55 Indian General Hospital was sent from Ceylon, with a staff of over 300.[63] When the influx of prisoners started, they had to fly in eighteen extra doctors, including many Indians and one woman – Captain Mrs E.M. Blanden.

The situation was urgent, with many of the new arrivals being severely under-nourished or suffering from diseases such as tuberculosis. At the peak in May, the hospital expanded to 1,150 beds, so huge was the demand. Fourteen men are buried in the UK from this time, in Brookwood, Thetford and Ipswich.[64] One man who was killed in an accident was cremated and his ashes sent home by air, a highly unusual occurrence.[65] Altogether, the record of the hospital testifies to the hard work of its doctors and nurses.

These men were released from prison but were still not at home, still in the army but with no fighting to do, and still marking time. So their commanders filled their time with leisure activities, including films, concerts, language classes, sports and trips.[66] A new organisation called *Fauji Dilkush Sabha*, whose name could be translated as 'Society to make the hearts of soldiers glad', organised concert parties.[67] They put on Indian shows with titles like 'Insaf of Jahangir' and '*Satya Harishandra* [sic]', as well as a variety show with a Russian dancer and juggling by Mr Amaraskara OBE.[68] Indian films like *Tulsi* and *Mahakavi Kalidas* were shown in local cinemas. Dr Chandra Gooneratne of the Indian YMCA gave lectures on 'The Folk Ways of the People' and 'His Experience in Brussels'.[69]

The men were also given plenty of opportunities to run off their surplus energy. In August, there was a three-day games meeting, with teams from each regiment competing in sports, including the quintessentially Indian game of kabaddi.[70] The 19 February saw Shivaji's birthday, so the Mahratta troops at Camp 50 celebrated in style, with some typical gymnastics including the Mallakhamba Pole.[71] Trips were organised to the FA Cup Final at Wembley, a garden party at the house of Miss Barret in Bishop's Stortford and the Vauxhall motor works in Luton.[72] Typical English weather struck the village fete at Much Hadham, however, to which the men had been given free tickets, and 'the gathering was dispersed due to heavy rain'.[73]

Every week, a party of sixty went to London, to a special leave centre at Dean Lodge in Roehampton (see Fig. 19).[74] Their busy programme included Big Ben and the National Gallery, Madame Tussauds, tea at the Indian Forces Club, while 'as many as possible will be taken to theatres'. Muslims could buy tinned halal meat from Shafi's Indian restaurant on Gerrard Street, run by brothers Yassim and Rahim Mohammed.[75] Eid al-Adha fell on 26 November in 1944, and some of the ex-POWs and camp staff 'served to swell the gathering' at Woking Mosque, Britain's oldest.[76] There was also a delegation led by Captain Bashir at the opening of the newest mosque, at London's Regent's Park.[77]

The birthday of Guru Nanak – the founder of Sikhism – was celebrated at a gurdwara in west London at the end of October 1944, attended by around twenty men from the camps. The report in the India Office files reads like something written by a police spy, concerned about nationalist sentiments among the men. The writer was most perturbed when one of the speakers said that he would rather see 'men in the uniform of their mother country and not of the British'.[78]

Not all was sweetness and light among the Indians in Britain that year. One of the camp staff wrote to his friend's English wife, 'England is an unfriendly place, particularly for us, the Indians'.[79]

Some locals were pleased to have such interesting neighbours for a short while. Bas Kybird was then aged 16 and enjoyed learning languages:

> Sometimes on a Saturday afternoon I would cycle to one of the camps, either at Didlington or Lyndford. I had made many friends of different creeds and castes among the Indian soldiers and enjoyed the challenge of making myself understood. I drank pint mugs of

tea, oddly with a pinch of salt. I ate chapattis with hard boiled eggs or jam. I went to the camp cinema and watched Indian films, learned a smattering of Urdu also how to write my name and address in Sanskrit. I even composed a short chant in Urdu seeking rain so we didn't have to play rugby at school![80]

In that first post-war summer, with a new Labour government and a new mood in the country, this young man showed the possibility of a new, more equal relationship with the Empire.

Among the measures taken to reassure the men that they were appreciated and valued were frequent visits by people of high status, including the Nepali Minister and King George VI.[81] The Commander-in-Chief Auchinleck visited, and contemplated flying the VCOs home as 'they are going to wield considerable influence when they get back to India'.[82]

In fact, many of the VCOs became extremely disillusioned during their time in the UK. They had been pleasantly surprised, as prisoners of the Germans, to be treated and paid like officers, so their treatment in England seemed like a demotion. An unnamed Punjabi officer wrote in his lengthy report on the East Anglian camps:

> I think that the Viceroy's Commission should be abolished in the Indian Army and instead we ought to create a very large number of scholarships for the sons of VCOs and give them free education at military schools like the ones in Jhelum and Jalandhar.[83]

VCOs in England were bored, and wanted more time for sightseeing, 'What are we to tell our families when we return when they ask what did you see in the Mother Country; we will have to reply, we saw camp 55, jungle and endless rain'.[84]

The British colonel who had commanded the Indian Section at Oflag 79 reckoned that they had been ill-treated by some British officers, who referred to them as 'bloody Indians', and concluded that the VCOs had 'lost a lot of respect they previously had for officers'.[85]

This ill-feeling came to a head at Glasgow Docks on 20 May. The SS *Ruys* troop ship was being loaded for a voyage to India, with 180 VCOs on its passenger list. When the VCOs discovered that they were to be sleeping on the troop deck while British warrant officers had been allocated cabins, most of them refused to embark.[86] Senior officers thought there would have been a mutiny if they had been ordered to embark, so they held back from giving the order. Soon after that, the quartermaster general agreed that all VCOs would have cabins in future. There was much heart-searching by the Britishers after this, with detailed analysis of the ringleaders, a list of 'VCOs who should be watched' and a 'secret and most immediate' report which stated that, having been treated as officers in the Oflag, 'they resent the fact that they are not being treated as officers now that they have obtained their freedom. They are, therefore, touchy in the extreme.'[87]

Given the discrimination shown towards the British warrant officers, this amounts to more than being 'touchy', and is a clear case of racism. This large group of VCOs was prepared to stand up for themselves and demand their rights, which threw the establishment into contortions. A very serious incident that was hushed up at the time, this near-mutiny was a dimming in the twilight of the Raj.

Another incident that garnered acres of coverage in the India Office filing cabinets was the story of Gurbux Singh.[88] On 6 June 1945, a local woman was 'cycling home about 11 pm along the Mildenhall Road when she was attacked by two Indian soldiers, who dragged her across a meadow and each man raped her'.[89]

Two soldiers were arrested. Kahan Singh was identified by the girl while the other – Gurbux Singh – was released and returned to his camp. Later, he was badly beaten up by two British warrant officers who were part of the camp guard. That night, the camp was in uproar, with some of the men coming to Gooneratne of the YMCA, asking for weapons.

Gurbux Singh was shipped home from Glasgow, where – according to a white British YMCA employee – the camp commander said, 'He is not sick, but just been beaten up but not been beaten up enough'. Kahan Singh was acquitted at the Old Bailey, the jury taking just ten minutes to reach their verdict.[90] A court of inquiry found that the two British guards should have been given a reprimand.

Gooneratne of the YMCA described it as a 'great tragedy', which has 'turned into an intense anti-British hatred', with soldiers regretting 'that they had not joined the German Legion'.[91] He continued:

The awful thing about all this is, that some men, after having risked their lives, bombed while in prison, starved very near to death, and spent three to five years in German Prison Camps, are going back 100% anti-British. The few who have kept clear away from all ideas of race conflicts have also changed their views radically ... As Prisoners they had a Protecting Power to appeal to, now, as supposedly Free men, they had none.

In due course, both Kahan Singh and Gurbux Singh rejoined their regiment in India, but were being 'watched since their return from leave'.[92] The sense from the British Establishment is clear. Despite the fact that neither man was found guilty, the two guards had done the right thing in keeping the men in their place, and the two Sikhs would be 'troublemakers' in future. With such attitudes evident, it is little wonder that Indian independence was so strongly on Indian minds.

These are two examples of racism in the system – there are others. The official discourse was one of continuing welcome in Britain, but these incidents point towards changing attitudes and behaviour all round. Prejudice against Indians lay not far beneath the surface, and such prejudice could result in racist action. Not all Indians were prepared to accept this any longer, and there was a concomitant decline in respect for old-fashioned British authority. Put together, these attitudes were a harbinger of what was to come soon after.

By the end of October 1945, all the POWs had gone and a total of 9,711 Indian POWs had come through the camps.[93] They sailed home in their thousands – the largest group of Indians to stay in Britain, the subjects of a unique transcultural experience. The escapers, the legionaries, the sick and the well, the Gurkhas, the Sikhs, the Muslims and the Hindus, all bound for Bombay.

They usually stopped in Egypt, where they stayed at the camps at Mina. As they sailed through the Red Sea, the Muslims among them looked to the port side, towards Medina and Mecca.[94] On one ship, they had a whipround for their saviours, the Red Cross, and collected over £21, which they handed over at Bombay, wrapped in a handkerchief.[95]

From the very first returns in July 1943, returning POWs were usually met with music and dignitaries at Bombay Docks.[96] There was a tea party organised in their honour, and gifts of cigarettes, a cigarette case and other comforts.[97] Mohd Yaqub of Jhelum had been in camps in Italy, France and Germany and said, 'All the time we thought only of our homes … Soon I shall see my wife and my little girl. They need no longer write to me now.'[98]

Back at home, traditional greetings were in order, 'I did my namastes to my parents in the customary and time-honoured way by touching their feet. I could see the tears of joy in their eyes at seeing their son arriving home safe and sound in mind and body.'[99]

The families were overjoyed. When Din Mohammed got home, his mother was 'almost blind crying for him'.[100] They were home. They could eat familiar food and see familiar sights, hear their own language around them and bask in the warm climate. But not all was the same. Just as no man ever steps in the same river twice, so for these men, 'the home the soldiers will return to can never be the one they left'.[101] The home had changed, and they had changed too.

The Indian government had laid down plans for the 'disposal' of returning POWs. They would all return to their regimental centre via a transit camp and then get three months' leave. They were predicted to be in 'a rather pleased and excited frame of mind' and had 'long been accustomed to conceal from authority their real feelings', so would need careful handling.[102]

One photograph from *Fauji Akhbar* around that time may reveal something of 'real feelings' (see Fig. 20). Two civilian women stand on the platform at Lahore railway station surrounded by ex-POWs returned from Germany, all garlanded. Nobody in the picture is smiling. Uncertainty about the future was everywhere in the summer of 1945.

Epilogue

The Greatest Escape?

I'd never heard of these POWs before – all those Great Escapes & never a brown face among them.[1]

So what was the experience of Indian POWs after their return home, the Épinal escapers and the others? The truth is that they weren't feted and greeted and welcomed back as heroes at the end of the war, nor with the passage of time.

Regimental Monthly Intelligence Reports were an essential government tool for taking the temperature of army and civilian opinion, and the reports from the Artillery Depot in Deolali are revealing. Unlike British servicemen (who were mostly conscripts), Indian soldiers were not demobilised quickly at the end of the war, and having seen British troops close up, they had many reasons to grouse about the comparison. The Artillery Depot reported grumblings about money, medals and general morale. A common complaint was 'why does the [Indian soldier] get less pay than the [British soldier] when both fight in the same war and we say we were better?'[2] In June 1945, the problem was more specific: some of the Épinal escapers (there were twenty-four from the artillery) had been waiting for their back pay over six months.[3]

There was also bad feeling about medals and awards. There is some evidence that the British were more generous at the end of the war than usual, in an effort to counteract the popularity of the Indian National Army and the general drift away from the Raj. Conversely, some ex-POWs in the artillery were disappointed not to receive the *Jangi Inam* – a category of gallantry award that carried a pension continuing to the next generation.[4] Unsurprisingly, in these conditions, morale among returning POWs was low.

Another report from Deolali made unfavourable comparisons between POWs coming back from Germany and those captured by the Japanese

(FEPOWs).[5] This contrast was repeated elsewhere. FEPOWS were seen as being more docile because they had been treated so much worse, while those from Europe were demanding promotions.

The whole picture was further complicated by press reports about the INA prisoners, 'Some apprehension is felt by all Ranks as a result in the press suggesting that INA personnel may be instated in the services by the new Government and that such men may be given seniority higher than that of loyal ex POWs'.[6]

All of this contributed to a post-war atmosphere leading to a series of upheavals in the military, which 'could not be insulated from the political changes'.[7] The men identified as 'black'— those who had joined the German or Japanese armies – were imprisoned in the Red Fort in Delhi. Three senior officers were put on trial for treason, found guilty but released soon after in the face of public pressure.[8] Shortly afterwards, the Royal Indian Navy at Bombay and Karachi mutinied, although they returned to their ships after a week.[9] The British grip on the South Asian military was loosening: being an ex-POW in India just after the war was not something that accrued respect or many chances for advancement.

There are very few sources of information on the long-term impact of their imprisonment on these men and few non-officers recorded their experience. One Épinal escapee interviewed in Switzerland talked about how he felt in the weeks since the bombing, 'I have never regained my inner happiness since'.[10] We can only hope that his inner happiness was restored with the healing passage of time.

Unlike in other Commonwealth countries, there do not seem to have been any ex-POW associations formed or newsletters established. Dr Santi Pada Dutt refused to tell his family why he had been awarded the MC, replying, 'Well, I just did my work and they gave it to me'.[11] His daughter, Leila Sen recalled:

My father never spoke about *any* of this to the very end of his life; and even then, not until I began probing him about his war experiences. As a child and a teenager I didn't question the source of the disturbing nightmares he suffered every so often, and by my late teens they occurred less frequently. I grew up with this man who, in my small world, was just my father – a wonderful father, but no more and no less. And only in our last years together did I come to realise that beyond being my parent he was also someone who had volunteered to do his best in a time of world turmoil and, little as that may have been,

I would find it archived in the museums and histories of countries other than his own. It will always amaze me and renew my appreciation for his humility and humanity.[12]

There were other long-term effects. Sahibzada Yaqub Khan had 'positively spartan ideas on food. The only time he ever mentioned his POW years was when he lectured over-indulgent me, on the virtues of eating less.'[13]

There were physical scars as well – Taj Mohd Khan of the 2nd Royal Lancers carried the marks of German bayonets.[14] Subedar Jit Singh Sarna from Rawalpindi bore mental scars and:

> … could not shrug off the memory of his stay in Oflag 79. The melancholy of those days was captured in a pencil sketch of his camp boots that Jit gifted his nephew in 1968. The sketch still hangs at the Sarnas' residence. Unable to forget the days of shame, Jit would cry before his family while recollecting how the Nazi soldiers would stop the train, force prisoners to defecate by the railway tracks in a row, and take photographs and laugh over it.[15]

Some ex-POWs reported positive impacts, however. Anwar Hussain Shah of the 22nd Animal Transport Company, who probably joined the German 950 Regiment, used to receive letters from Germany, offering him jobs. His family considered that he had gained:

> … knowledge and experience from his time in army and prison. He became disciplined. He had an ocean of social, political and financial knowledge. He was a great intellectual. He learned history and had expertise on our national poet Allama Iqbal. All the knowledge he gained was from his time in the prison.[16]

Many prisoners had learnt languages. At the Bengal Sappers & Miners' HQ at Roorkee after the war, 'there were men who could carry on a conversation in German, French and Italian as well as Urdu and English'.[17] The Italian filmmaker Roberto Rossellini was visiting India in the 1950s and got stuck one night on a highway. When a truck didn't stop to his waving, he swore at the driver in Italian. To his surprise, the Sikh driver poked his head out to shout back at him in the same language. The driver had spent several years in an Italian camp and had used his time wisely.[18] More generally, the veterans of Stalags and Oflags became building blocks in post-war South Asian societies – generals, ambassadors, farmers, teachers – bringing back what they had learnt in Europe, their enhanced political and social awareness helping to build their new countries.

Apart from Anwar Hussain Shah, others stayed in touch by letter, at least for a short while. Jules Perret mentioned letters from Indians who had sheltered in Étobon.[19] Sohan Singh was taken prisoner in North Africa at the age of 18 and spent three years in Annaburg. He stayed in touch with the farmer he'd worked for in Germany, writing to him in passable German. A local historian from Annaburg started to visit him in India and newspapers in Germany carried his reports. Singh always wished to return to Germany but was unable to.[20]

Others did manage to return to Europe, as Yaqub Khan did in 1985 when he was Pakistan's Foreign Minister, giving a speech in Italian.[21] R.G. Salvi also went back to Italy, taking his wife Hansa with him, to see the people who had sheltered him over the winter of 1943–44. Hansa writes of the trip as if it were a pilgrimage, visiting old hiding places and 'following our Indian custom of sitting for a while on the steps of the temples that we visit, revering them and trying to establish a rapport with those that lead us to [god]'.[22] As they left, she had a realisation that 'I owe them more than I can ever repay. But it worries me no longer for I realise that these very obligations are the eternal link between us.'[23] This sense of gratitude must have been widespread among those Épinal escapers who had passed through Étobon and other French villages.

Other prisoners – like Barkat Ali – never left Europe. Their physical remains are buried in cemeteries, scattered in rivers or fields, or still lying hidden in a forest or under a post-war building. Of the 6,000 European graves and memorials to Indian soldiers on the Commonwealth War Graves Commission website, there are 248 named soldiers whom I have identified as POWs (although they are not marked as POWs by the Commission).[24] They represent the counterpoint to the British graves in Pune, Rawalpindi and across South Asia – Empire soldiers far from home.

The French national cemetery at Épinal is a large one, on the hills to the east of the town. There is a large Christian civil section, a smaller Jewish section and a large enclosure at the top for French military graves, mostly from the First World War. Right up in the top corner is a row of limestone headstones, conforming to the standards of the

Commonwealth War Graves Commission. There are seventy-one in total, all Indians. Sixty-six of them are dated 11 May 1944: they died during the air raid. Of those, eleven stones bear the inscription 'A soldier of the Indian Army 1939–1945 is honoured here' – meaning that those bodies were never identified.

There are Muslims and Gurkhas here, Hindus and Sikhs. Some are very young – Kartal Singh of the Bengal Sappers & Miners is recorded as being just 16, so could have been as young as 14 when he was captured. The bodies of the Sikhs and Hindus were cremated, and the ashes scattered in the Canal des Grands Moulins, and their stones stand as memorials.[25] Seven birch trees are arranged nearby in a circle, and as I photographed the graves, a blackbird settled on one of the headstones. Life continues among the dead.

Those seventy-one graves are not the whole story, however. In late 1945, an Indian Military Mission opened in Berlin, charged with tracing missing POWs and locating graves.[26] From August to December 1946, they supervised excavations of bomb craters at Épinal. Sixty-four bodies were found, but most were not identified. The mission completed its work in 1946 with 125 men still listed as missing.[27] The work of locating them continues.

In 1954, a grave marked '*Un Français Inconnu*' ('an unknown Frenchman') was dug up and found to be wearing British khaki. In due course, he was identified as Dafadar Jodha Ram from Chauki Kankari, near Hoshiarpur, and he was later reburied at Épinal.[28]

More recently, the headstone of a soldier from the Baluch Regiment was discovered in a ditch in Waregem in Belgium.[29] It turned out be a duplicate of that of Salim Makhmad, killed on 11 May in the bombing of Épinal. How it came to be in that ditch, 400km north-west of Épinal, is yet to be established.

The memories continue to haunt. When the authorities in Épinal started excavations for a new gendarme barracks next to the site of the camp in the 1970s, several bodies of Indian soldiers were discovered.[30] In the woods near Chenebier, a landowner who was planning to sell a parcel of woodland changed his mind when he looked at the raised mounds among the beech trees, thinking that there might still be Indian bodies buried there.[31]

The connection between north-east France and South Asia feels strongest in Étobon. The anguish of the residents for their lost thirty-nine continued long after the war and was recognised by French and other governments.

There were other villages that suffered in a similar way, in France, South Asia and Poland, but there are two things that make Étobon unique – Jules Perret's writing, and the unequalled assistance that the villagers gave to the Épinal escapers. Both of these are remembered and commemorated in the village itself.

But are the Indians remembered in the wider region? And is Étobon remembered in South Asia?

In the first years after the war, the memory was strong. The memorial to the thirty-nine was officially inaugurated on 7 September 1947, and the village was awarded the *Croix de Guerre* and the *Légion d'Honneur*, with representatives from India and Pakistan attending the ceremonies (see Fig. 22). Prior to that was a ceremony in October 1946, before the memorial was ready, and before Partition. Colonel Hayaud Din represented the Indian Army, and Sir Samuel Runganadhan – the last High Commissioner of India to London – gave a speech of thanks, presenting a cheque for £1,000 to the memorial fund, and a smaller cheque for the establishment of a library to serve Étobon and Chenebier.[32]

The remembrance continues in the village, with an annual commemoration every 27 September. On the front of the presbytery, where so many Indians sheltered and ate soup, is a plaque recognising the building as a 'house of charity, welcome, resistance and faith' in the 'sombre hours' from 1940–44.

The governments of Britain, India and Pakistan maintained their connection for a few years. In 1948, the Pakistan government showed interest in erecting a memorial, in addition to the stone at Étobon put there in 1947.[33] Nothing further was done. The memorial stone and the gift of money from the pre-Partition Indian government became a substitute for anything else in Épinal, Étobon or elsewhere. As time and tide moved on, the urge to memorialise these events ebbed away.

Perret's talents as a writer and *annaliste* did not go unrecognised. His wartime diaries were first published in 1949, in an edition edited by the Swiss writer Benjamin Vallotton and entitled *Ceux d'Étobon*.[34] Nearly thirty years later, his grandson Philippe – who had been with him as a boy at that very first encounter – published a longer version, with illustrations, deposited at the local archives. Philippe's impassioned plea is on the first page, 'I wish these writings will always remain in the family, however sad the remembrance of those dearly departed, for their memories. Save them!!!'[35]

Philippe Perret's thoughts and actions go to the heart of the process I experienced in researching this book. He yearns for the presence of his father, Jacques, and his grandfather, Jules, and all those who died on 27 September. And he knows that there is a way to keep their memory alive: by writing and depositing in archives. 'Save them!' he cries – save these people by saving their writings.

So why has there been no account of the Great Épinal Escape, and why is there nothing in English about Étobon? The greatest escape of the Second World War is simply unknown on the internet, by historians or by the general public. Unravelling how that has happened is not an exact science, and I am not a scientist. The standard line is that when it comes to writing about twentieth-century people from South Asia – especially those from 'subordinate' classes – we are faced with a shortage of material. The novelist Amitav Ghosh wrote, 'The only people for whom we can begin to imagine a properly individual human existence are the literate and the consequential: those who have the means to inscribe themselves upon history.'[36]

People without such means – those who are illiterate or inconsequential – are therefore unimaginable as proper humans. An example of the vacuum of documents concerns a camp called Hafen Arbeiter Abteilung – the work detachment at a harbour, where 1,250 Indians were working in September 1943.[37] It has proved impossible to find any more information about this large group of POW workers. Not only are these men unknown and forgotten, their camp has disappeared into the depths of forgetting.

Elsewhere, memories do linger, stories and the fragments of stories do exist. My hope is that the process of finding them and piecing them together will enable us to imagine a properly individual human existence for these prisoners.

The officers – British and Indian – among these prisoners were from a ruling class, accustomed to money and power. Not being required to work, they had time to plan escapes, to write, draw, learn and paint, and to keep journals. The skill of literacy acts as a doorway to memory. If you can write, you can enter the archives from the *other* side – the side of those who deposit, who contribute.

There is privilege at work here – this was not a level playing field. The preference in this book has been towards the words of Indians themselves, and wherever possible, the other ranks. One great stroke of luck was finding Virk's book on the Postal Service, which contained Mukandan's fantastic account.[38] These are probably the best writings on Indian POW life by a non-officer: hardly surprising, given that postal workers are literate, organised and interested in records.

Forgetting is a process, not a single act.[39] The German Egyptologist Aleida Assmann has identified seven types of forgetting, among which is 'Selective Forgetting'.[40] She explains that cultures and societies choose – in a complex and repeating process – what is forgotten and what is not. What fits a society will be remembered, what mis-fits will be left aside or overlooked. In Britain, the story is about Colditz, in South Asia, Bose and the INA. There is a gap in the middle, between those two poles of popular history, where the Épinal escapers slip through, not quite right for either society.

The national myths of Britain, India and Pakistan seem not to want or need stories of brown-skinned prisoners in Europe – they simply do not fit. However, as politics, society and culture move on, so the criteria for selection evolve. This makes possible a process of re-remembering, with one frame of memory replacing another, and memories that were previously excluded being 're-appropriated by the group'.[41]

The world changes, the nations change, and so the memories that we need also change. This opens up the possibility of agency – the implication of re-remembering or un-forgetting embedded within it. E.P. Thompson wrote that history is 'a gigantic act of reparation'.[42] By re-remembering the Indians of Épinal, and the French men and women who helped them along the way, we can help in this process of making amends.

The frame of memory operating in Britain with regard to camps and escapes has long been dominated by the power of books, television and film. *The Wooden Horse*, *Colditz* and *The Great Escape* remain the dominant tropes here. In the post-war period there was a kind of official or mainstream version of the camps, focused on a tight circle of themes and events. Stories were told and retold. The original 1950s book on *Colditz Castle* was made into a film which led to a TV series, remembered by men like Ben Macintyre, who wrote a new book which then became a new TV series.[43] But if a story has never been told once, it never enters that cycle of telling and retelling.

There is another, simpler, explanation for the British forgetting of these men: racism. Although there is no single example of a particular story or person being repressed or erased due to racism, Britain was certainly a racist society in the 1940s and afterwards. There was racism in the armed forces, the media, history departments in schools and universities, across society and in all institutions. All the agencies that might have remembered the Épinal escapers were tainted by racism and operated within a racist system. As a white British historian with no direct experience of racism myself, I am less likely to understand it on the personal, experiential level, but it is clear to me that part of the reason these men are not remembered in Britain is due to that racism in society, stretching from the 1940s until now.

Some British *kriegies* carried stories of Indians they had met at Lamsdorf or elsewhere. Jack Date from Carlow in Ireland kept his war log with the names and addresses of nine Indians that he had met in Lamsdorf. Decades later, his sister shared them via Facebook.[44] The haircut incident involving Harbans Singh at Campo 57 in Italy is still remembered by Australian POWs and their descendants and has assumed legendary status. One Aussie corresponded with Singh after the war, saying, 'It is with fond memories that I pay tribute to a staunch friend, a brave man and a soldier loyal to Britain. I am proud to call him brother.'[45] Neither of these men – of course – were British.

In France, very different pressures exist around collective memory and the chances of the Épinal story being reclaimed. Being part of the Resistance became a badge of honour for many French men and women, and there is still a feeling that forgetting the Resistance is a form of betrayal. In towns like Belfort and Épinal, there are still sensitivities about allegiances and activities during the period from 1940 to 1944, and local historians often get involved in research about the period for highly personal reasons.

The memory of the passage of the Indians during that extraordinary summer lives long in some villages, although it is often mixed with the story of the atrocities committed by the 950 Regiment as it traversed the region at the same time. In Étobon, there is still a desire to have the story of their thirty-nine martyrs more widely known, and the Indian guests are a part of that story. Charlotte Biediger from Chagey – who had escorted so many Indians – took the names and addresses of four of them and wrote to them after the war.[46] She received no replies.

In South Asia there are many elements that militate against recovery of memories. There may be resistance from family members. If a prisoner had joined the German army – as was the case in one interview

– relatives may be taciturn about telling a British historian his story.[47] Researchers are not always trusted:

> There's been a considerable demand … for war medals and ribbons and decorations and other assorted memorabilia of the two world wars. And I believe that teams of suspicious strangers pretending to be historians and 'researchers' have been going around, befooling the local farmers, and carrying away all kinds of stuff that had belonged to ancestors or relatives, at really ridiculous prices … there's a sinister side to military historical research here.[48]

Replies to a tweet seeking stories in India in March 2023 were often willing, but vague and unsure, for example:

> My grandfather fought in WW II. The story goes that the family received news he was dead. Being Catholics they conducted [a requiem mass a month after the death]. A year or two later he returned … He brought a statue of Our Lady of Fathima supposedly from Germany. The stories of these brave men, our ancestors, deserve to be told.[49]

There is a paradox embedded here: we should tell their stories, and yet we don't know their stories.

In some families, however, the memory of the ex-prisoner is preserved. In one village in Jhelum, families of ex-POWs live in neighbouring houses. When I asked one woman why she had kept photos and documents while others had not, she said, 'This is our love for him. He was our ideal. So you keep everything of your ideal close with you. This is our precious heritage.'[50]

These neighbours also had keepsakes – one had a *rehal* (a Qur'an stand) that her grandfather made in Germany; another had a worn, repaired rentenmark note dated 1937.[51] The grandson of Chanu Khan remembered, 'He received many medals that used to fill his both hands. My father used to play with those medals'.[52]

Such physical, material artefacts – the writer Aanchal Malhotra suggests – can serve to distil 'an enormous event down to something that is graspable' by acting as 'a reservoir of memory and experience, its physical weight outweighed by the emotional weight cached into it over the years'.[53] This emotional weight can make a deep impression on later generations, evoking distant times and faraway places.

In May 2023 I travelled to Rohtak to meet Jai Lall's family, who still live in his native village of Madina, deep in the sugar, wheat and dairy belt west of Delhi. Watermelon vines creep along the walls, citrus trees line the roads and potatoes grow in flat fields, irrigated by the waters of the Sutlej and Jumna rivers. In 2023, the people were mostly Hindus, but before the war there were many Muslim families hereabouts, long since departed across the border. Men from all communities joined the army, and in fact, this area had one of the highest enlistment rates in the country: Jai Lall was one among many thousands.

This proved to be the only interview with the family of a non-officer that I conducted in India.[54] They remembered him well in this agricultural village and they have kept documents, artefacts and photos for over thirty years since his death. The family are proud of his memory, happy to host us and eager to talk. After all, he had been awarded the Indian Order of Merit (IOM) – the second-highest medal available at the time.

I met his three sons, Jagdish, Suresh and Samsher. When they told their father's story, it was much the same as that related in *Fauji Akhbar* – this was the version handed down within the village. According to them, their father had been hiding in a French haystack in May 1944, Denise had been passing by with a dog, who smelt the fugitive and barked. When she saw his face, it was the mole by his nose that struck her, and it was love at first sight.

In due course, he came back from Europe without his wife. His fellow POW, Karam Singh, not realising Jai Lall had escaped, had written a letter saying he was dead, so when his mother saw him she didn't recognise him. 'Oh, you are my son!' she exclaimed, seeing through the beard and hearing his voice.

He was discharged from the army in October 1946, and went back to his life as a farmer and carpenter, sitting every evening with his friends playing *tash* and smoking *huqqa* while they talked of old times. He died in 1991, at the age of 70.

As part of the IOM award, he was given 350 acres of land to farm – he was now well-off. Jai Lall told his family that not only did he marry Denise in France, but they had two children together, a boy and a girl. The sons told me:

> He wanted to bring [Denise] to India. But our grandmother refused this. She said it is against our values as the girl is a *Angrezz* [foreigner]

and they eat *mass-mitti* [non-vegetarian food]. At that time children used to do everything their parents wanted them to do. People had *log lihaz* [respect] and *sabhyata* [civilisation] back then. So, once my grandmother said no to the marriage with French girl, he decided not to bring her here.

According to his sons, Jai Lall was deeply unhappy about this, and returned twice to France to visit his French children. He also sent them a portrait photo of him touching his ear, a gesture which in India means 'I'm sorry in block capitals'.[55] After he died, the family were visited by two men claiming to be from the state government and wanting to look at his IOM. They took it away and it was never seen again. Only the certificate remains, signed in 1949 by the prime minister's secretary, granting a pension to his widow, Saroj, until her death and referencing his 'outstanding qualities as a brave soldier'.[56]

More than thirty years after his death, there is still a large photo of Jai Lall in his son Suresh's house, and the memory is alive. This was a man who was loved and respected during his lifetime and revered after his death. They kept many of the significant documents safely in trunks, worn by folding and unfolding. Although he never learned to read and write, he was fluent in many languages; he was a successful farmer, who was sought after for advice and loved in the village. From everything that can be gleaned about his time in Europe, he was clearly a clever, brave, risk-taking young sepoy, who made the most of his life in those far countries. He was also charming, with piercing blue eyes and a mole that people remembered. For the young Jai Lall, prison and war were a chance for growth, adventure, novelty. He took the opportunities of this crazy war and made himself into something new, reinventing himself as a captain in the army. Those few weeks between 11 May 1944 and his arrival in England in the autumn may have been a time when he was truly free.

But was he the father of two French babies? The register in the *Mairie* in Bouligney carries no record of births by Denise Naidet during 1944 or 1945. She did marry in 1947, to a man called Marcel Raillard, and they had two sons.[57] It is possible that she had another baby while she was in Paris in 1945 and gave that baby up for adoption, but I have been unable so far to trace anything there. It remains a mystery.

The varied angles on his story are as fascinating as the story itself, each revealing something of the teller. Everyone has a stake. The journalist

writing in *Fauji Akhbar* and the officers who approved his medal wanted
to keep up the prestige of the army, to buttress the crumbling Empire.
Perhaps they also bought into the popular British view of the French as
unreliable and incapable of sustained combat, and therefore easily led by
an Indian corporal with a large helping of gumption. The Naidet family
wish to retain the idea of French agency for events and bolster the story
of the Resistance as saviours in 1944. Meanwhile, Jai Lall's family in
India wish to preserve his memory as a war hero, while acknowledging
his transgressions with Denise.

And the truth? The real story? It may never be known. As Jules Perret
says, 'It is difficult to always write the truth, nothing but the truth.'[58]

★★★

There are few physical memorials to the Indian Army in South Asia,
and those that exist stop at 1919, like the memorial in Bangalore to the
61st Pioneers. There are privately funded local memorials, though.
Épinal escaper Lakha Singh Grewal funded and built a gurdwara in
Chandigarh with his brothers to thank God for their safe return.[59]

There is increasing memorialisation of the INA, especially in India.
In Palampur, in Himachal Pradesh, a statue to Bose was unveiled in
2021, together with a memorial carrying a list of 131 names of men
who joined him.[60] In the Red Fort in Delhi, at the entrance to the INA
museum, you will find the identity card of Narayan Singh, who rose
to the rank of *Obergefreiter* (lance corporal) in the German army. The
discourse is that this card – together with a photograph of Bose shaking
hands with Hitler – is something for modern Indians to be proud of.

Nowhere is there a list of men who died on the other side – no local
or national government is interested in sponsoring a memorial to the
pre-Partition Indian Army. One Indian officer said, 'We who served
with the British must be traitors.'[61] He was being ironic, but there is
more than a trace of bitterness there. If Bose was on the right side,
then Mukandan and Grewal and Barkat Ali were all on the wrong side,
the logic says.

Of course, public opinion is more nuanced than that, and things are
changing. When Raghu Karnad started his research into his three relatives' experience in the war, he 'hadn't thought Madras could even be
mentioned in the same book as Pearl Harbor'.[62] He knew little of the

Indian contribution, as most of his readers know little, but by the end of the process they knew much more.

Modern South Asia is a product of the process of Partition, of which the Second World War was an essential element. Perhaps the Second World War is forgotten because it is too complicated to deal with the loyalties and rivalries, the rights and wrongs. The British Indian Army is like an embarrassing grandfather that you can't quite explain or understand, so you ignore him. Or it is something that is too distant in time, in miles or in spirit. People are disconnected, 'The only army most Pakistanis recognise today is the Pakistan Army ... and their memories rarely stretch beyond the 1965 Indo-Pakistani War.'[63]

When historian Srinath Raghavan joined the Indian Army as a cadet fifty years after Partition, his instructors told him that Indian military history began with the first Indo-Pak conflict in Kashmir.[64] Raghavan did not know the significance of place names like Kohima, Keren and Cassino – Second World War battles with a large Indian presence. His education had not covered them, as 'this was a history that neither country wanted much to recall. The nation-states of India and Pakistan needed new histories for self-legitimisation. And so they sought to gloss over the war years of common mobilisation and sacrifice.'[65]

Even the military seemed reluctant to keep the memory alive at the start of the twenty-first century. That is also changing. During the research for this book, I visited nine regimental centres in India and talked to countless Indian Army officers, and in 2018, I met many officers and men of the Pakistan Army. In most cases, these men (and one woman) were interested in stories of prisoners in Europe and keen to help. Whatever the political changes in 1947, there were significant continuities in the army between 1939 and 1948 – most of the personnel were the same and also the regiments, buildings and equipment. An army evolves slowly, careers can span several decades, and ex-POWs became very senior figures in both armies. In this way, an army embodies the memory of its earlier self.

The *kriegie* privates and NCOs are more likely to have been forgotten, although the Army Service Corps Museum in Bangalore now has a panel devoted to Jai Lall, and other centres plan to update their records. Once again, they will have to put up with 'one of the most galling legacies of empire ... that its story has so far been told almost entirely by the former colonial rulers'.[66]

Things are different in Europe, however. More and more places in the UK have commemorated the men of the Indian Army. The Chattri Memorial on the hills above Brighton was opened in 1921, the Peace Garden in Woking goes back to 1917, the statue of a Sikh soldier in Birmingham was erected in 2015, and the first ever memorial to the whole of the British Indian Army will be put in Kelvingrove Park in Glasgow in 2024.[67] The Commonwealth Memorial Gates in London were eventually inaugurated in 2002, with one of the prime movers behind the campaign being Chanan Singh Dhillon, POW and camp leader at Limburg.[68]

There is one memorial to the Épinal escapers, however – in a surprising location. About 500m from France, by a roundabout next to the River Allaine, in the border town of Boncourt, you can find a panel to the '*soldats indiens*', erected in 2018. It is part of a trail round the town called '*Chemin de la liberté*', which commemorates the crossing of refugees of many nations during the Second World War.[69] Perhaps in due course, this solitary panel will inspire other places to remember the Épinal escapers and the fortitude of Jules Perret and hundreds more like him.

Memorialised or not, these men – the 15,000 Indian POWs, the 500 successful Épinal escapers and the countless men and women and children who helped them – are not well remembered. They should be. They are no less worthy of record than the Americans and Britishers at Colditz and Stalag Luft III. For the sake of their families, and to set right the historical record, their stories should be told and retold.

Barkat Ali died right on the Swiss frontier and is buried in Vevey. Jai Lall fell in love and had unimaginable adventures. Mukandan kept meticulous notes and wrote them all up after the war.

These men were all individuals, all with loves and lives and needs. Not just regimental numbers, more than the sum of those numbers, more than a single sepoy among 2.5 million. There was no single story. Just as their routes from Épinal varied, so too their lives varied. We only have names for most of them, but for some of them there is enough evidence to assemble a biography, to give them the dignity of telling their story. To tell that story is to be honest, to forget them is to be untrue to what happened.

This is a story about agency. About taking action, control. They seized the moment. After years of sitting, they walked. How many would do the same?

Men who were thought of as powerless became makers of their own destinies when they stepped away from the rubble and started the long walk to the border stones. Even if they didn't make it, they tried. Their stories are stories of determination, resilience and dogged, hard slog.

Everything that a white British prisoner did – learning languages, playing music, falling in love, digging tunnels – they also did. They had ski lessons in Switzerland. They joined the *Maquis*. Everything you can imagine, everything that you saw on *Colditz* or *The Great Escape*. They did it all.

May the unknown become known.

Appendix 1

The 500 Épinal Escapers

The names and ranks of the 500 who made it to Switzerland from Épinal are shown here, arranged by regiment or corps. Names are spelt as found in the sources – mostly WO 344/360 in the National Archives in Kew. Much more information will be available on the 'Indian POWs in Europe' database.

Infantry

1st Punjab Regiment
Ali Zaman	Sepoy
Bostan Khan	Sepoy
Mohd Ayub	Naik
Mohd Zaman	Sepoy
Painda Khan	Sepoy

2nd Punjab Regiment
Amir Afsar	Coy Havildar Major
Gurbachan Singh	Lance Naik
Kartar Singh	Sepoy
Mohd Afsar	Sepoy
Tambarh Budh Singh	Sepoy
Tarlok Singh	Sepoy

5th Mahratta Light Infantry
Amre Bhagwan	Naik
Babaji Sakpal	Water carrier
Baburao Ghodpade	Naik
Baburao Kadam	Naik
Bhagat Rao Kadam	Coy Havildar Major
Dagdu Mahamulkar	Havildar
Dattaram Khanvilkar	Havildar
Deoram Dhamne	Sepoy
Ganpatrao Tawde	Sepoy

Laxman Chalke	Naik
Marute Dhamale	Cook
Pandurang Kadam	Coy QM Havildar
Raghunath Patil	Havildar
Rajaram Shinde	Havildar
Ramu Jadhwo	Sepoy
Shankar Shinde	Sepoy
Shanker Raskar	Naik
Shripatrao Gaikwad	Coy Havildar Major
Siddu Shinde	Lance Naik
Soma Ghadi	Sepoy
Subdar Sawant	Coy QM Havildar
Tatyasab Sawant	Coy QM Havildar
Trimbak Dongre	Sepoy
Tukaram Shelke	Naik
Tuko Mian	Sepoy

6th Rajputana Rifles

Afsar Zaman	Coy Havildar Major
Amar Singh	Rifleman
Bhagwaranam Ram	Rifleman
Bihari Ram	Coy Havildar Major
Chandegi Ram	Naik
Chandgi Ram	Naik
Chatar Singh	Rifleman
Dalip Ram	Rifleman
Dayaram	Rifleman
Dhanna Ram	Rifleman
Hanumana Ram	Naik
Jaisa Ram	Naik
Jhandu Ram	Rifleman
Kehri Ram	Cook
Khiali Ram	Naik
Mangu Ram	Naik
Maru Ram	Rifleman
Mohd Aslam	Sepoy
Nanha Ram	Rifleman
Pat Ram	Rifleman
Ram Sarup	Rifleman
Ratti Ram	Rifleman
Ratti Ram	Rifleman
Sanwal Ram	Lance Naik
Sanwal Ram	Rifleman
Shiv Karan Ram	Lance Naik
Shribux Singh	Havildar
Subhachand	Rifleman
Tokh Ram	Havildar

Umrai Singh	Naik
Zalim Singh	Sepoy

7th Rajput Regiment

Babu Khan	Havildar
M. Wahabkhan	Havildar
Manawar Khan	Havildar
Nurab Dullah Khan	Havildar
Yasin Khan	Sepoy

8th Punjab Regiment

Bakhshish Singh	Havildar
Fazal Hussain	Naik
Mohd Fazal	Sepoy
Mohd Iqbal Khan	Sepoy
Rae Chanan Singh	Sepoy
Sadhu Singh	Sepoy

9th Jat Regiment

Balu Ram	Sepoy
Budh Ram	Sepoy
Inder Singh	Havildar
Janpal Singh	Havildar
Kewal Singh	Naik
Lachhman Singh	Sepoy
Ram Bhagat	Lance Naik
Rattan Singh	Sepoy
Sultan Mohd	Naik
Yad Ram	Naik

10th Baluch Regiment

Abdul Aziz	Lance Naik
Allaha Bakhsh	Lance Naik
Badshah Wali	Sepoy
Chaudhari Khan	Havildar
Fateh Mohd	Sepoy
Fateh Sher	Naik
Faujun	Lance Naik
Ghanam Rang	Sepoy
Ghulam Mohd	Sepoy
Ghulam Rabbani	Naik
Gul Ghuffar	Sepoy
Gulzar Khan	Havildar
Hazrat Shah	Naik
Ibrahim	Sepoy
Kher Hussain	Sepoy
Mehar Mohd	Sepoy

Mohd Aslam	Sepoy
Mohd Hussain	Sepoy
Mohd Sarwar	Havildar
Mohd Shafi	Sepoy
Mohd Siddiq Khan	Havildar
Mohd Yaqub Khan	Sepoy
Mohd Zamn	Havildar
Musharraf Khan	Sepoy
Najab Din	Lance Naik
Niwaz Khan	Havildar
Pir Bux	Naik
Rajwali	Havildar
Ram Parkash	Naik
Saraj Din	Lance Naik
Taza Gul	Sepoy
Yaqin Gul	Sepoy

11th Sikh Regiment

Abdul Karim	Naik
Amir Abdullah Khan	Havildar
Athwal Gurmit Singh	Havildar
Bachan Singh	Sepoy
Dew Bhan Singh	Sepoy
Dhaliwal Gurbaks Singh	Sepoy
Dial Baktauer Singh	Sepoy
Fazal Karim	Naik
Hakam Singh	Sepoy
Inder Singh	Havildar
Ingehra Ram Singh	Coy Havildar Major
Kangas Lachhman Singh	Sepoy
Kartar Singh	Naik
Kishan Singh	Cook
Mohd Niwaz Khan	Havildar
Nahl Bhagat Singh	Naik
Panun Darshan Singh	Sepoy
Shah Sowar	Naik
Sohan Singh	Sepoy
Surain Singh	Water carrier
Thakar Singh	Sepoy

12th Frontier Force Regiment

Alimat Shah	Lance Naik
Bad Shah Khan	Sepoy
Dhariwal Bachan Singh	Sepoy
Feroz Khan	Havildar
Kant Bachint Singh	Havildar

Nagahia Singh	Sepoy
Nakhan Singh	Naik
Rattansingh	Sepoy
Sakah Rursingh	Sepoy
Sarwar Khan	Sepoy

13th Frontier Force Rifles

Ahmed Khan	Naik
Alam Gul	Havildar
Ali Akbar	Sepoy
Alim Hussain	Sepoy
Arjansingh	Sepoy
Asghar Khan	Havildar
Asla Chattar Singh	Bn Havildar Major
Badshah Nur	Naik
Basant Ram	Havildar
Chinar Gul	Sepoy
Dalip Singh	Sepoy
Daud Khan	Naik
Durga Singh	Coy Havildar Major
Fateh Khan	Sepoy
Feroz Khan	Lance Naik
Garewal Masto Singh	Sepoy
Ghulam Jaffar	Havildar
Jan Beg	Havildar
Jaqub Khan	Havildar
Kamar Gul	Sepoy
Khabib Shah	Sepoy
Khadmir	Naik
Khazan Singh	Sepoy
Lal Singh	Naik
Lash Kari Khan	Sepoy
Mohd Shafi	Sepoy
Muzaffar Khan	Havildar
Pegham Shah	Naik
Pirat Khan	Sepoy
Roghan Ali	Naik
Sher Raz Gul	Lance Naik
Wazir Khan	Sepoy
Zar Gul	Sepoy

15th Punjab Regiment

Gulzar Khan	Coy Havildar Major
Mohd Khan	Sepoy
Reham or Rahim Din	Sepoy

16th Punjab Regiment

Amir Zaman	Bn Havildar Major
Atta Mohd	Naik
Dost Mohd	Lance Naik
Mohd Azan	Sepoy
Shah Mohd	Sepoy
Surkharu Khan	Sepoy
Yaqub Khan	Naik

18th Royal Garhwal Rifles

Bhopal Sing Negi	Rifleman
Bhopal Singh Sauntiyal	Havildar
Jagat Singh Negi	Rifleman
Sital Singh	Rifleman

Gurkhas

3rd Gurkha Rifles

Badri Ram	Barber
Ghale Bel Bahadur	Rifleman
Kir Bahadur Gurung	Rifleman
Nanda Kishor	Barber
Parsuram Gurung	Rifleman
Rudraman Pun	Cook

4th Gurkha Rifles

Balbir Bura	Naik
Balu Bura	Naik
Budh Singh Rana	Coy QM Havildar
Dhanprashad Gurung	Rifleman
Kharak Bahadur Gurung	Cook
Kharkajit Pun	Rifleman
Lalkaji Gurung	Rifleman
Narain Singh Kanwar	Havildar
Nathu Ram Thapa	Rifleman
Pahar Singh Gurung	Havildar
Ram Bahadur	Rifleman
Sane Sirki	Bn Havildar Major
Sarabjit Thapa	Rifleman
Sherbahadur Sahi	Rifleman
Tejbahadur Gurung	Havildar

5th Gurkha Rifles

Bhimbahadur Gurung	Naik
Bombahadur Thapa	Rifleman
Sete Gurung	Lance Naik

7th Gurkha Rifles

Asbahadur Limbu	Naik
Chanderbahadur Limbu	Naik
Chandraprasad Limbu	Rifleman
Jaimardan Rai	Rifleman
Jit Bahadur Rai	Lance Naik
Manbahadur Limbu	Rifleman
Rattanbahadur	Rifleman
Rikhi Dhan Rai	Naik
Sharandhoj Rai	Rifleman

8th Gurkha Rifles

Anu Pun	Coy QM Havildar
Bal Bahadur Gurung	Rifleman
Bishan Singh Thapa	Rifleman
Dal Bahadur Pun	Rifleman
Dhan Bahadur Gurung	Rifleman
Durga Prasad	Barber
Ganja Singh Thapa	Cook
Hastabahadur Gurung	Rifleman
Inderjang Rana	Havildar
Kharak Bahadur Gurung	Naik
Manbahadur	Rifleman
Raj Bahadur Gurung	Rifleman
Ramasharan Sahi	Havildar
Shippujan	Barber
Tejbahadur Gurung	Naik

9th Gurkha Rifles

Chan Khatri Singh	Rifleman

Cavalry

13th Connaught's Lancers

Taj-Ud-Din	L/Dafadar

18th King Edward VII Cavalry

Hazari Lall	Sowar
Heri Singh	Sowar
Manke Ram	Sowar
Sarup Singh	L/Dafadar

2nd Royal Lancers

Abdul Hamid	Sepoy
Abdul Rahim	Sowar
Abhe Ram	Sowar
Ami Lal	Sowar
Bhagwan Singh	Sowar
Bhalaram Singh	Sowar
Bhola Singh	L/Dafadar
Chander Singh	L/Dafadar
Dalip Singh	L/Dafadar
Dalipsingh	Sowar
Dayaram	Sowar
Duli Chand	Sowar
Fateh Singh	Sowar
Fazal Matin	Sowar
Ganeshi Ram	L/Dafadar
Ganpat Singh	Sowar
Gopal Singh	Sowar
Govind Ram	Sowar
Hashmat Ali Khan	Sepoy
Hazari Singh	Sowar
Herisingh	L/Dafadar
Hira Singh	Sowar
Israr Hussain Khan	Sowar
Jagan Singh	Sowar
Jage Ram	DEF
Jage Ram	L/Dafadar
Jodha Singh	Sowar
Jot Ram	L/Dafadar
Jugti Ram	DEF
Karamsingh	L/Dafadar
Khazan Singh	Naik
Moti Ram	L/Dafadar
Mubarik Ali	Naik
Nafe Singh	Sowar
Noshe Ali	Sepoy
Parbhu Singh	Sowar
Pat Ram	Sowar
Pat Ram	Sowar

Pirbhu Singh	Sowar
Pokhar Singh	Sowar
Rae or Rai Singh	L/Dafadar
Ram Mehr	L/Dafadar
Ramji Lal	Sowar
Ramnarain	Sowar
Rattan Singh	Sowar
Rattan Singh	Sowar
Rawat Singh	L/Dafadar
Risal Singh	L/Dafadar
Risal Singh	Sowar
Roshan Singh	L/Dafadar
Shankar Lal	Sowar
Sher Singh	Coy QM Daf
Sukhe Singh	L/Dafadar
Tota Ram	Sowar
Zile Singh	L/Dafadar

Prince Albert Victor's Own Cavalry

Alam Gir Khan	L/Dafadar
Amar Singh	Sowar
Assa Singh	Sowar
Barkat Ali	Naik
Dost Mohd	L/Dafadar
Harbans Singh	Sowar
Hardiyal Singh	Sowar
Mohd Amin	Naik
Mohd Hayat	Naik
Mohd Khan	Sepoy
Mohd Zaman	Sowar
Pal Singh	Sowar
Sandgu Bhaghel Singh	Sepoy
Sandhu Beant Singh	Dafadar
Santasingh	Sowar
Sohansingh	Sowar
Sowar Pritam Singh	Sowar

21st King George V Horse

Ghulam Sarwar	Sepoy
Kapur Singh	S.D.M.
Sher Ali Khan	L/Dafadar
Sher Mohd Khan	Sowar

Other Arms

Army Remount Dept

Abdul Aziz	Sepoy
Ashiq Ali Khan	Sepoy
Ghulam Rasul	Groom
Hakam Ali Khan	Sepoy
Hakam Khan	Sepoy
Mohd Khan	Sepoy
Mohd Sahin	Sepoy
Sher Mohd	Sepoy

Bengal Sappers & Miners

Abdul Rehman	Sepoy
Atta Mohd	Cook
Fazal Elahi	Sepoy
Firdos Khan	Sepoy
Harbans Singh	Havildar
Islam Ullah Khan	Naik
Mehar Khan	Sepoy
Mehar Shah	Lance Naik
Mohd Areef	Sepoy
Mohd Hussain	Sepoy
Mohd Shafi	Sepoy
Mohindar Singh	Sepoy
Nazar Mohd	Sepoy
Pir Bux	Sepoy
Samundar Khan	Sepoy

Bombay Sappers & Miners

Akbar Ali Shah	Havildar
Chanan Singh	Naik
Dhariwal Basakha Singh	Sepoy
Gajansingh	Sepoy
Ganpat Jadhao	Naik
Karam Singh	Sepoy
Mohd Sadiq	Sepoy
Nawab Khan	Sepoy
Nur Ul Haq	QM Havildar
Razam Shah	Lance Naik
Sarjib Singh	Sepoy

Madras Sappers & Miners

B. Boriah	Havildar
Nasaraya Kattarpali	Coy Havildar Major
Premaya or Premiyya	Sapper
Ramaswamy Thevar	Naik
Ramayya or Ramian J.	Sapper
S. Apparao	Havildar

Indian Army Corps of Clerks

Digambar Kirwe	Naik
Havel Singh	Sepoy
Rati Ram	Sepoy
V.S. Sivon	Warrant Officer

Indian Army Medical Corps

B.B. Bhattacharjee	Havildar
Ghulab Khan	Sepoy
Jai Bahadur Chattri	Sepoy
Khan Mohd	Naik
Mir Ahmed	Sepoy
Nadar Khan	Sepoy
Sher Dil Khan	Sepoy
Sohbat Ali	Sepoy

Indian Hospital Corps

Bhundu	Sweeper

Indian Army Ordnance Corps

Abdul Bashir	Lance Naik
Autar Singh	Naik
Haripada Bandopadhya	Havildar Clerk
Karam Elahi	Sepoy
Mohd Afsar	Naik
Mohd Amin	Company QM
Mohd Feroz	Coy Havildar Major

Indian Artillery

Aman Ullah Shah	Havildar
Bhura Ram	Naik
Chhana Yaqub	Water Carrier
Dalip Singh	Naik
Fateh Baz	Havildar
Fateh Mohd	Havildar
Fazal Hussain	Sepoy

Ganeshi Lall	Naik
Ghazi Khan	Naik
Ghulam Abbas	Havildar
Ghulam Hussain	Sepoy
Ghulam Mohd	Sepoy
Hukma Singh	Havildar
Karnail Singh	Sepoy
Kehar Singh	Havildar
Maha Bux Singh	Havildar
Maula Bakhsh	Havildar
Mohd Ghazan	Havildar
Mohd Khan	Sepoy
Mohd Yusaf	Havildar
Niazahmed Shah	Naik
Rup Chand	Sepoy
Sarae Sadhu Singh	Havildar

Indian General Service Corps

Allah Ditta	Cook (Mess)
Jatwan	Cook (Mess)
Sebastian D'Souza	Mess Waiter

Indian Pioneer Corps

Abdul Rehman	Havildar
Abdullah Khan	Sepoy
Amir Khan	Sepoy
Ayub Khan	Havildar
Dost Mohd	Battalion QM
Ilam Ram	Sepoy
Mohd Elahi	Naik

Indian Postal Service

Ganpat Rao Tawde	Havildar Clerk
Mahadeo Kadam	Naik
Rajnikant R. Dave	Havildar Clerk
Sidhamaya Swammy	Naik

Indian Signal Corps

Anup Singh	Signalman
Balwant Singh	Signalman
Bhagat Singh	Naik
Chain Singh	Signalman
Dure Iman	Naik
Ghulam Mohd	Lance Naik
Gurdit Chirne Singh	Signalman

Ishar Singh	Signalman
Jit Singh	Lance Naik
Mohd Akbar	Havildar
Mohd Fazal	Havildar
Mohd Sadiq	Naik
Mohd Yaqub Khan	Naik
Mohd Zarait Khan	Sepoy
Samundar Khan	Naik
Sultan Sharaf	Lance Naik
Sumal Bachan Singh	Signalman
V.V. Subbaraya Sarma	Naik

Royal Indian Army Service Corps

Abdul Karim	Naik
Abdul Manan	Driver
Abdul Samad	Sepoy
Abdullah Khan	Lance Naik
Alaf or Allah Din	Driver
Ali Mohd	Sepoy
Atwal Gurdial Singh	Naik
Bashir Ahmed	Sepoy
Darshan Singh	Sepoy
Desai Madhusudan	Naik SM
Deviki Nandan	Sepoy
Dharmavir Sharma	Naik SM
Didar Singh	Sepoy
Diwan Singh	Naik
Edwin Kesar Dass	Lance Naik
Faiztalab	Naik
Fazal Dad	Naik
Fazal Elahi	Sepoy
Ghulam Haidar	Sepoy
Ghulam Sarwar	Lance Naik
Gul Khan	Driver
Gurbachan Singh	Lance Naik
Hari Ram	Sepoy
Hehngar Chuhar Singh	Sepoy
Iqbal Mohd Khan	Sepoy
Jan Mohd Khan	Lance Naik
Jasod Singh	Naik
Jaswant Singh	Sepoy
Jiwan Khan	Sepoy
Joginder Singh	Sepoy
Lakha Singh Grewal	Sepoy
Mahbub Hussain	Sepoy
Manga Khan	Naik

Maskin Khan	Driver
Misri Khan	Lance Naik
Mohan K.Thakur	Naik SM
Mohd Anwar	Lance Naik
Mohd Ashraf	Driver
Mohd Aslam	Sepoy
Mohd Ayub	Sepoy
Mohd Dalil	Sepoy
Mohd Faraz Khan	Naik
Multan Khan	Lance Naik
Narain Singh	Lance Naik
Niaz Ali Shah	Driver
Omparkash Bhardwaj	Jemadar
Partap Singh	Sepoy
Pritam Singh	Sepoy
Pritam Singh	Sepoy
Qasim Shah	Driver
Sandhu Gurdial Singh	Lance Naik
Sardar Khan	Lance Naik
Sardar Khan	Sepoy
Saudagar Khan	Driver
Shivdayal Pershad	Naik
Sohan Singh	Sepoy
Zafar Ali	Sepoy

Appendix 2

Before and After Épinal

The seventeen Indian POWs who reached Switzerland before Épinal are listed here, in order of their crossing the border:

Name	Rank	Unit
Hari Raj Singh	Jemadar/Adjt	2nd Royal Lancers
Ram Pratap Singh	Jemadar	2nd Royal Lancers
Mohd Gulsher Khan	Lance Dafadar	2nd Royal Lancers
Mohd Siddiqkhan or Saddiq Khan	Sowar	2nd Royal Lancers
Amar or Umar Singh	Sowar	2nd Royal Lancers
Dipchand	Sowar	2nd Royal Lancers
Harbuxsingh or Harbakhash Singh	Lance Naik	Royal Indian Army Service Corps (3rd Motor Brigade Field Ambulance)
Birendar Nath Mazumdar	Captain	Royal Army Medical Corps
Daryao Singh	Sowar	2nd Royal Lancers
Lakhi Ram	Jemadar	2nd Royal Lancers
Bhondu Khan	Sepoy	35 Field Sqn, Bengal Sappers & Miners
Hussain or Hassan Khan	Lance Naik	35 Field Sqn, Bengal Sappers & Miners
Sardarsingh	Sowar	2nd Royal Lancers
Sobha Ram	Lance Dafadar (acting)	2nd Royal Lancers
Mahmud Khan	Sepoy	Royal Indian Army Service Corps (22nd Animal Transport Company)
Ghulam Qadar or Kadar	Sepoy	3/7 Rajput Regiment
Abdul Matlab	Cook	2/7 Gurkha Rifles

The Three Who Reached Switzerland in 1945

Name	Rank	Unit
Mohd Ramzan	Blacksmith Sepoy	Indian Army Ordnance Corps
Jasin Shah	Sepoy	–
Kalangher Chan	Sepoy	–

Acknowledgements

The process of researching and writing this book was truly a collaborative one. I spent many months at desk four on the top floor of the Library of the University of Exeter, and I am very grateful to the library and cleaning staff for their smiles and warm welcomes. Yimei Chen made the map for me, a task I could never have done.

Elsewhere in the UK, many archive staff were generous with their time and help finding documents. I'm especially grateful to Doug Henderson at the excellent Gurkha Museum in Winchester; to Derek Law, who helped me trace stories of lascars; and to Ian 'John' Shuttleworth for translation help. Sophy Antrobus gave valuable feedback on an early chapter draft.

The generosity and welcome shown by the people of north-east France to the Épinal escapers was echoed by their descendants' kindness and warmth towards me eighty years later. Jacques Grasser showed me round Épinal, while Mme Large, Claude and Joelle Demet, Rolland and Giselle Naidet and Jean-Noël Naidet made wonderful interviewees. Philippe Perret provided priceless material from his grandfather, Jules. Edith Eccher and Anne Kleiber gave me a whole day on the frontier, showed me the routes, sent me reams of useful material and made my job easy, and Michel Colney welcomed me into his house. I will treasure the memory of a sunny eve of St Jean in Héricourt, eating sausages and telling stories with Claude Canard, Raymond Berdah and Victor Schwach. Claude, in particular, was subsequently very generous with sending sources.

Archivists in Switzerland have been incredibly helpful. Thanks go to Fabrizio Bensi at the ICRC in Geneva and many people at the Swiss Federal Archives in Berne, especially Guido Koller and Luca Krämer. Thomas Schmid at Dorfarchiv Adelboden and Peter Klopfenstein provided a set of amazing skiing photos. Emanuele Redolfi at the Ticino Archives gave the warmest welcome, and Zeno Ramelli gave excellent help on Ticinese matters. For hospitality and translation in Geneva, I thank Justine Melero and her family.

In Pakistan, I am once again grateful to Major General Syed Ali Hamid, my friend Omer Tarin, who never says no and who read a draft manuscript, and to Zeenut Ziad. Waqar Ahmed and Sabur made possible my village interviews in 2018, which I have drawn on for this book.

I spent three months in India conducting research and many people there made my work easier. Rhys and Maithreyi Hughes put me up for several weeks, which made it all possible. At the regimental centres that I visited, I am particularly grateful to Lieutenant Colonel Shivam Agarwal of the Garhwals, Colonel Martin of the Mahrattas, and Major Ramya at the Service Corps. Gautam Hazarika supplied me with numerous links to INA papers, saving me much frustration. Teesta Guha Sarkar and Saburi Sumran at Pan Mac India welcomed me warmly and looked after me. Samar Salvi and Shireen Vakil – both descended from POWs – were fascinating to talk to, and provided material, as did Leila Sen.

Interviewing Jai Lall's family was a highlight of the whole trip. I thank them, and Colonel Dilbag Dabas, who was determined to find them, interpreted so ably and put everything in context. Prashant Sharma translated the audio. Thanks also to those who contributed to the extraordinary twitterstorm that happened in the search for Jai Lall. Arun Swaminathan made my last night in India very memorable. Sonia Wigh gave me great feedback on the draft manuscript at just the right moment.

A very special thanks goes to the wonderful folk at the United Service Institution of India in Delhi. I stayed there for several weeks. They gave me enormous help in getting access to the regimental centres, and I made extensive use of their digitised back catalogue of *Fauji Akhbar*. Thanks to everyone there, but in particular, to Saanjana Goldsmith, Shefali Oberoi and their generous, warm *saheb*, Rana Chhina.

People without whom none of this would have been possible, I leave till last. Katherine Douglass introduced me to the whole Étobon story, helped me along the way, and toured me round the region. Claire Hopkins at The History Press guided and nudged me sensitively. Clare Grist and Donald Taylor accommodated me and fed me many times, encouraged me and listened to my stories. My two children, Alex and Hans, transcribed, translated, listened, accompanied and generally supported me all the way through. And my wife Rebecca continues to be the best person I could ever wish to meet.

Bibliography

A Note on Sources

For much of what I have written there is only a single source. Although the main theme of the book is well attested in multiple places, the stories of individual soldiers are often only to be found in one place: an archival document, a medal recommendation or a memoir. This is the nature of research into the stories of subordinate classes in South Asia. Without Virk's book on the Indian Post Office (and Mukandan's account, in particular), my book would be much less.

Primary Sources

British Archives
Churchill Archives, Cambridge: Leo Amery papers.
The Gurkha Museum, Winchester.
Hansard online.
Imperial War Museum, London.
India Office Records, the British Library, London.
The National Archives, Kew, London.

French Archives
Archives Départementales de la Haute-Saône, Vesoul.
Archives Départementales des Vosges, Épinal.
Service Historique de la Défense, Vincennes.
Archives Départementales du Territoire de Belfort.
Société d'Émulation de Montbéliard.

Swiss Archives
Archives of the International Committee of the Red Cross (ICRC), Geneva.
Berne Historical Museum.
Photo Archives of the International Committee of the Red Cross (ICRC), Geneva.
Swiss Federal Archives (BAR), Berne.

German Archives
Bundesarchiv-Militär, Freiburg.

Indian Archives
Centre for Armed Forces Historical Research at the United Service Institution of
 India, Delhi.
Garhwal Regimental Museum, Lansdowne.
National Archives of India, New Delhi.
Nehru Memorial Museum & Library, Delhi.

Newspapers and Periodicals

United Kingdom
Bury Free Press & Post.
Lancashire Daily Post.
Northern Whig.
Picture Post.
The Times.

France
Figaro.
Le Nouvelliste.
Le Pays.
Les Lettres Françaises.
Liberté de l'Est.

Switzerland
Corriere Del Ticino.
Gazzetta Ticinese.
Giornale Del Popolo.
L'Eco Di Locarno.
Le Franc-Montagnard.
L'illustré.
Le Jura.

India
Fauji Akhbar.
Times of India.

Pakistan
Friday Times.

Interviews Conducted by Ghee Bowman

Aaliyah Gilani, Fizza Bibi; Saboor & Ghayur Gilani, 2018.

Citizens of Étobon: Marianne Peret-Stuart & her husband, Jean; Collette Beltran; Josselyne Jeand'heur; M. Pernon; Jacques Croissant; Claude Demet; M. le Maire, Daniel Philippe Perret, 2017.

Claude Canard and Raymond Berdah, 2023.

Dilbag Dabas, 2023.

Dr Qausar, 2022.

Jacques Grasser, 2023.

Jagdish, Suresh and Samsher – Jai Lall's family, 2023.

Jean-Noël Naidet, 2023.

Katherine Douglass, 2023.

Leila Sen, 2022.

Madame Large, 2023.

Michel Colney, Anne Kleiber and Edith Eccher, 2023.

Micky Denehy, 2023.

Muhammed Yunis and Gul Mubarak, 2018.

Nazar Hussain, Abdul Ghafour, Ghulam Rasul, Allah Yar Hussain and Ghulam Abbas Mumtaz, 2018.

Nighat, Waqas Ahmed and Robina, 2018.

Rolland Naidet, 2023.

Sajad, 2018.

Senior officer of the Bombay Sappers & Miners, 2023.

Senior officer of the Rajput Rifles, 2023.

Shireen Vakil, 2023.

Veteran's family in Madina, 2023.

Yoder family, 2023.

Zeenut Ziad, 2018.

Zeno Ramelli, 2022.

Interviews Conducted for Imperial War Museum

Birendra Nath Mazumdar, 1996, Imperial War Museum, 16800.

Cyril Vincent McCann, 1990, Imperial War Museum, 4689.

Edward Neville Mumford, 1982, Imperial War Museum, 6363.

Interviews Conducted by Others

Yves le Bris by Michel Colney.

Denise Dieny by Edith Eccher, 2023.

Jacqueline Stouff by Michel Colney.

Heidi Swierczynska by Wolfgang von Arx and Rahel Grütter, 2016.

Unpublished Theses

Empey, William Stewart, 'The Effect of Change of Environment on the Incidence and Type of Tuberculosis in Indian Troops' (unpublished MD, Queens University Belfast, 1942).

Grütter, Rahel, 'Egerkingen Im Zweiten Weltkrieg' (unpublished Maturaarbeit, Kantonsschule Olten, 2018).

TV and Radio Broadcasts

Colditz, directed by Brian Degas (BBC, 1972).
Long March to Freedom, directed by Stephen Saunders (Netflix, 2011).

Films

Danger Within, directed by Don Chaffey (British Lion Films, 1959).
La Grande Illusion, directed by Jean Renoir (World Pictures, 1937).
Nos Patriotes, directed by Gabriel Le Bomin (France 3 cinéma, 2017).
Soldats Étrangers En Suisse, directed by Adolf Forter (Gloria Films, 1945).
The Colditz Story, directed by Guy Hamilton (British Lion Films, 1955).

Private Collections

Hexley collection.
Hukam Dad Khan collection.
Jai Lall family collection.
Lynne Gray-Ross collection.
Muneeza Shamsie collection.
Perret collection.
Varun Khanna collection.

Emails and Social Media

Sebastian Cox, 14 October 2016.
Kay Laracy, 2 January 2022.
Savie Karnel, 16 March 2022.
@nomhossain, 16 March 2022.
Leila Sen, 4 November 2022.
A.J. Grewal, 13 May 2023.
Vincent Coulon, 9 June 2023.
Jean-Claude Grandhay, 26 June 2023.
Patrick Invernizzi, July 2023.
George Hay and Nick Bristow, 10 July 2023.

@Vanguard_WW2, 12 July 2023.
Omer Tarin, August 2023.

Published Primary Sources

'Around the Camp', *The Clarion: Lamsdorf Camp Newsletter*, June 1943, p.13.
'August Sports', *The Clarion: Lamsdorf Camp Newsletter*, Autumn 1943, p.4.
Brief History of the 11th Sikh Regiment (Military Star, 1944).
Caesar, Julius, *The Conquest of Gaul*, trans. by S.A. Handford (London: Penguin, 1982).
Godden, Rumer, *Bengal Journey* (Calcutta: Longman, 1945).
Holland, Robert W., *Adversis Major: A Short History of the Educational Books Scheme of the Prisoner of War Department of the British Red Cross Society and Order of St John of Jerusalem* (London: Staples Press, 1949).
Horner, Gordon, *For You the War Is Over* (London: Falcon Press, 1948).
'The Id El Adzha in England', *Islamic Review*, 1945, p.70.
MacMunn, George, *The Martial Races of India* (London: Sampson Low, Marston, 1932).
Prisoner of War Magazine, June 1943.
'Report of the International Committee of the Red Cross on its Activities during the Second World War' (Geneva: International Committee of the Red Cross, 1948).
Shepherd, Claude, *War Record of the Indian Comforts Fund* (London, 1946).
Sorabji, Cornelia (ed.), *Queen Mary's Book for India* (London: Harrap, 1943).
Wikeley, James Masson, *Recruiting Handbooks for the Indian Army: Punjabi Musalmans* (Calcutta: Government of India, 1915).
Yeats-Brown, Francis, *Martial India* (London: Eyre & Spottiswoode, 1945).

Secondary Sources: Articles and Book Sections

Biddiss, Michael, 'Gobineau and the Origins of European Racism', in *Racism*, ed. by Martin Bulmer and John Solomos (Oxford: Oxford University Press, 1999).
Davis, Gerald H., 'Prisoners of War in Twentieth-Century War Economies', *Journal of Contemporary History*, 12.4 (1977) pp.623–34.
Dewan, A., 'The Famous Indian Mass Escape from Épinal', *United Service Institution of India Journal*, LXXV.320 (1945) pp.318–21.
Douds, G.J., 'The Men Who Never Were: Indian POWs in the Second World War', *South Asia: Journal of South Asian Studies*, 27.2 (2004) pp.183–216.
Ferguson, Niall, 'Prisoner Taking and Prisoner Killing in the Age of Total War', *War in History*, 11.2 (2004) pp.148–92.
Ghosh, Amitav, 'The Slave of MS H6', in *Subaltern Studies VII* (New Delhi: Oxford University Press, 1992) pp.159–214.
Harfield, Alan, 'Indian Army Corps of Clerks', *Journal of the Society for Army Historical Research*, 81 (2003) pp.291–94.
Hastings, Macdonald, 'The POWs Fly Home', *USI Journal* (1945) pp.304–06.
Hitchcock, Laurence William, 'In German Hands', *RIASC Journal*, XIV (1946) pp.8–17.
Indian Artillery Newsletter (1950).
Khan, Suleman, 'Report by a VCO on Victory Parade in London', *USI Journal* (1947) pp.304–06.

Lloyd, Christopher, 'Enduring Captivity: French POW Narratives of World War II', *Journal of War & Culture Studies*, 6.1 (2013) pp.24–39.

Luchessa, Christian, 'Il Ticino Dei Campi: L'internamento Dei Rifugiati Militari Durante La Seconda Guerra Mondiale', *La Memoria Delle Alpi Nella Seconda Guerra Mondiale* (2005) pp.36–44.

Naidu, Sarojini, 'The Gift of India', *The Living Age* (1916) p.258.

Newman, P.H., 'The Prisoner-of-War Mentality', *The BMJ*, 4330 (1944) pp.8–10.

Omissi, David E., 'Europe Through Indian Eyes: Indian Soldiers Encounter England and France, 1914–1918', *The English Historical Review* (2007).

Overy, Richard, 'Introduction', in *Bombing, States and Peoples in Western Europe, 1940–1945*, ed. by Claudia Baldoli, Andrew Knapp and Richard Overy (London: Continuum, 2011) pp.1–20.

Perret, Charles, 'Étobon 1943–1944: *Supplément Au Bulletin Numéro 10 de La Société d'Histoire et Archéologie de l'Arrondissement de Lure* (Lure, 1991).

Spivak, Gayatri Chakravorty, 'Can the Subaltern Speak', in *Marxism and the Interpretation of Culture*, ed. by Cary Nelson and Lawrence Grossberg (Urbana, Illinois: University of Illinois Press, 1988).

Thapar, Romila, 'Theory of Aryan Race in India', *Social Scientist*, 24.1/3 (1996) pp.3–29.

Wylie, Neville, 'Muted Applause? British Prisoners of War as Observers and Victims of the Allied Bombing Campaign over Germany', in *Bombing, States and Peoples in Western Europe, 1940–1945*, ed. by Claudia Baldoli, Andrew Knapp and Richard Overy (London: Continuum, 2011) pp.256–78.

Secondary Sources: Books

Laurie and Cecilia Norman (eds.), *A History of the Royal Bombay Sappers and Miners, 1939 to 1947* (UK: The Royal Bombay Sappers & Miners Officers' Association, 1999).

Abhyankar, M.G., *Valour Enshrined: A History of the Maratha Light Infantry 1768–1947* (New Delhi: Orient Longman, 1971).

Ahmed, Rafiuddin, *History of the Baluch Regt, 1939–1956* (Abbottabad: Baloch Regimental Centre, 1998).

Baker, Philip (ed.), *Lamsdorf in Their Own Words: The True Story of a Prisoner-of-War Camp* (Prisoner of War Museum, 2020).

Baldoli, Claudia, and Andrew Knapp, *Forgotten Blitzes: France and Italy under Allied Air Attack 1940–45* (London: Continuum, 2012).

Barnett, Alex, *Hitler's Digger Slaves: Caught in the Web of Axis Labour Camps* (Loftus, NSW: Australian Military History Publications, 2001).

Barr, James, *A Brief History of the Mahratta Light Infantry* (Bombay: Claridge, 1945).

Basu, Shrabani, *Spy Princess: The Life of Noor Inayat Khan* (New Delhi: Lotus, 2006).

Beard, Mary, *SPQR: A History of Ancient Rome* (London: Profile, 2015).

Bhalla, J.S., *History of the Remount and Veterinary Corps 1794–1987* (New Delhi: Additional Directorate General, Remount and Veterinary, Quartermaster General's Branch, Army Headquarters, 1988).

Bowker, John (ed.), *The Oxford Dictionary of World Religions* (Oxford: OUP, 1997).

Bowman, Ghee, *The Indian Contingent: The Forgotten Muslim Soldiers of Dunkirk* (Cheltenham: The History Press, 2020).

Brickhill, Paul, *The Great Escape* (London: Faber & Faber, 1951).

Buckledee, Harry, *For You the War Is over: A Suffolk Man Recounts His Prisoner of War Experiences* (Sudbury: Don Fraser, 1994).

Caskie, Donald, *The Tartan Pimpernel* (Oxford: Isis, 2008).

Cecil, Robert, *The Myth of the Master Race: Alfred Rosenberg and Nazi Ideology* (London: Batsford, 1972).

Churches, Ralph, *A Hundred Miles as the Crow Flies* (Adelaide: RF Churches, 1996).

Churchill, Winston, *The Hinge of Fate: The Second World War*, IV (London: Weidenfeld and Nicolson, 2015).

Clutton-Brock, Oliver, *Footprints on the Sands of Time: RAF Bomber Command Prisoners of War in Germany 1939–45* (Grub Street, 2003).

Cobban, Alfred, *A History of Modern France, Vol. 3: 1871–1962* (Harmondsworth: Penguin, 1965).

Colney, Michel, *À Boncourt, de l'Autre Côté de La Frontière* (Strasbourg: CSV, 2007).

— *François Bourquenez – Agent de Renseignement à La Frontière Suisse* (Strasbourg: CSV, 2012).

Cross, J.P., and Buddhiman Gurung, *Gurkhas at War. In Their Own Words: The Gurkha Experience 1939 to the Present* (London: Greenhill, 2002).

Daladier, Edouard, *Prison Journal* (Boulder: Westview, 1995).

Davall, E., *Les Troupes Françaises Internées En Suisse a La Fin de La Guerre Franco-Allemande En 1871* (Berne: Government of Switzerland, 1873).

Deedes, Ralph B., *Historical Record of the Royal Garhwal Rifles Volume II: 1923–1947* (Lansdowne: Garhwal Regimental Centre, 1995).

Dhillon, A.I.S., *The Garhwalis: The Garhwal Rifles Regimental Officers Handbook*, 2nd edn (Lansdowne: Garhwal Regimental Centre, 2008).

Dhillon, Gurbakhsh Singh, *From My Bones* (New Delhi: Aryan Books International, 1998).

Dunn, Clive, *Permission to Speak* (London: Hutchinson, 1986).

Filose, A.A., *King George V's Own Central Indian Horse*, II (Edinburgh: Blackwood, 1950).

Finck, Heinz Dieter, and Michael T. Ganz, *Bourbaki Panorama* (Zurich: Werdverlag, 2000).

Floege, Ernest Frederic, *Un Petit Bateau Tout Blanc: La Resistance Française, Vue Par Un Officier Américain Parachuté Deux Fois En France Occupée* (Le Mans: Commerciale, 1962).

Foot, M.R.D, and J.M. Langley, *MI9: Escape and Evasion 1939–1945* (London: Bodley Head, 1979).

Freeman, Roger A., *The Mighty Eighth: A History of the Units, Men and Machines of the US 8th Air Force* (London: Cassell, 2000).

Gillies, Midge, *The Barbed-Wire University: The Real Lives of Allied Prisoners of War in the Second World War* (London: Aurum, 2011).

Gould, Tony, *Imperial Warriors: Britain and the Gurkhas* (London: Granta, 2000).

Grandhay, Jean-Claude, *La Haute-Saône dans la Deuxième Guerre Mondiale* (Paris: ERTI, 1989).

Gundevia, Y.D., *Outside the Archives* (Bombay: Sangam, 1984).

Gupta, Diya, *India in the Second World War: An Emotional History* (London: Hurst, 2023).

Hartog, Rudolf, *The Sign of the Tiger* (Delhi: Rupa, 2001).

Hasan, Mushirul, *Roads to Freedom: Prisoners in Colonial India* (Delhi: OUP, 2016).

Hubble, Nick, *Mass Observation and Everyday Life: Culture, History, Theory* (Basingstoke: Palgrave Macmillan, 2006).

Issar, Satish K., *General S.M. Shrinagesh* (New Delhi: Natraj, 2009).

Jackson, Ashley, *The British Empire and the Second World War* (London: Bloomsbury, 2006).

Jha, U.C., and Sangamitra Choudhury, *Protection of Prisoners of War: The Third Geneva Convention and Prospective Issues* (Delhi: Vij Books, 2021).

Jones, Alan (trans.), *The Qur'an* (Exeter: Gibb Memorial Trust, 2007).

Karnad, Raghu, *Farthest Field: An Indian Story of the Second World War* (Noida, Uttar Pradesh: William Collins, 2015).

Khan, Shaukat Hayat, *The Nation That Lost Its Soul: Memoirs of a Freedom Fighter* (Lahore: Jang, 1995).

Khan, Yasmin, *The Great Partition: The Making of India and Pakistan* (New Haven: Yale University Press, 2007).

— *The Raj at War: A People's History of India's Second World War* (London: Bodley Head, 2015).

Kindersley, Philip, *For You the War Is Over* (Tunbridge Wells: Midas, 1983).

Kundu, Apurba, *Militarism in India: The Army and Civil Society in Consensus* (London: Tauris, 1998).

Lal, P., *The Ramayana of Valmiki* (Delhi: Vikas, 1981).

Levy, Harry, *Dark Side of the Sky* (Barnsley: Pen and Sword, 1996).

Lindsell, R.A., *A Short History of Queen Victoria's Own Madras Sappers and Miners during World War II, 1939–1945* (Bangalore: Hosali, 1950).

Mabon, Armelle, *Prisonniers de Guerre 'Indigènes': Visages Oubliés de La France Occupée* (Paris: la Découverte, 2010).

Macintyre, Ben, *Colditz: Prisoners of the Castle* (London: Penguin Viking, 2022).

Mackay, J.N., *A History of 4th Prince of Wales's Own Gurkha Rifles, Vol. III: 1938–1948* (Edinburgh: Blackwood, 1952).

MacKenzie, S.P., *The Colditz Myth* (Oxford: Oxford University Press, 2004).

Makepeace, Claire, *Captives of War : British Prisoners of War in Europe in the Second World War* (New York: Cambridge University Press, 2017).

Malhotra, Aanchal, *Remnants of a Separation: A History of the Partition through Material Memory* (Gurugram: Harper Collins, 2017).

Martin, J.J., *Les Vosges Martyres: 1940–1944* (Paris: Comité d'Assistance aux sinistrés vosgiens, 1945).

Masani, Zareer, *Indian Tales of the Raj* (London: BBC, 1987).

Mattin, Pierre, *Souviens-Toi ! Les Années Noires Dans Deux Deux Vallées Du Sundgau 1938–1945*, three vols (Editions CSV, 2013).

Mayer, S.L. (ed.), *Signal: Hitler's Wartime Picture Magazine* (Feltham: Bison, 1976).

Miller, David, *Mercy Ships: The Untold Story of Prisoner-of-War Exchanges in World War II* (London: Continuum, 2008).

Milton, Giles, *The Ministry of Ungentlemanly Warfare* (John Murray, 2016).

Moore, Bob, *Prisoners of War, Europe: 1939–1956* (Oxford: Oxford University Press, 2022).

Moore, Bob, and Kent Fedorowich (eds), *Prisoners of War and their Captors in World War II* (Oxford: Berg, 1996).

Moore-Gilbert, Bart, *The Setting Sun: A Memoir of Empire and Family Secrets* (London: Verso, 2014).

Moorehead, Caroline, *Dunant's Dream: War, Switzerland, and the History of the Red Cross* (New York: Carroll & Graf Pub., 1999).

Morton-Jack, George, *The Indian Empire at War: From Jihad to Victory, the Untold Story of the Indian Army in the First World War* (London: Little, Brown, 2018).

Naravane, A.S., *A Soldier's Life in War and Peace* (Delhi: APH Publishing Corporation, 2004).

Naravane, Vijaya, *The Uniform and I* (Delhi: Army Educational Stores, 1969).

Nichol, John, and Tony Rennell, *The Last Escape: The Untold Story of Allied Prisoners of War in Germany 1944–45* (London: Penguin, 2003).

Padgaonkar, Dileep, *Under Her Spell: Roberto Rossellini in India* (New Delhi: Viking, 2008).

Palit, D.K., *History of the Regiment of Artillery, Indian Army* (London: Leo Cooper, 1972).

Pearson, G., *Brief History of the K.G.V's Own Bengal Sappers and Miners Group, R.I.E.* (Roorkee, 1947).

Pennington, William, *Pick Up Your Parrots and Monkeys ... and Fall in Facing the Boats* (Cassell, 2003).

Perret, Jules, and Benjamin Vallotton, *Ceux D'Étobon*, trans. by Katherine Douglass (Montbeliard: Impr. de Metthez frères, 1949).

Quinn, Malcolm, *The Swastika: Constructing the Symbol* (London: Routledge, 1994).

Raghavan, Srinath, *India's War: The Making of Modern South Asia, 1939–1945* (London: Penguin, 2016).

Ramelli, Zeno, *Campi Di Lavoro e Lavoro Nei Campi: L'internamento Militare in Ticino Durante La Seconda Guerra Mondiale (1940–1945)* (Locarno: Armando Dado, 2022).

Reid, Pat, *The Colditz Story* (London: Hodder & Stoughton, 1952).

Rollings, Charles, *Prisoner of War* (London: Ebury Press, 2007).

Roy, Franziska, Heike Liebau, and Ravi Ahuja (eds), *When the War Began We Heard of Several Kings: South Asian Prisoners in World War I Germany* (New Delhi: Social Science Press, 2011).

Salik, Siddiq, *The Wounded Pride* (Lahore: Wajidalis, 1984).

Salvi, R.G., *Whom Enemies Sheltered* (Bombay: Bharatiya Vidya Bhavan, 1983).

Samuel, Raphael, *Theatres of Memory*, three vols (London: Verso, 1994).

Scheck, Raffael, *Hitler's African Victims: The German Army Massacres of Black French Soldiers in 1940* (Cambridge: Cambridge University Press, 2008).

— *Love between Enemies: Western POWs and German Women in WW2* (Cambridge: CUP, 2021).

Singh, Harbakhsh, *In the Line of Duty: A Soldier Remembers* (New Delhi: Lancer, 2000).

Singh, Khushwant, *Train to Pakistan* (Gurgaon: Penguin, 2009).

Singh, Mohan, *Soldiers' Contribution to Indian Independence* (New Delhi: Army Educational Stores, 1974).

Smith, Graham, *When Jim Crow Met John Bull: Black American Soldiers in World War II Britain* (London: Tauris, 1987).

Stockbridge, Ian, *Book of Remembrance: The Merchant Navy World War Two* (London: Numast, 2003).

Streets, Heather, *Martial Races* (Manchester: Manchester University Press, 2004).

Sundar, C.R., *General PP Kumaramangalam: His Life and Times* (Chennai: Sundar, 2018).

Talwar, Sushil, *Indian Recipients of the Military Medal* (New Delhi: KW Publishers, 2017).

Tanner, Stephen, *Refuge from the Reich: American Airmen and Switzerland During World War II* (London: Greenhill, 2000).

Thomas, Gabe, *Milag: Captives of the Kriegsmarine: Merchant Navy Prisoners of War Germany, 1939–1945* (Glamorgan: Milag Prisoner of War Association, 1995).

Ungerer, Tomi, *Tomi: A Childhood under the Nazis* (Enfield: Tomico, 1998).

Vartier, Jean, *Histoires Secrètes de l'Occupation En Zone Interdite (1940–1944)* (Paris: Hachette, 1972).

Vaughan, *A History of the 2nd Royal Lancers (Gardner's Horse): From 1922–1947* (London: Sifton Praed, 1951).

Virk, D.S., *Indian Army Post Offices in the Second World War* (New Delhi: The Army Postal Service Association, 1982).

Visram, Rozina, *Asians in Britain: 400 Years of History* (London: Pluto, 2002).

—, *Ayahs, Lascars and Princes: Indians in Britain 1700–1947* (London: Pluto, 1986).

Vourkoutiotis, Vasilis, *The Prisoners of War and German High Command: The British and American Experience* (Basingstoke: Palgrave Macmillan, 2003).

Winter, Jay, *Sites of Memory, Sites of Mourning: The Great War in European Cultural History* (Cambridge: Cambridge University Press, 1998).

Websites

'41-28738 Meat Around the Corner', American Air Museum in Britain: www.americanairmuseum.com/archive/aircraft/41-28738 [accessed 11 July 2023].

von Arx, Guido, 'Internierte Aus Einer Fremden Welt – Als Es in Egerkingen Ein Lager Mit Indischen Sikhs Gab', trans. by Ian Shuttleworth, Solothurner Zeitung (Solothurn, 24 January 2016): www.solothurnerzeitung.ch/solothurn/thal-gaeu/internierte-aus-einer-fremden-welt-als-es-in-egerkingen-ein-lager-mit-indischen-skihs-gab-ld.1531684

Assmann, Aleida, 'Forms of Forgetting', Herengracht 401 (2014): h401.org/2014/10/forms-of-forgetting/ [accessed 1 September 2023].

Castres, Eduoard, 'Bourbaki Panorama at Luzern': www.bourbakipanorama.ch/ [accessed 19 August 2022].

Chowdhury, Srimoyee, 'Historian Searches for Indian World War II Prisoner. Twitter on Alert', *India Today* (2023): https://www.indiatoday.in/trending-news/story/historian-searches-for-indian-world-war-ii-prisoner-twitter-on-alert-2358698-2023-04-11

'Commonwealth War Graves Commission' (2019) www.cwgc.org/ [accessed 8 October 2019].

'Crew 55 – Assigned 754th Squadron – October 1943', 458th Bombardment Group (H): www.458bg.com/crew55goldsmith.htm [accessed 11 July 2023].

'Facebook Group for Stalag VIII-B Lamsdorf': www.facebook.com/groups/828123490592144

Field, A.E., 'Get a Hair Cut', Campo 57 Gruppignano: www.grupignano.com/camp-life.html

France Actualité, 'Voyage Du Maréchal Pétain à Nancy, Épinal et Dijon', L'INA Éclaire l'actu (1944): www.ina.fr/ina-eclaire-actu/video/afe86002730/voyage-du-marechal-petain-a-nancy-epinal-et-dijon

'FREE! Prisoners of War Released by the "Desert Rats" Stalag XIB and 357 – 1945' (British Movietone, 1945): www.youtube.com/watch?v=eOtbjd0eN4c

ICRC, 'Convention Relative to the Treatment of Prisoners of War. Geneva, 27 July 1929', International Humanitarian Law Databases: ihl-databases.icrc.org/en/ihl-treaties/gc-pow-1929?activeTab=historical

Joshi, Vandana, 'The Making of a Cosmopolitan Jangi Qaidi: A Leaf from Sohan Singh's Prison Notebook Written in Annaburger Stammlager D/Z in German Captivity during the Second World War (1942–45)', Das Moderne Indien in Deutschen Archiven (2020): www.projekt-mida.de/reflexicon/the-making-of-a-cosmopolitan-jangi-qaidi/ [accessed 18 December 2021].

Kybird, Bas, 'Memories of Methwold', Joe Masons Page (2013): joemasonspage.wordpress.com/2013/07/16/ [accessed 16 December 2022].

'La Résistance: Une Évidence', *L'Est Republicain*, 3 March 2011: https://www.estrepublicain.fr/haute-saone/2011/03/03/la-resistance-une-evidence

'Lamsdorf Museum', Central Museum of Prisoners-of-War: www.cmjw.pl/en/muzeum2/

Marly, Anna, 'La Complainte Du Partisan': www.youtube.com/watch?v=uTMe6-6VSuQ

'Netaji's Statue Unveiled in Palampur', *Tribune*, 23 January 2021: www.tribuneindia.com/news/himachal/netajis-statue-unveiled-in-palampur-202810

Pathé, 'Indian Army Special Newsreel (1940)': www.youtube.com/watch?v=yq6E1luxLQQ&t= [accessed 25 May 2017].

'Quand Boncourt Était Terre de Passage', Radio Fréquence Jura (2022): www.rfj.ch/rfj/Actualite/Region/20221118-Quand-Boncourt-etait-terre-de-passage.html

Sarna, Jit Singh, 'Indian Army History Thread', Bharat Rakshak (2007): forums.bharat-rakshak.com/viewtopic.php?f=3&t=2623&start=40 [accessed 26 July 2019].

'Sikh Soldier Statue in Smethwick Honours WW1 Dead', *BBC News* (2018): www.bbc.co.uk/news/uk-england-birmingham-46083728

Singh, Anita, 'New Colditz TV Series Highlights "appalling Racism" of British Officers', *The Telegraph*, 3 June 2023: www.telegraph.co.uk/news/2023/06/03/tv-series-dismantle-colditz-mythology-racism-brit-officers/

Stafford, Edna, 'Repatriating Allied Prisoners of War in France 1945', *BBC People's War* (2019): www.bbc.co.uk/history/ww2peopleswar/stories/91/a2301391.shtml [accessed 18 December 2019].

Sward, Susan, 'Santi Pada Dutt: Obituary', *SFGate* (2001): www.sfgate.com/news/article/Santi-Pada-Dutt-2960799.php

'The Chattri Memorial': www.brighton-hove.gov.uk/libraries-leisure-and-arts/parks-and-green-spaces/chattri-memorial

'The Wartime Logbook of Patrick Brady': www.kbrady.com/milag_logbook.htm? [accessed 3 August 2023].

'The Woking Peace Garden': www.visitsurrey.com/things-to-do/the-peace-garden-p1463921

Tiwari, Vidushi, 'Why is Scotland Building a Memorial for Indian and Pakistani Soldiers?', STV (2023): news.stv.tv/scotland/why-is-scotland-building-a-memorial-for-indian-and-pakistani-soldiers-at-glasgows-kelvingrove-museum

'Trois Itinéraires Didactiques Pour Trois Siècles d'histoire': www.boncourt.ch/files/424/Curiosit%C3%A9s/210705_RISp_IT_80x110-Vdef.pdf

Verbauwhede, Levi, 'Grafsteen van Noord-Indische soldaat uit WO I gevonden naast bouwwerf: "Geen idee hoe dit hier terechtkomt"', 18 August 2023: www.nieuwsblad.be/cnt/dmf20230818_94968918

'Vevey (St Martin's) Cemetery', Commonwealth War Graves Commission: www.cwgc.org/visit-us/find-cemeteries-memorials/cemetery-details/54344/vevey-st-martin-s-cemetery/ [accessed 4 September 2023].

'Wie Ein Indischer Soldat Im Zweiten Weltkrieg Nach Adelboden Kam', Zeitblende (Schweizer Radio und Fernsehen, 2022): www.srf.ch/audio/zeitblende/wie-ein-indischer-soldat-im-zweiten-weltkrieg-nach-adelboden-kam?id=12133598

Notes

Prologue

1. R.G. Salvi, *Whom Enemies Sheltered* (Bombay: Bharatiya Vidya Bhavan, 1983), p.xiv.
2. 'Daily Weather Reports 1944_05', Met Office: digital.nmla.metoffice.gov.uk/ IO_dfbaf491-55d0-42a0-bbb0-c9c6e205a321/ [accessed 19 October 2023].
3. 'The Tragedy of Stalag Luft III', *The Times*, 20 May 1944, p.5.
4. 'Prisoners of War: Indian POWs and Escapees' (1945), India Office Records at the British Library, IOR/L/WS/1/1536.
5. I wrote a brief account of the Épinal escape in my first book: Ghee Bowman, *The Indian Contingent: The Forgotten Muslim Soldiers of Dunkirk* (Cheltenham: The History Press, 2020).
6. Paul Brickhill, *The Great Escape* (London: Faber & Faber, 1951); *The Great Escape*, directed by John Sturges (United Artists, 1963).
7. There was also a successful escape of 105 privates and NCOs from Stalag 306 in Yugoslavia led by an Australian private, related in Ralph Churches, *A Hundred Miles as the Crow Flies* (Adelaide: RF Churches, 1996).
8. Some writers prefer to call this army the 'British Indian Army', but I have stuck to the historical term, in common with most historians, such as Srinath Raghavan, *India's War: The Making of Modern South Asia, 1939–1945* (London: Penguin, 2016).

Chapter 1

1. Sarojini Naidu, 'The Gift of India', *The Living Age*, 289.3747 (1916) p.258.
2. George MacMunn, *The Martial Races of India* (London: Sampson Low, Marston, 1932) gives a good impression of how it was seen at the time; for a more current critique, see Heather Streets, *Martial Races* (Manchester: Manchester University Press, 2004).
3. Gandhi in 'Harijan', quoted in Diya Gupta, *India in the Second World War: An Emotional History* (London: Hurst, 2023) p.11.
4. Interview with Leila Sen, 2022.
5. Mohan Singh, *Soldiers' Contribution to Indian Independence* (New Delhi: Army Educational Stores, 1974) p.42.
6. Francis Yeats-Brown, *Martial India* (London: Eyre & Spottiswoode, 1945) p.13.
7. 'Hindou, Indische Internierte', Swiss Federal Archives, E5791 1000949 991.

8. 'Indore Cadets 1918–19', India Office Records at the British Library, IOR/L/MIL/7/19018.

9. 'Short Service Commissions in Indian Medical Service', India Office Records at the British Library, IOR/L/MIL/7/14343.

10. 'Report of the International Committee of the Red Cross on Its Activities during the Second World War' (Geneva: International Committee of the Red Cross, 1948), p.283; 'Traitement Des Prisonniers de Guerre Indiens – Germany', Swiss Federal Archives, E2001-02_1000_114_280.

11. 'Traitement Des Prisonniers de Guerre Indiens – Germany', Swiss Federal Archives, E2001-02_1000_114_280.

12. 'Stalag IIIA: July 43–44', trans. by Fiona Schroeder (1945), Bundesarchiv, Germany, RH 49/40.

13. Interview with Leila Sen. This episode also appears in Masters' book, *The Road Past Mandalay*, pp.18–20.

14. 'Medal Recommendation for Santi Pada Dutt', the National Archives, Kew, England, WO-373-47-535.

15. Susan Sward, 'Santi Pada Dutt: Obituary', SFGate (2001): www.sfgate.com/news/article/Santi-Pada-Dutt-2960799.php

16. Rozina Visram, *Ayahs, Lascars and Princes: Indians in Britain 1700–1947* (London: Pluto, 1986) p.222.

17. *Ibid.*, p.52.

18. Rozina Visram, *Asians in Britain: 400 Years of History* (London: Pluto, 2002) p.346.

19. Visram, *Ayahs, Lascars and Princes*, p.191.

20. 'Indian Soldiers and Seamen in Europe Well Cared For', *Fauji Akhbar*, 5 October 1940, p.15, United Services of India.

21. Gabe Thomas, *Milag: Captives of the Kriegsmarine: Merchant Navy Prisoners of War Germany, 1939–1945* (Glamorgan: Milag Prisoner of War Association, 1995) p.275.

22. 'Seamen Released from Germany', *Times of India*, 19 February 1940.

23. For a full account of the 22nd Company, see Bowman, *The Indian Contingent*.

24. 'Report on Stalag VIIIB Lamsdorf' (1945), the National Archives, Kew, England, WO 224/27.

25. Gerhard L. Weinberg, *A World at Arms: A Global History of World War II* (Cambridge: Cambridge University Press, 1994) p.211.

26. Shaukat Hayat Khan, *The Nation That Lost Its Soul: Memoirs of a Freedom Fighter* (Lahore: Jang, 1995) pp.44–53.

27. Ashley Jackson, *The British Empire and the Second World War* (London: Bloomsbury, 2006) p.97.

28. Weinberg, *A World at Arms*, p.348.

29. Pathé, 'Indian Army Special Newsreel (1940)': www.youtube.com/watch?v=yq6E1luxLQQ&t= [accessed 25 May 2017].

30. 'Indischer Flüchtling, Sikh, Beant Singh Im Lager Schönenwerd' (1944), Swiss Federal Archives, J1.257#1997/157#71*.

31. Syed Ali Hamid, *Sahabzada Yaqub Khan: Pursuits and Experiences as Prisoner of War* (Karachi: Paramount, 2022) p.32.

32. Vaughan, *A History of the 2nd Royal Lancers (Gardner's Horse): From 1922–1947* (London: Sifton Praed, 1951) p.186.

33. *Ibid.*, p.91.

34. *Ibid.*, p.189.

35. M.G. Abhyankar, *Valour Enshrined: A History of the Maratha Light Infantry 1768–1947* (New Delhi: Orient Longman, 1971) p.293.

36. Vaughan, *A History of the 2nd Royal Lancers*, p.186.

37. D.K. Palit, *History of the Regiment of Artillery, Indian Army* (London: Leo Cooper, 1972) p.70.

38. C.R. Sundar, *General P.P. Kumaramangalam: His Life and Times* (Chennai: Sundar, 2018) pp.72–77.

39. Hansard, 'Hansard House of Commons Debate: Libyan Battle and Bombing of Germany' HC Deb 2 June 1942, Vol. 380, cc528-34; 'Indian Artillery Newsletter', 1950.

40. J.N. Mackay, *A History of 4th Prince of Wales's Own Gurkha Rifles, Vol. III: 1938–1948* (Edinburgh: Blackwood, 1952) p. 70; A.D. Fitzgerald, 'A Summarised History of the 13th Frontier Force Rifles during the Second World War, 1939–1946' (1985) p.2, Imperial War Museum, London, LBY K 89/96.

41. 'Old Record Card for Bhopal Sing Negi' (1931), Garhwal Regimental Museum, Lansdowne; 'Pension Record Card for Bhopal Sing Negi' (1946), Garhwal Regimental Centre, Lansdowne.

42. A.I.S. Dhillon, *The Garhwalis: The Garhwal Rifles Regimental Officers Handbook*, 2nd edn (Lansdowne: Garhwal Regimental Centre, 2008) pp.1–19.

43. Ralph B. Deedes, *Historical Record of the Royal Garhwal Rifles, Vol. II: 1923–1947* (Lansdowne: Garhwal Regimental Centre, 1995) p.104.

44. Hamid, *Sahabzada Yaqub Khan: Pursuits and Experiences as Prisoner of War*, p.18.

45. R.G. Salvi, *Whom Enemies Sheltered* (Bombay: Bharatiya Vidya Bhavan, 1983) p.26. Indian brigades typically comprised two Indian battalions and one British.

46. Abhyankar, *Valour Enshrined*, p.281.

47. *A History of the Royal Bombay Sappers and Miners, 1939 to 1947* (1999) p.181.

48. D.S. Virk, *Indian Army Post Offices in the Second World War* (New Delhi: The Army Postal Service Association, 1982) p.336.

49. Tony Gould, *Imperial Warriors: Britain and the Gurkhas* (London: Granta, 2000) pp.236–37.

50. J.P. Cross and Buddhiman Gurung, *Gurkhas at War. In Their Own Words: The Gurkha Experience 1939 to the Present* (London: Greenhill, 2002) p.313.

51. 'Indian POW List', 1945, the National Archives, Kew, England, WO 344/360.

52. '7th Gurkha Rifles, 2nd Bn Digest of Service 1907–42', Gurkha Museum, Winchester.

53. James Barr, *A Brief History of the Mahratta Light Infantry* (Bombay: Claridge, 1945) p.1.

54. *Ibid.*, p.65.

55. Abhyankar, *Valour Enshrined*, p.310.

56. Winston Churchill, *The Hinge of Fate: The Second World War*, IV (London: Weidenfeld and Nicolson, 2015) p.487.

57. Raghavan, *India's War*, pp.357–59; *Brief History of the 11th Sikh Regiment* (Military Star, 1944) p.41.

58. Syed Ali Hamid, 'Prisoners of Aversa', *Friday Times*, 9 February 2019: www.thefridaytimes.com/2019/02/09/prisoners-of-aversa/

59. Weinberg, *A World at Arms*, p.222.

60. 'Indian POWs and CSDIC', 1945, India Office Records at the British Library, IOR/L/WS/1/1516; 'Correspondence of Colonel Sidney Henry Powell and Eva Mary Bell with Indian Prisoners of War in Germany', 1941, India Office Records at the British Library, mss EUR F172/148; J.S. Bhalla, *History of the Remount and Veterinary Corps 1794-1987* (New Delhi: Additional Directorate General, Remount and Veterinary, Quartermaster Generals Branch, Army Headquarters, 1988) p.130.

61. 'Part I to XIII – CSDIC(I) Red Fort Delhi Report No. 801-900', p.377, National Archives of India, PP_000002998623.

62. Clive Dunn, *Permission to Speak* (London: Hutchinson, 1986) p.85; 'POWs in Greece Lists', 1941, the National Archives, Kew, England, FO 916/213.

63. Korinth Mai 1941, Deutsches Historisches Museum, Germany, ba110792.

64. Visram, *Asians in Britain*, p.347; Ian Stockbridge, *Book of Remembrance: The Merchant Navy World War Two* (London: Numast, 2003) p.91.

65. *Signal: Hitler's Wartime Picture Magazine*, edited by S.L. Mayer (Feltham: Bison, 1976).

66. Weinberg, *A World at Arms*, p.716.

67. R.A. Lindsell, *A Short History of Queen Victoria's Own Madras Sappers and Miners during World War II, 1939–1945* (Bangalore: Hosali, 1950) p.13.

68. Interview with Micky Denehy, 2023. Denehy went on to become a tailor, making clothes for escapees in Oflag IX, A/H Spangenberg.

69. 'Traitement Des Prisonniers de Guerre Indiens – Germany', Swiss Federal Archives, E2001-02_1000_114_280; Commonwealth War Graves Commission, 2019: www.cwgc.org/ [accessed 8 October 2019].

Chapter 2

1. Interview with Birendra Nath Mazumdar, 1996, Imperial War Museum, 16800.

2. 'Medal Recommendation for Shriniwas Raghavendra Kulkarni', the National Archives, Kew, England, WO-373-46-67.

3. Syed Ali Hamid, 'Uninvited Guests: How Indian Prisoners Of War Lived In Italian Prison Camps During The Second World War', *The Friday Times*, 23 September 2021: www.thefridaytimes.com/2021/09/23/uninvited-guests-how-indian-prisoners-of-war-lived-in-italian-prison-camps-during-the-second-world-war/; 'Traitement Des Prisonniers de Guerre Indiens – Germany', Swiss Federal Archives, E2001-02_1000_114_280.

4. Cross and Gurung, *Gurkhas at War. In Their Own Words*, pp.142–43.

5. Virk, *Indian Army Post Offices in the Second World War*, p.332.

6. *Ibid.*, pp.336–39.

7. *The Oxford Dictionary of World Religions*, edited by John Bowker (Oxford: OUP, 1997) p.348.

8. Virk, *Indian Army Post Offices in the Second World War*, p.340.

9. *Ibid.*, p.335.
10. 'Rest Camps, Prisoners of War (Indian Army)', India Office Records at the British Library, IOR L/WS/1/916.
11. Virk, *Indian Army Post Offices in the Second World War*, pp.340–41.
12. 'List of All POWs in Italy', 1943, the National Archives, Kew, England, WO 392/21.
13. A.S. Naravane, *A Soldier's Life in War and Peace* (Delhi: APH Publishing Corporation, 2004) p.106.
14. Sherbahadur Limbu, 'After Tobruk – the Many', 7 Gurkha Rifles Regimental Journal, 1–5 (1939), p.29.
15. Interview with Leila Sen.
16. Hamid, 'Uninvited Guests: How Indian Prisoners Of War Lived In Italian Prison Camps During The Second World War', *The Friday Times*, 23 September 2021.
17. Limbu, 'After Tobruk – the Many', *7 Gurkha Rifles Regimental Journal*, 1–5 (1939), p.29.
18. A.S. Naravane, *A Soldier's Life in War and Peace*, p.107.
19. Balbir Rai, 'Postcards Home from Subedar Balbir Rai', Gurkha Museum, Winchester, 7 GR/402. He addresses his wife as '*subedarni*', the feminised version of his rank, a common practice in the Indian Army.
20. 'Reports on Visit of Swiss Legation to Campo 91 Avezzano', 1942, Swiss Federal Archives, E2001_02_1000114_664.
21. Virk, *Indian Army Post Offices in the Second World War*, p.333.
22. *Ibid.*, pp.341–42.
23. 'MI9 Questionnaire to Ex POWs Iliff – Kumaramangalam', 1944, the National Archives, Kew, England, WO 208/5442.
24. Bowker, *The Oxford Dictionary of World Religions*, p.348.
25. Alex Barnett, *Hitler's Digger Slaves: Caught in the Web of Axis Labour Camps* (Loftus, NSW: Australian Military History Publications, 2001); A.E. Field, 'Get a Hair Cut', Campo 57 Gruppignano: www.grupignano.com/camp-life.html
26. 'Traitement Des Prisonniers de Guerre Indiens – Germany', Swiss Federal Archives, E2001-02_1000_114_280.
27. Weinberg, *A World at Arms*, pp.597–600.
28. Virk, *Indian Army Post Offices in the Second World War*, p.333.
29. M.R.D. Foot and J.M. Langley, *MI9: Escape and Evasion 1939–1945* (London: Bodley Head, 1979) pp.156–57.
30. 'H.Q. Allied P.W. Repatriation Unit', 1944, the National Archives, Kew, England, WO 170/3746.
31. Salvi, *Whom Enemies Sheltered*.
32. 'Medal Recommendation for Naik Mohd Khan', the National Archives, Kew, England, WO-373-64-258.
33. Bilbir Rai, 'Capture & Escape', *7 Gurkha Rifles Regimental Journal*, 3 (1947) pp.42–46.
34. Foot and Langley, *MI9: Escape and Evasion 1939–1945*, p.66.
35. Donald Caskie, *The Tartan Pimpernel* (Oxford: Isis, 2008).
36. 'FRANCE F(D) Frontstalag – Frontstalags in France', ICRC Archives, Geneva.

37. Therese Bonney, 'British Troops inside a Vichy Prison', *Picture Post*, 12.13 (1941), pp.17–21.

38. 'Four Indians at Saint-Hippolyte-Du-Fort, 1941', ICRC Photo Archives, Geneva, V-P-HIST-03440-24.

39. 'Prisonniers En France : Camps de D à P', Swiss Federal Archives, BG 017 05-095_G17_51 – 94 Fr I.

40. 'FRANCE F(D) Frontstalag – Frontstalags in France', ICRC Archives, Geneva.

41. 'Correspondence Powell and Bell', India Office Records at the British Library, mss EUR F172/148.

42. *Ibid*.

43. Weinberg, *A World at Arms*, p.433.

44. Information on Qasim Shah comes from 'Hindou, Indische Internierte', Swiss Federal Archives, E5791 1000949 991; 'War Diary, HQ Force K6, 1942', the National Archives, Kew, WO 179/5881; 'List of All POWs in Italy', the National Archives, Kew, England, WO 392/21; 'War Diary, HQ Force K6, 1943', the National Archives, Kew, WO 179/5882.

45. 'Correspondence Powell and Bell', India Office Records at the British Library, mss EUR F172/148.

46. Virk, *Indian Army Post Offices in the Second World War*, p.343.

47. 'Censors Reports', 1944, India Office Records at the British Library, IOR/L/PJ/12/578.

48. 'Medal Recommendation for Ram Sharan Sahi', the National Archives, Kew, England, WO-373-64-71; 'Karteikarten (A-Z) Mit Persönlichen Und Militärischen Daten, Angaben Zum Grenzübertritt, Aufenthaltsorte, Repatriierung (z.T. Mit Passfotos)', Swiss Federal Archives, E5791 1988 6 1.

49. 'Medal Recommendation for Mohindar Singh', the National Archives, Kew, England, WO-373-64-257.

50. A.S. Naravane, *A Soldier's Life in War and Peace*, p.158.

Chapter 3

1. Poem by Ghalib, quoted in Siddiq Salik, *The Wounded Pride* (Lahore: Wajidalis, 1984).

2. Jai Bahadur, 'Letter from Mohamed Afzal to General Barrow', 25 August 1941, Imperial War Museum, London, 23628.

3. Bandleader Jimmy Howe had served the dual function of band boy and stretcher bearer in a Scottish regiment until captured in France in 1940: Sarah Coggrave, 'An Interview with Major James Howe', Sound & Vision Blog (2020): blogs.bl.uk/sound-and-vision/2020/11/an-interview-with-major-james-howe.html

4. '22 Mule Company RIASC Daily Orders Part II DGIMS', 1941, National Archives of India, DGIMS 8/9/4/1941.

5. 'Indian POW List', 1945, the National Archives, Kew, England, WO 344/360.

6. A good summary of POW camps can be found in Vasilis Vourkoutiotis, *The Prisoners of War and German High Command: The British and American Experience* (Basingstoke: Palgrave Macmillan, 2003).

7. Report of the ICRC, p.232.

8. 'Frontstalag 315 Épinal', 1944, the National Archives, Kew, WO 224/61.

9.   *Prisoners of War and Their Captors in World War II* edited by Bob Moore and Kent Fedorowich (Oxford: Berg, 1996) p.1.
10.   Ferguson, Niall, 'Prisoner Taking and Prisoner Killing in the Age of Total War', *War in History*, 11.2 (2004) pp.148–92 (p.164).
11.   G.J. Douds, 'The Men Who Never Were: Indian POWs in the Second World War', *South Asia: Journal of South Asian Studies*, 27.2 (2004) pp.183–216 (p.185).
12.   The main source for my database was 'Indian POW List', compiled in 1944 by the British, based on information from the Germans. It was of course not 100 per cent accurate, with over 100 duplicates, and no mention of most of the 500 men who made it to Switzerland, the National Archives, Kew, England, WO 344/360.
13.   Interview with Shireen Vakil, daughter of Jimmy Vakil, 2023.
14.   'Medal Recommendation for Sarto Pacheco', the National Archives, Kew, England, WO-373-46-90.
15.   Interview with Zeenut Ziad, daughter of Anis Ahmad Khan, 2018.
16.   'Karteikarten', Swiss Federal Archives, E5791 1988 6 1.
17.   'Spangenberg Oflag IX A/H', the National Archives, Kew, England, FO 916/19.
18.   Mohan Singh, *Soldiers' Contribution to Indian Independence*, p.41.
19.   P. Lal, *The Ramayana of Valmiki* (Delhi: Vikas, 1981) pp.188–91.
20.   *The Qur'an*, trans. by Alan Jones (Exeter: Gibb Memorial Trust, 2007) p.467. See also Sura 2, Verse 190 and Sura 76, Verses 8–9.
21.   Colonel Jacob, quoted in Bart Moore-Gilbert, *The Setting Sun: A Memoir of Empire and Family Secrets* (London: Verso, 2014) p.226.
22.   George Morton-Jack, *The Indian Empire at War: From Jihad to Victory, the Untold Story of the Indian Army in the First World War* (London: Little, Brown, 2018) pp.307–10.
23.   Mushirul Hasan, *Roads to Freedom: Prisoners in Colonial India* (Delhi: OUP, 2016) p.244.
24.   'Censors Reports for Middle East, August 1942–April 1943', India Office Records at the British Library, IOR/L/PJ/12/654.
25.   T.W.P. Hexley, 'Movements of No. 22 Animal Transport Company (M) from Approximately 20th May 1940 to 25th June 1940', p.9, private collection. The phrase is Hexley's rendition of the Urdu '*Izzati wali Qaid*', or 'honourable imprisonment'.
26.   'Prisonniers En Allemagne, Juin 1944–Janvier 1945', Swiss Federal Archives, B G 017 05-026 G17/13 – 20 All VII.
27.   'War Diary, HQ Force K6, 1942', the National Archives, Kew, WO 179/5881.
28.   The site now holds a museum, as well as a thriving tourist industry. 'Lamsdorf Museum', Central Museum of Prisoners of War: www.cmjw.pl/en/muzeum2/
29.   *Lamsdorf in their own Words: The True Story of a Prisoner-of-War Camp*, edited by Philip Baker (Prisoner of War Museum, 2020).
30.   'Stalag VIIIB Lamsdorf', the National Archives, Kew, England, WO 224/27.
31.   'Indian Army Clerk Outwits Gestapo', *Times of India*, 2 May 1945, p.4.
32.   Ben Macintyre, *Colditz: Prisoners of the Castle* (London: Penguin Viking, 2022); interview with Birendra Nath Mazumdar; '950 Regiment (Free Indian Legion) of the Wehrmacht: History and Interrogation of Former Members', 1945, the National Archives, Kew, England, WO 106/5881.

33. 'Killing and Ill-Treatment of Indian POWs in European Theatre of War: Disposal of Cases and Cases Referred to JAG India', 1942, the National Archives, Kew, England, WO 311/41.

34. 'Recommendation for Award for Ganpat Ram', 1945, the National Archives, Kew, England, WO 373/101/539.

35. 'Traitement Des Prisonniers de Guerre Indiens – Germany', Swiss Federal Archives, E2001-02_1000_114_280.

36. Thomas, *Milag: Captives of the Kriegsmarine*, pp.viii, 112; for a fascinating picture of what the camp looked like, refer to 'The Wartime Logbook of Patrick Brady': www.kbrady.com/milag_logbook.htm? [accessed 3 August 2023].

37. Report of the ICRC, p.553.

38. Midge Gillies, *The Barbed-Wire University: The Real Lives of Allied Prisoners of War in the Second World War* (London: Aurum, 2011) p.36; *Adversis Major: A Short History of the Educational Books Scheme of the POW Department*, edited by Robert Holland (London: Staples Press, 1949) p.78.

39. March 1945 report in 'Allemagne Marlag Ilag Nord', p.11, ICRC Archives, Geneva.

40. March 1944 report, *ibid.*

41. 'Private Papers of Captain H.W. Jones', Imperial War Museum, London, Documents: 14774.

42. Vourkoutiotis, *The Prisoners of War and German High Command*, p.138.

43. Report of the ICRC, pp.69–70.

44. *Ibid.*, p. 232.

45. 'Stalag VC Malschbach', 1945, the National Archives, Kew, England, WO 224/19A.

46. *Ibid.*

47. Lady Amery, 'Indian Comforts Fund Papers and Correspondence', Churchill Archive, Cambridge, England, AMEL 6/3/140; Claude Shepherd, *War Record of the Indian Comforts Fund* (London, 1946).

48. Shepherd, *War Record of the Indian Comforts Fund*, p.21.

49. *Ibid.*

50. 'Food Parcels for Indian Prisoners', *Fauji Akhbar*, October 1941, Imperial War Museum.

51. ICRC, 'Convention Relative to the Treatment of Prisoners of War. Geneva, 27 July 1929', International Humanitarian Law Databases: ihl-databases.icrc. org/en/ihl-treaties/gc-pow-1929?activeTab=historical

52. Vourkoutiotis, *The Prisoners of War and German High Command*, p.5.

53. 'Reports on Visits of Swiss Legation to Campo No. 29, Veano (Piacenza)', 1942, Swiss Federal Archives, E2001_02_1000114_638.

54. 'Allemagne WK XII Stalag XIIA, XIID, XIIF', ICRC Archives, Geneva.

55. Interview with Muhammed Yunis and Gul Mubarak, 2018.

56. Letters to Adeliza Amery, Churchill Archive, Cambridge, England, AMEL 6/3/120.

57. Airgram from Jemadar Siddiq Ahmed to Mrs Colvin, 10 May 1942, Imperial War Museum, London, 23628.

58. 'Censors Reports for Middle East, August 1942–April 1943', India Office Records at the British Library, IOR/L/PJ/12/654.
59. ICRC.
60. 'Allemagne WK V Stalag VC, D,E', ICRC Archives, Geneva.
61. Bowman, *The Indian Contingent*, p.125. Muslims do not actually need a prayer leader but may pray by themselves.
62. 'Stalag VC Malschbach', 1945, the National Archives, Kew, England, WO 224/19A.
63. Report of the ICRC, p.275.
64. 'Censors Reports', India Office Records at the British Library, IOR/L/PJ/12/654.
65. Virk, *Indian Army Post Offices in the Second World War*, pp.341–42.
66. 'Traitement Des Prisonniers de Guerre Indiens – Germany', Swiss Federal Archives, E2001-02_1000_114_280.
67. 'Indian Prisoners of War in Germany Welfare', the National Archives, Kew, England, FO 916/870.
68. Vijaya Naravane, *The Uniform and I*, p.129.
69. Vourkoutiotis, *The Prisoners of War and German High Command*, pp.146–47.
70. Report of the ICRC, p.135.
71. 'Captain H.W. Jones', Imperial War Museum, London, documents: 14774.
72. David E. Omissi, 'Europe Through Indian Eyes: Indian Soldiers Encounter England and France, 1914–1918', *The English Historical Review* (2007) p.375; *When the War Began We Heard of Several Kings: South Asian Prisoners in World War I Germany*, edited by Franziska Roy, Heike Liebau and Ravi Ahuja (New Delhi: Social Science Press, 2011) p.5.
73. ICRC.
74. 'Traitement Des Prisonniers de Guerre Indiens – Germany', Swiss Federal Archives, E2001-02_1000_114_280.
75. 'Mail to Indian Prisoners of War', Swiss Federal Archives, E2200.56-06_1000_646 2565.
76. 'Letters from Indian Prisoners of War', Imperial War Museum, London, 23628.
77. Mrs Bell was the widow of a colonel in the 27th Punjabis who had died in 1916. She had had a regular column in *Fauji Akhbar* since 1924. In 1941, she was awarded the *Kaiser-i-Hind* medal for her services. 'Question of the Grant of Honours to Certain Members of the Indian Contingent in Europe', 1941, National Archives of India, 18(5) – H/41.
78. Letter from R.R. Dave to Mrs Bell, 6 February 1943, Imperial War Museum, London, 23628.
79. Harbakhsh Singh, *In the Line of Duty: A Soldier Remembers* (New Delhi: Lancer, 2000) p.157.
80. 'Indian Prisoners Reach Britain', *Times of India*, 18 October 1944, p.5.
81. 'Private Papers of E. Randolph', p.47, Imperial War Museum, London, documents 3504.
82. 'Around the Camp', *The Clarion: Lamsdorf Camp Newsletter*, June 1943, p.13.
83. 'August Sports', *The Clarion: Lamsdorf Camp Newsletter*, autumn 1943, p.4.
84. 'Allemagne WK XII Stalag XIIA, XIID, XIIF', ICRC Archives, Geneva.

85. 'Captain H.W. Jones', Imperial War Museum, London, Documents: 14774.
86. 'Censors Reports for Middle East, August 1942–April 1943', India Office Records at the British Library, IOR/L/PJ/12/654.
87. Foot and Langley, *MI9: Escape and Evasion 1939–1945*, p.249.
88. Gordon Horner, *For You the War Is Over* (London: Falcon Press, 1948).
89. 'Rest Camps', India Office Records at the British Library, IOR L/WS/1/916.
90. Virk, *Indian Army Post Offices in the Second World War*, p.336.
91. 'Stalag VC Malschbach', 1945, the National Archives, Kew, England, WO 224/19A.
92. 'Letter from Bhim Singh to Mrs Bell', 11 September 1943, Imperial War Museum, London, 23628.
93. Vijaya Naravane, *The Uniform and I*, p.176.
94. 'Captain H.W. Jones', Imperial War Museum, London, Documents: 14774.
95. 'Allemagne Marlag Ilag Nord', ICRC Archives, Geneva.
96. Virk, *Indian Army Post Offices in the Second World War*, pp.344–45.
97. Article 31, ICRC.
98. Vourkoutiotis, *The Prisoners of War and German High Command*, p.199; Gerald H. Davis, 'Prisoners of War in Twentieth-Century War Economies', *Journal of Contemporary History*, 12.4 (1977) pp.623–34 (p.626).
99. Letter from Roda Khan to Colonel McRae, 21 September 1941, Imperial War Museum, London, 23628.
100. 'Indians Admired by German Guards', *Fauji Akhbar*, October 1941, Imperial War Museum.
101. 'Censors Reports for Middle East, August 1942–April 1943', India Office Records at the British Library, IOR/L/PJ/12/654.
102. 'Stalag VC Malschbach', 1945, the National Archives, Kew, England, WO 224/19A.
103. 'Killing and Ill-Treatment of Indian POWs in European Theatre of War: Disposal of Cases and Cases Referred to JAG India', 1942, the National Archives, Kew, England, WO 311/41.
104. Vourkoutiotis, *The Prisoners of War and German High Command*, pp.181–82.
105. C.A. Bayly, *The Birth of the Modern World, 1780–1914: Global Connections and Comparisons* (Oxford: Blackwell, 2003) p.397.
106. A.S. Naravane, *A Soldier's Life in War and Peace*, p.72.
107. Interview with Cyril Vincent McCann, 1990, Imperial War Museum, 4689.
108. 'Private Papers of L.H. Harcus', p.31, Imperial War Museum, London, documents 4689.
109. Harry Buckledee, *For You the War Is Over: A Suffolk Man Recounts His Prisoner of War Experiences* (Sudbury: Don Fraser, 1994) p.44.
110. Canadian Bill Jackson quoted in S.P. MacKenzie, *The Colditz Myth* (Oxford: Oxford University Press, 2004) pp.275–76.
111. Article 9, ICRC.
112. Vourkoutiotis, *The Prisoners of War and German High Command*, p.38.
113. Moore and Fedorowich, *Prisoners of War and their Captors in World War II*, p.4.
114. A.S. Naravane, *A Soldier's Life in War and Peace*, p.158.

115. Chapter 12 in Bob Moore, *Prisoners of War, Europe: 1939–1956* (Oxford: Oxford University Press, 2022); Raffael Scheck, *Hitler's African Victims: The German Army Massacres of Black French Soldiers in 1940* (Cambridge: Cambridge University Press, 2008).

116. Mayer, *Signal: Hitler's Wartime Picture Magazine*.

117. David Killingray, 'Africans and African Americans in Enemy Hands', in *Prisoners of War and Their Captors in WW2*, edited by Moore and Fedorowich (Oxford: Berg, 1996) pp.181–204.

118. MacKenzie, *The Colditz Myth*, p.277.

119. Private Alfred Bryant in Charles Rollings, *Prisoner of War* (London: Ebury Press, 2007) p.89.

120. 'Prisoners of War: Indian PoWs and Escapees', 1945, India Office Records at the British Library, IOR/L/WS/1/1536.

121. 'Mohd Gulsher Khan', Swiss Federal Archives, E4264 1985 196 14516.

122. Armelle Mabon, *Prisonniers de Guerre 'Indigènes': Visages Oublies de La France Occupée* (Paris: la Découverte, 2010) p.115.

123. 'Harbaksh Singh', Swiss Federal Archives, E4264 1985 196 16699.

124. Bowker, *The Oxford Dictionary of World Religions*, p.996.

125. 'Wie Ein Indischer Soldat Im Zweiten Weltkrieg Nach Adelboden Kam', Zeitblende (Schweizer Radio und Fernsehen, 2022): www.srf.ch/ audio/zeitblende/wie-ein-indischer-soldat-im-zweiten-weltkrieg-nach- adelboden-kam?id=12133598 (I am grateful to Silvan Zemp for alerting me to this wonderful story).

Chapter 4

1. *La Grande Illusion* directed by Jean Renoir (World Pictures, 1937).

2. Tomi Ungerer, *Tomi: A Childhood under the Nazis* (Enfield: Tomico, 1998) p.132.

3. Julius Caesar, *The Conquest of Gaul*, trans. by S.A. Handford (London: Penguin, 1982) pp.42–57.

4. Georges Gygax, *La Glorieuse Epopée d'un Hameau de Haute-Saône*, trans. by Hannah Michel-Bowman, *L'illustré* (Lausanne, 1948) p.21.

5. Jules Perret and Benjamin Valotton, *Ceux D'Étobon*, trans. by Katherine Douglass (Montbéliard: Impr. de Metthez frères, 1949) pp.16–17.

6. Jay Winter, *Sites of Memory, Sites of Mourning: The Great War in European Cultural History* (Cambridge: Cambridge University Press, 1998), p.128.

7. Interview and tour of Épinal with Jacques Grasser, 2023.

8. Virk, *Indian Army Post Offices in the Second World War*, p.345.

9. 'Frontstalag 315 Épinal', the National Archives, Kew, WO 224/61.

10. 'Indian Prisoners of War: Charente', 1944, the National Archives, Kew, England, WO 229/73/13.

11. 'Hindou, Indische Internierte', Swiss Federal Archives, E5791 1000949 991.

12. 'Frontstalag 315 Épinal', the National Archives, Kew, WO 224/61.

13. Virk, *Indian Army Post Offices in the Second World War*, p.345.

14. 'Frontstalag 315 Épinal', the National Archives, Kew, WO 224/61.

15. *Ibid*.

16. Virk, *Indian Army Post Offices in the Second World War*, pp.345–46.

17. 'Frontstalag 315 Épinal', the National Archives, Kew, WO 224/61.
18. *Ibid.*
19. Virk, *Indian Army Post Offices in the Second World War*, p.345.
20. February 1944 report in 'Frontstalag 315 Épinal', the National Archives, Kew, WO 224/61 pp.10–11.
21. 'Frontstalag 315 Épinal', the National Archives, Kew, WO 224/61.
22. A. Dewan, 'The Famous Indian Mass Escape from Epinal', *United Service Institution of India Journal*, LXXV.320 (1945) pp.318–21.
23. Alan Harfield, 'Indian Army Corps of Clerks', *Journal of the Society for Army Historical Research*, 81 (2003) pp.291–94 (p.292).
24. 'Indian POWs and Escapees', India Office Records at the British Library, IOR/L/WS/1/1536.
25. 'Karteikarten', Swiss Federal Archives, E5791 1988 6 1.
26. 'Frontstalag 315 Épinal', the National Archives, Kew, WO 224/61.
27. Report of the ICRC, p.199.
28. 'Correspondence, Recommendation for Honours and Awards', National Archives of India, PP_000002999103.
29. 'Rapatriement Du Personnel Sanitaire et Des Aumoniers', Swiss Federal Archives, E2001-02_1000_114_696.
30. The little that I know about Dr Seal comes from the ICRC reports, 'Frontstalag 315 Épinal', the National Archives, Kew, WO 224/61, and 'Allemagne Marlag Ilag Nord', ICRC Archives, Geneva. He appears in the Indian Army List of January 1942, but not in that of October 1945. So, he either didn't return from Europe, or left the army immediately upon return.
31. 'Frontstalag 315 Épinal', the National Archives, Kew, WO 224/61.
32. *Ibid.*
33. Virk, *Indian Army Post Offices in the Second World War*, p.336.
34. William Stewart Empey, 'The Effect of Change of Environment on the Incidence and Type of Tuberculosis in Indian Troops' (unpublished MD, Queens University Belfast, 1942).
35. Bowman, *The Indian Contingent*, pp.150–51.
36. Commonwealth War Graves Commission.
37. *Ibid.* This figure is still provisional, as there may be others of whom the CWGC is unaware.
38. Morton-Jack, *The Indian Empire at War*, p.400.
39. ICRC.
40. 'Traitement', Swiss Federal Archives, E2001-02_1000_114_280; 'H.Q. Allied P.W. Repatriation Unit', the National Archives, Kew, England, WO 170/3746.
41. 'Private Papers of The Reverend (Captain) J.H. King', Imperial War Museum, London, Documents: 18647. I am grateful to Bill Robertson for this source.
42. Report of the ICRC, p.303.
43. Interview with Sajad, 2018.
44. 'Indian Prisoners of War in Germany Welfare', the National Archives, Kew, England, FO 916/870.
45. 'Frontstalag 221 Rennes', the National Archives, Kew, England, WO 224/59.

46. 'H.Q. Allied P.W. Repatriation Unit', the National Archives, Kew, England, WO 170/3746.
47. *Ibid.*
48. Article 69, ICRC.
49. David Miller, *Mercy Ships: The Untold Story of Prisoner-of-War Exchanges in World War II* (London: Continuum, 2008) p.18.
50. Interview with Leila Sen.
51. 'Letter from Yasin Khan to Colonel McCleverty', 18 October 1943, Imperial War Museum, London, 23628.
52. 'Great Welcome for Repatriated Indians', *Fauji Akhbar*, 24 October 1944, p.18, United Services of India.
53. Miller, *Mercy Ships*.
54. 'Frontstalag 315 Épinal', the National Archives, Kew, WO 224/61.
55. *Ibid.*
56. Interview and tour of Épinal with Jacques Grasser.
57. 'Frontstalag 315 Épinal', the National Archives, Kew, WO 224/61.
58. Malcolm Quinn, *The Swastika: Constructing the Symbol* (London: Routledge, 1994).
59. *Ibid.*, p.5.
60. Quoted in Ungerer, *Tomi: A Childhood under the Nazis*, p.73.
61. L/WS/1/1516, quoted in Douds, 'The Men Who Never Were', p.193.
62. Interview with a senior officer of the Rajput Rifles, 2023.
63. Quinn, *The Swastika*, p.142.
64. 'Hindou, Indische Internierte', Swiss Federal Archives, E5791 1000949 991.
65. 'Rapports de Visite Müller Losone et Leysin', ICRC Archives, Geneva, B G 002 185.

Chapter 5

1. Maurice Gillet, 'A Propos Du Bombardement Du 23 Mai 1944', trans. by Hannah Michel-Bowman, *Liberté de l'Est*, 23 May 1984.
2. Claudia Baldoli and Andrew Knapp, *Forgotten Blitzes: France and Italy under Allied Air Attack 1940–1945* (London: Continuum, 2012) p.28.
3. *Ibid.*, p.36.
4. *Ibid.*, p.29.
5. Stephen Tanner, *Refuge from the Reich: American Airmen and Switzerland during World War II* (London: Greenhill, 2000) p.155.
6. Baldoli and Knapp, *Forgotten Blitzes*, p.29.
7. Roger A. Freeman, *The Mighty Eighth: A History of the Units, Men and Machines of the US 8th Air Force* (London: Cassell, 2000) p.140; Baldoli and Knapp, *Forgotten Blitzes*, p.9.
8. Baldoli and Knapp, *Forgotten Blitzes*, p.3.
9. *Ibid.*, p.13.
10. Gillet, 'A Propos Du Bombardement Du 23 Mai 1944'. This is reinforced by a war diary entry by the local Resistance leader, reporting there were 130 locomotives at Épinal Station at the time. Quoted in Jean-Claude Grandhay, *La Haute-Saône dans la Deuxième Guerre Mondiale* (Paris: ERTI, 1989) pp.146–47.

11. Freeman, *The Mighty Eighth*, p.141; 'Report on Operation 350: Mulhouse, Épinal, Belfort and Chaumont Marshalling Yards and Orleans/Bricy Airfield, 11 May (Am)', the National Archives, Kew, England, AIR 40/625.

12. 'Target File for Épinal', 1944, the National Archives, Kew, England, AIR 51/217/943.

13. 'Monthly Statement of Camp Locations (by Areas) of Imperial Prisoners of War', July 1944, forwarded by Sebastian Cox, 'Email from Air Historical Branch', 14 October 2016.

14. Report of the ICRC, p.316.

15. *Ibid.*, p.306.

16. 'Report on Operation 350', the National Archives, Kew, England, AIR 40/625.

17. Baldoli and Knapp, *Forgotten Blitzes*, p.34.

18. Freeman, *The Mighty Eighth*, pp.140–41.

19. 'Report on Operation 350', the National Archives, Kew, England, AIR 40/625.

20. *Ibid.*

21. '41-28738 Meat Around the Corner', American Air Museum in Britain: www.americanairmuseum.com/archive/aircraft/41-28738 [accessed 11 July 2023]. 'Feathering' was a deliberate step taken by a pilot to increase gliding distance in the case of engine failure.

22. Tanner, *Refuge from the Reich*, p.2.

23. 'Crew 55 – Assigned 754th Squadron – October 1943', 458th Bombardment Group (H), p.55: www.458bg.com/crew55goldsmith.htm [accessed 11 July 2023].

24. Interview and tour of Épinal with Jacques Grasser.

25. 7 June report by Épinal's Director of Passive Defense, in 'Compte Rendu Bombardements', 1944, Archives Départmentales des Vosges, Épinal, 16 W 17.

26. *Ibid.*

27. 'Bombardement d'Épinal En Mai 44: Liste Des Tués et Blessés', Archives Départmentales des Vosges, Épinal, 5 W 1.

28. 'Compte Rendu Bombardements', Archives Départmentales des Vosges, Épinal, 16 W 17.

29. Neville Wylie, 'Muted Applause? British Prisoners of War as Observers and Victims of the Allied Bombing Campaign over Germany', in *Bombing, States and Peoples in Western Europe, 1940–1945*, edited by Claudia Baldoli, Andrew Knapp and Richard Overy (London: Continuum, 2011) pp.256–78.

30. Jean Vartier, *Histoires Secrètes de l'Occupation En Zone Interdite (1940–1944)* (Paris: Hachette, 1972) p.283; Gillet, 'A Propos Du Bombardement Du 23 Mai 1944'.

31. Richard Overy, 'Introduction', in *Bombing, States and Peoples in Western Europe, 1940–1945*, ed. by Claudia Baldoli, Andrew Knapp and Richard Overy (London: Continuum, 2011) pp.1–20 (pp.2–3).

32. Perret and Vallotton, *Ceux D'Étobon*, p.41.

33. Michel Colney, *François Bourquenez – Agent de Renseignement à La Frontière Suisse* (Strasbourg: CSV, 2012) p.215.

34. Vourkoutiotis, *The Prisoners of War and German High Command*, p.51.

35. Dewan, 'The Famous Indian Mass Escape from Épinal', p.318; letter from Bhagat Ram dated 18 May; 'Frontstalag 315 Épinal', 1944, the National Archives, Kew, England, WO 224/61.
36. Virk, *Indian Army Post Offices in the Second World War*, p.346.
37. 'Correspondence, Recommendation for Honours and Awards', National Archives of India, PP_000002999103.
38. 'Recommendation for Award for Ganpatrao Tawde', 1945, the National Archives, Kew, England, WO 373/101/528.
39. Letter from Bhagat Ram to ICRC, 1944, the National Archives, Kew, England, WO 224/61.
40. 'Prisoner of War Camps Germany', pp.19–20, National Archives of India, PP_000002998237.
41. 'Rapports de Visite Müller Losone et Leysin', ICRC Archives, Geneva, B G 002 185.
42. Vaughan, *A History of the 2nd Royal Lancers*, pp.190–91.
43. Charles Perret, 'Étobon 1943–1944'; Supplément Au Bulletin Numéro 10 de La Société d'Histoire et Archéologie de l'Arrondissement de Lure' (Lure, 1991), p.27.

Chapter 6

1. J.C. Kumarappa, *Stone Walls and Iron Bars* (Allahabad: New Literature, 1946), p.6.
2. MacKenzie, *The Colditz Myth*, p.327.
3. L/WS/1/1536, quoted in Douds, *The Men Who Never Were*, p.194.
4. 'Indian Escapees from German Prisoner of War Camps', 1942, the National Archives, Kew, England, WO 208/808. In fact, it seemed the case was trumped up by two men from his village who had joined the Legion and wanted revenge against him.
5. 'Recommendation for Award for Ghasi Khan and Ghulam Abbas', 1945, the National Archives, Kew, England, WO 373/64/64.
6. Vourkoutiotis, *The Prisoners of War and German High Command*, pp.104–06.
7. MacKenzie, *The Colditz Myth*, pp.322–23.
8. Michel Colney, *À Boncourt, de l'Autre Côté de La Frontière* (Strasbourg: CSV, 2007) p.38.
9. Vartier, *Histoires Secrètes de l'Occupation en Zone Interdite*, pp.285–86.
10. Virk, *Indian Army Post Offices in the Second World War*, p.346.
11. J.J. Martin, *Les Vosges Martyres: 1940–1944* (Paris: Comité d'Assistance aux sinistrés vosgiens, 1945).
12. Vartier, *Histoires Secrètes de l'Occupation en Zone Interdite*, pp.286–87.
13. Interview with Jacqueline Stouff. Many French used the word 'Hindu' as a generic name for Indians. I have kept their original words.
14. 'Recommendation for Award for Bhan Singh', 1945, the National Archives, Kew, England, WO 373-101-518.
15. Interview with Michel Colney, Anne Kleiber and Edith Eccher, 2023; Dewan, 'The Famous Indian Mass Escape from Épinal'.
16. Dewan, 'The Famous Indian Mass Escape from Épinal', p.319.
17. 'Hindou, Indische Internierte', Swiss Federal Archives, E5791 1000949 991.

18. '29 Field Ambulance War Service Diary', 1941, the National Archives, Kew, England, WO 177/2117.
19. 'Indian POWs and Escapees', India Office Records at the British Library, IOR/L/WS/1/1536.
20. 'Un Prisonnier Hindou Se Noie Dans Le Doubs', *Le Franc-Montagnard*, 20 May 1944.
21. 'Vevey (St Martin's) Cemetery', Commonwealth War Graves Commission: www.cwgc.org/visit-us/find-cemeteries-memorials/cemetery-details/54344/vevey-st-martin-s-cemetery/ [accessed 4 September 2023].
22. 'Angehörige Anderer Nationen. Todesfälle', Swiss Federal Archives, E5791 1000 949 3500.
23. Virk, *Indian Army Post Offices in the Second World War*, pp.333–34.
24. *Ibid.*, p.334.
25. Rafiuddin Ahmed, *History of the Baluch Regt, 1939–1956* (Abbottabad: Baloch Regimental Centre, 1998) pp.112–14. After the war, he went on to become a jemadar in the Pakistani Army. I am grateful to Major General Syed Ali Hamid for bringing his story to my attention.
26. 'Rapports de Visite Müller Losone et Leysin', ICRC Archives, Geneva, B G 002 185.
27. Email from Vincent Coulon, 9 June 2023.
28. Dewan, 'The Famous Indian Mass Escape from Épinal', p.319.
29. *Ibid.*
30. Interview with Michel Colney, Anne Kleiber and Edith Eccher.
31. 'Médaille de la Résistance: Propositions', Archives Départmentales de la Haute-Saône, Vesoul, 71 W 12.
32. 'Propositions Pour Attribution de la Médaille de la Résistance', Archives Départmentales du Territoire de Belfort, 99 W 229.
33. 'Propositions de Demandes de Médéilles', Archives Départmentales du Territoire de Belfort, 99 W 217.
34. Dewan, 'The Famous Indian Mass Escape from Épinal', p.320. The *Maquis* was the rural arm of the French Resistance.
35. 'Recommendation for Award for Ganpatrao Tawde', the National Archives, Kew, England, WO 373/101/528.
36. Pierre Mattin, *Souviens-Toi ! Les Années Noires Dans Deux Vallées Du Sundgau 1938–1945*, Vol. 1 (Editions CSV, 2013) p.193.
37. 'Indian Prisoners Escape', *Times of India*, 25 May 1944, p.7; 'Escaped Indian Prisoners', *Times of India*, 29 May 1944, p.5.
38. '7000 Broke out of Hun Camp', *Lancashire Daily Post*, 23 May 1944.

Chapter 7
1. 'Edition Jules Perret WEB' (diary), trans. by Ghee Bowman, p.101, Archives Départementales de la Haute-Saône, Vesoul, 9 J 14.
2. Interview with Katherine Douglass, 2023.
3. Charles Perret, 'Étobon 1943–1944', p.27.
4. Jules Perret diary, pp.87–88.
5. *Ibid.*, p.89.

6. *Ibid.*
7. Charles Perret, 'Étobon 1943–1944', p.26.
8. Charles Renaud, letter from *Mairie* of Montreal to Jules Perret, 15 January 1946, private collection.
9. Jules Perret diary, p.90.
10. *Ibid.*, p.91.
11. This 'officer' may have been Jemadar Omparkash Bhardwaj of the RIASC, who crossed into Switzerland on 17 May. Jules Perret diary, p.91.
12. *Ibid.*
13. *Ibid.*, p.92.
14. Interview with citizens of Étobon: Marianne Peret-Stuart and her husband Jean, Collette Beltran, Josselyne Jeand'heur, M. Pernon, Jacques Croissant, Claude Demet, M. le Maire, Daniel Philippe Perret, 2017.
15. Charles Perret, 'Étobon 1943–1944', p.27.
16. *Ibid.*, pp.27–28.
17. Jules Perret diary, p.92.
18. 'Karteikarten', Swiss Federal Archives, E5791 1988 6 1.
19. Jules Perret diary, pp.92–93 It is likely that the 'Chinese or Tibetan' soldiers were Gurkhas.
20. Interview with Claude Canard and Raymond Berdah, 2023.
21. Jules Perret diary, p.93.
22. *Ibid.*, pp.94–95.
23. Charles Perret, 'Étobon 1943–1944', pp.29–30.
24. Vartier, *Histoires Secrètes de l'Occupation en Zone Interdite*, p.279.
25. Interview with Madame Large, 2023.
26. 'Le Village Martyr d'Étobon et le Village Frère de Chenebier Sont à l'honneur', unidentified French newspaper, 1947; Vartier, *Histoires Secrètes de l'Occupation en Zone Interdite*, p.291.
27. Jules Perret diary, p.100.
28. *Ibid.*
29. Charles Perret, 'Étobon 1943–1944', pp.31–32.
30. *Ibid.*
31. *Ibid.*
32. Jules Perret diary, pp.158–59.

Chapter 8

1. *La Grande Illusion.*
2. Perret and Vallotton, *Ceux D'Étobon*, p.49, 27 May.
3. 'Porrentruy', *Le Jura*, 25 May 1944.
4. 'Hindou, Indische Internierte', Swiss Federal Archives, E5791 1000949 991.
5. 'Medal Recommendation for Farid Mohd & Mubarak Ali', the National Archives, Kew, England, WO-373-101-541.
6. February 1944 report in 'Frontstalag 315 Épinal', the National Archives, Kew, WO 224/61.
7. 'Ex-Prisoner of War', *Fauji Akhbar*, 8 May 1945, p.20, United Services of India.

8.   Commonwealth War Graves Commission.
9.   Douglass.
10.   Interview with Claude Canard and Raymond Berdah.
11.   'Quelque Souvenirs d'il y a 60 Ans', *L'Est Républicain*, 2005.
12.   Interview with Yoder family, 2023.
13.   'Quelque Souvenirs d'il y a 60 Ans', *L'Est Républicain*, 2005.
14.   Interview with Denise Dieny, 2023.
15.   Mattin, *Souviens-Toi*, Vol. 1, pp.167–68.
16.   Interview with Denise Dieny.
17.   'Quand Boncourt Était Terre de Passage', Radio Fréquence Jura (2022): www.rfj.ch/rfj/Actualite/Region/20221118-Quand-Boncourt-etait-terre-de-passage.html
18.   The last line of *La Grande Illusion* is 'Don't shoot – they're in Switzerland'.
19.   Tanner, *Refuge from the Reich*, p.127.
20.   Marcel Quain, quoted in Colney, *À Boncourt, de l'Autre Côté de La Frontière*, p.166.
21.   Colney, *À Boncourt, de l'Autre Côté de La Frontière*, p.171.
22.   Interview with Birendra Nath Mazumdar.
23.   Interview with Michel Colney, Anne Kleiber and Edith Eccher.
24.   Interview with Yves le Bris.
25.   Colney, *François Bourquenez*, pp.214–15.
26.   'Karteikarten', Swiss Federal Archives, E5791 1988 6 1.
27.   'Indian Prisoners Escape', *Times of India*, 25 May 1944.
28.   Dewan, 'The Famous Indian Mass Escape from Épinal', pp.320–21.
29.   Colney, *À Boncourt, de l'Autre Côté de La Frontière*, p.171.
30.   *Ibid.*, pp.163–65.
31.   *Ibid.*, p.166.
32.   'Indian POWs and Escapees', India Office Records at the British Library, IOR/L/WS/1/1536.
33.   'Escaped Indian Prisoners', *Times of India*, 29 May 1944.
34.   Colney, *À Boncourt, de l'Autre Côté de La Frontière*, pp.171–72.
35.   'Hindou, Indische Internierte', Swiss Federal Archives, E5791 1000949 991.
36.   Colney, *À Boncourt, de l'Autre Côté de La Frontière*, p.173.

Chapter 9
1.   'Indian Soldiers in France', *Times of India*, 24 August 1944, p.4.
2.   'François Michel De Champeaux', Service Historique de la Défense, Vincennes, GR 8YE 140204; see also Bowman, *The Indian Contingent*, p.41.
3.   Alfred Cobban, *A History of Modern France, Vol. 3: 1871–1962* (Harmondsworth: Penguin, 1965) p.198.
4.   Giles Milton, *The Ministry of Ungentlemanly Warfare* (John Murray, 2016) pp.263–5.
5.   Mabon, *Prisonniers de Guerre 'Indigènes'*, p.116; *Nos Patriotes*, directed by Gabriel Le Bomin (France 3 cinéma, 2017).
6.   'Indian Soldiers in France', *Times of India*, 24 August 1944, p.4.
7.   Email from Jean-Claude Grandhay, 26 June 2023.

8. Bowman, *The Indian Contingent*, pp.134–41, 190–91; Raghavan, *India's War* pp.246–55.
9. 'French Treatment of Indian Ex POWs', 1944, the National Archives, Kew, England, FO 371/49116; Georges Raves, 'J'ai vu Les Héros de L' Inde Libre ', *Figaro*, 29 September 1944.
10. Rudolf Hartog, *The Sign of the Tiger* (Delhi: Rupa, 2001) pp.135–48.
11. His name was Ganpat Kadam. 'Indian Prisoners of War: Charente', the National Archives, Kew, England, WO 229/73/13.
12. Vartier, *Histoires Secrètes de l'Occupation En Zone Interdite*, p.292.
13. Jules Perret diary, p.93.
14. Perret and Vallotton, *Ceux D'Étobon*, 23 May.
15. 'Indian Escapees from German Prisoner of War Camps', the National Archives, Kew, England, WO 208/808.
16. 'Medal Recommendation for Nadir Khan', the National Archives, Kew, England, WO-373-101-519.
17. Stockbridge, *Book of Remembrance: The Merchant Navy World War Two*, p.208.
18. 'Indian P.O.Ws Freed via Russia', *Fauji Akhbar*, 3 April 1945, p.20, United Services of India.
19. 'Five Years in Prison, Now Back in India', *Fauji Akhbar*, 8 May 1945, p.20, United Services of India.
20. 'Indian Prisoners of War Back Home from Europe: Some of Our Jawans had Fought with the Maquis', *Fauji Akhbar*, 2 January 1945, p.17, United Services of India.
21. 'Karteikarten', Swiss Federal Archives, E5791 1988 6 1.
22. The sources for Jai Lall's story do not always align (and in some cases, his name is spelled with one 'l'). This account is based on all of them: 'Medal Recommendation for Jai Lal', the National Archives, Kew, England, WO 373/64/245; interview with veteran's family in Madina, 2023; interview with Jean-Noël Naidet, 2023; interview with Rolland Naidet, 2023; 'Jai Lal', *Fauji Akhbar*, 17 July 1945, p.5, United Services of India; 'Indian Led Frenchman to Freedom', *Fauji Akhbar*, 29 May 1945, p.19, United Services of India.
23. 'Jai Lal', *Fauji Akhbar*, 17 July 1945, p.5.
24. Interview with Jean-Noël Naidet.
25. 'Jai Lal', *Fauji Akhbar*, 17 July 1945, p.5.
26. 'La Résistance: Une Évidence', *L'Est Republicain*, 3 March 2011: www.estrepublicain.fr/haute-saone/2011/03/03/la-resistance-une-evidence
27. Interview with Jean-Noël Naidet.
28. 'La Résistance: Une Évidence', *L'Est Republicain*, 3 March 2011.
29. Interview with Rolland Naidet.
30. 'Jai Lal', *Fauji Akhbar*, 17 July 1945, p.5.
31. Note dated 28 April 1945 from Lieutenant Colonel Benbow, Indian Army Liaison Officer with SHAEF, 'Indian PWs', 1945, the National Archives, Kew, England, WO 229/73/15.
32. 'Jai Lal', *Fauji Akhbar*, 17 July 1945, p.5.
33. Lieutenant Colonel Benbow, 'Indian PWs', the National Archives, Kew, England, WO 229/73/15.

34. 'German and Italian Attempts to Suborn Indian Prisoners of War. Activities of Central Free Indian Bureau in Berlin and Rome, June 1942–Aug 1945', the National Archives, Kew, England, WO 208/802.
35. 'Medal Recommendation for Vishram Rao Shinde', the National Archives, Kew, England, WO-373-101-529.
36. Douds, *The Men Who Never Were*, p.210.
37. Rafiuddin Ahmed, *History of the Baluch Regt, 1939–1956*, pp.114–15.
38. Raffael Scheck, *Love Between Enemies: Western POWs and German Women in WW2* (Cambridge: CUP, 2021) pp.104–05.
39. There is one Shakti Singh in the database, a sepoy with the 7 Rajput Regiment, 'Indian POW List', the National Archives, Kew, England, WO 344/360.
40. 'Ernest [Ernst] Frederick FLOEGE, Aka Jean FONTAINE, Aka Paul FONTAINE', the National Archives, Kew, England, HS 9/520/8.
41. Harkabahadur Rai, 'With the Free French', *7 Gurkha Rifles Regimental Journal* (1939) pp.30–31.
42. *Ibid.*
43. Ernest Frederic Floege, *Un Petit Bateau Tout Blanc; La Résistance Française, Vue Par un Officier Américain Parachute Deux Fois en France Occupée* (Le Mans: Commerciale, 1962) pp.206–07. Floege does not mention the name of this particular '*hindou*', but all the evidence says that this was Harkabahadur.
44. 'Ernest [Ernst] Frederick FLOEGE', the National Archives, Kew, England, HS 9/520/8, p.8.
45. 'POW Rec Camps', 1944, India Office Records at the British Library, IOR/L/WS/2/43.
46. 'Medal Recommendation for Harkabir Rai', the National Archives, Kew, England, WO-373-64-91. His name sometimes appears in this format.
47. 'Indian Prisoners of War: Charente', the National Archives, Kew, England, WO 229/73/13.
48. 'Indian POWs and CSDIC', India Office Records at the British Library, IOR/L/WS/1/1516.

Chapter 10
1. The motto of Geneva, meaning 'After Darkness, Light': www.unige.ch/math/EnsMath/EM_fr/coin.html
2. Y.D. Gundevia, *Outside the Archives* (Bombay: Sangam, 1984) p.131.
3. Report of the ICRC, p.32.
4. E. Davall, *Les Troupes Françaises Internées en Suisse a la Fin de la Guerre Franco-Allemande En 1871* (Berne: Government of Switzerland, 1873) pp.258, 295.
5. *Ibid.*, p.56.
6. Heinz Dieter Finck and Michael T Ganz, *Bourbaki Panorama* (Zurich: Werdverlag, 2000).
7. Caption in Eduoard Castres' 'Bourbaki Panorama at Luzern': www.bourbakipanorama.ch/ [accessed 19 August 2022].
8. Davall, *Les Troupes Françaises Internées*, p.113.
9. *Ibid.*, p.49.

10. 'Hindou, Indische Internierte: Die Indischen Militaerfluechtlinge', 1944, Swiss Federal Archives, E5791 1000949 991.
11. Report of the ICRC, p.223.
12. Tanner, *Refuge from the Reich*, p.56.
13. *Ibid.*, p.72.
14. *Ibid.*, p.73.
15. *Swiss History*, Bern Historical Museum.
16. *Ibid.*
17. Caroline Moorehead, *Dunant's Dream: War, Switzerland, and the History of the Red Cross* (New York: Carroll & Graf Pub., 1999) p.xxvii; *Swiss History*, Bern Historical Museum.
18. Moorehead, *Dunant's Dream*, p.xxx.
19. *Queen Mary's Book for India*, edited by Cornelia Sorabji (London: Harrap, 1943) p.75.
20. From a book published in 1956, Khushwant Singh, *Train to Pakistan* (Gurgaon: Penguin, 2009) p.39.
21. 'Hindou, Indische Internierte', Swiss Federal Archives, E5791 1000949 991.
22. For example, James Masson Wikeley, *Recruiting Handbooks for the Indian Army: Punjabi Musalmans* (Calcutta: Government of India, 1915).
23. *Soldats Etrangers En Suisse*, directed by Adolf Forter (Gloria Films, 1945).
24. Report of the ICRC, p.557.
25. *Soldats Etrangers En Suisse*.
26. Foot and Langley, *MI9: Escape and Evasion 1939–1945*, p.19.
27. Tanner, *Refuge from the Reich*, p.17.
28. Report of the ICRC, p.564.
29. Interview with Edward Neville Mumford, 1982, Imperial War Museum, 6363: www.iwm.org.uk/collections/item/object/80006184
30. *Soldats Etrangers En Suisse*.
31. 'Military Attache's Report on British POW's Stay in Switzerland', 1944, the National Archives, Kew, England, WO 208/3481; Foot and Langley, *MI9: Escape and Evasion 1939–1945*, p.132.
32. Tanner, *Refuge from the Reich*, p.140; 'Termination of Use of Adelboden Church by Escapees', the National Archives, Kew, England, FO 371/39880.
33. 'Marking Time, A Weekly Newspaper For British Troops in Switzerland', Swiss Federal Archives, E5791 1000 949 2631.
34. 'Prisonniers En Allemagne, Juin 1944–Janvier 1945', Swiss Federal Archives, B G 017 05-026 G17/13 – 20 All VII.
35. 'Karteikarten', Swiss Federal Archives, E5791 1988 6 1.
36. 'Indian POWs and Escapees', India Office Records at the British Library, IOR/L/WS/1/1536.
37. 'Medal Recommendation for Lakhi Ram', the National Archives, Kew, England, WO-373-64-79.
38. 'Indian Prisoners of War Back Home from Europe: Some of Our Jawans Had Fought with the Maquis', *Fauji Akhbar*, 2 January 1945, p.17.
39. 'Indian POWs and Escapees', India Office Records at the British Library, IOR/L/WS/1/1536.

40. These statistics are mainly drawn from the Swiss record cards, 'Karteikarten', Swiss Federal Archives, E5791 1988 6 1; 'Heimschaffungen USA Und Briten', Swiss Federal Archives, E5791 1000 949 922.

41. 'Historical Record of MI9, IS9, RAF Intelligence Course B, Awards Bureau and Screening Commission', p.14, the National Archives, Kew, England, WO 208/3242.

42. Army observer report, reported in Raghavan, *India's War*, p.434.

43. Mattin, *Souviens-Toi*, Vol. 1, pp.194–95.

44. *Ibid.*, pp.194–95.

45. *Soldats Etrangers En Suisse*.

46. Interview with Edward Neville Mumford.

47. 'Hindou, Indische Internierte', Swiss Federal Archives, E5791 1000949 991.

48. *Ibid.*

49. 'Britische Internierte', Swiss Federal Archives, E5791 1000 949 941.

50. 'Hindou, Indische Internierte', Swiss Federal Archives, E5791 1000949 991.

51. 'Heimschaffungen', Swiss Federal Archives, E5791 1000 949 922.

52. 'Hindou, Indische Internierte', Swiss Federal Archives, E5791 1000949 991.

53. This section draws particularly on two sources: Rahel Grütter, 'Egerkingen Im Zweiten Weltkrieg' (unpublished Maturaarbeit, Kantonsschule Olten, 2018); and Guido von Arx, 'Internierte Aus Einer Fremden Welt – Als Es in Egerkingen Ein Lager Mit Indischen Sikhs Gab', trans. by Ian Shuttleworth, Solothurner Zeitung (Solothurn, 24 January 2016): www.solothurnerzeitung. ch/solothurn/thal-gaeu/internierte-aus-einer-fremden-welt-als-es-in- egerkingen-ein-lager-mit-indischen-skihs-gab-ld.1531684

54. Guido von Arx, 'Internierte Aus Einer Fremden Welt – Als Es in Egerkingen Ein Lager Mit Indischen Sikhs Gab', trans. by Ian Shuttleworth, Solothurner Zeitung (Solothurn, 24 January 2016): www.solothurnerzeitung.ch/solothurn/ thal-gaeu/internierte-aus-einer-fremden-welt-als-es-in-egerkingen-ein-lager- mit-indischen-skihs-gab-ld.1531684

55. *Ibid.*

56. *Ibid.*

57. Castres, 'Bourbaki Panorma at Luzern': www.bourbakipanorama.ch

58. Grütter, 'Egerkingen im Zweiten Weltkrieg' (unpublished Maturaarbeit, Kantonsschule Olten, 2018).

59. Interview with Heidi Swierczynska, 2016.

60. Guido von Arx, 'Internierte Aus Einer Fremden Welt'.

61. *Ibid.*

62. *Ibid.*

63. 'Porrentruy', *Le Jura*, 25 May 1944.

64. *Soldats Etrangers En Suisse*.

65. 'Hindou, Indische Internierte', Swiss Federal Archives, E5791 1000949 991.

66. *Ibid.*

Chapter 11
1. Salvi, *Whom Enemies Sheltered*, p.125.

2. 'Compte Rendu Bombardements', Archives Départmentales des Vosges, Épinal, 16 W 17.
3. Gillet, 'A Propos Du Bombardement Du 23 Mai 1944'.
4. Interview and tour of Épinal with Jacques Grasser.
5. Gillet, 'A Propos Du Bombardement Du 23 Mai 1944'.
6. Baldoli and Knapp, *Forgotten Blitzes*, p.120.
7. Gillet, 'A Propos Du Bombardement Du 23 Mai 1944'.
8. France Actualité, 'Voyage Du Maréchal Pétain à Nancy, Épinal et Dijon', *L'INA Éclaire l'actu* (1944): www.ina.fr/ina-eclaire-actu/video/afe86002730/voyage-du-marechal-petain-a-nancy-epinal-et-dijon
9. Overy, 'Introduction', in *Bombing, States and Peoples in Western Europe, 1940–1945*, ed. by Claudia Baldoli, Andrew Knapp and Richard Overy, p.17.
10. Interview and tour of Épinal with Jacques Grasser.
11. 'Frontstalag 315 Épinal', the National Archives, Kew, WO 224/61.
12. 'Les Pauvres Victimes Des Bombardements', *Le Nouvelliste*, 27 May 1944.
13. 'FRANCE F(D) Frontstalag – Frontstalags in France', ICRC Archives, Geneva.
14. *Ibid*.
15. 'Shooting on Recapture of Four Indian Prisoners of War near Stalag 315, Épinal, France, 15 July 1944', the National Archives, Kew, England, WO 311/906.
16. *Ibid*.
17. Email from George Hay and Nick Bristow to Ghee Bowman, 10 July 2023.
18. Commonwealth War Graves Commission.
19. 'Shooting on Recapture', the National Archives, Kew, England, WO 311/906.
20. Dewan, 'The Famous Indian Mass Escape from Épinal', pp.319–20.
21. 'Karteikarten', Swiss Federal Archives, E5791 1988 6 1.
22. 'Part I to XIII – CSDIC(I) Red Fort Delhi Report No. 801–900', p.85.
23. This section is based on the work of local journalist Hubert Bernard, published in Vartier, *Histoires Secrètes de l'Occupation En Zone Interdite*, pp.290–91. Unfortunately, no Indian account has been found, although their leader may have been Shivdeo Singh, mentioned in Chapter 8.
24. Gillet, 'A Propos Du Bombardement Du 23 Mai 1944'.
25. 'German and Italian Attempts', the National Archives, Kew, England, WO 208/802.
26. Interview with Zeno Ramelli in Geneva, 2022.
27. Christian Luchessa, 'Il Ticino Dei Campi: L'internamento Dei Rifugiati Militari Durante La Seconda Guerra Mondiale', *La Memoria Delle Alpi Nella Seconda Guerra Mondiale* (2005) pp.36–44 (p.36).
28. Salvisberg, 'Final Report Ticino Sector', 1945, Swiss Federal Archives, E5791 1000949 2370.
29. 'Britische Internierte', Swiss Federal Archives, E5791 1000 949 941.
30. 'Anche Gli Indiani', *Gazzetta Ticinese*, 16 June 1944, p.3.
31. 'Un'altra Caroyana Di Indiani', *Giornale Del Popolo* (Lugano, 23 June 1944) p.3.
32. 'Internés Hindous et Chypriotes', ICRC Archives, Geneva, B G 002 149.
33. Interview with Edward Neville Mumford.

34. Salvisberg, 'Final Report Ticino Sector', 1945, Swiss Federal Archives, E5791 1000949 2370.
35. Zeno Ramelli, *Campi Di Lavoro*, p.143.
36. 'Internés Hindous et Chypriotes', ICRC Archives, Geneva, B G 002 149.
37. Interview with Edward Neville Mumford.
38. 'Indian Escapees from German Prisoner of War Camps', the National Archives, Kew, England, WO 208/808.
39. Interview with Birendra Nath Mazumdar.
40. *Ibid*.
41. 'Internés Hindous et Chypriotes', ICRC Archives, Geneva, B G 002 149.
42. Ramelli, *Campi Di Lavoro*, p.142.
43. 'Rapports de Visite Müller Losone et Leysin', ICRC Archives, Geneva, B G 002 185.
44. Email from Patrick Invernizzi to Ghee Bowman, July 2023.
45. 'Karteikarten', Swiss Federal Archives, E5791 1988 6 1.
46. The information in this section is from Ramelli, *Campi Di Lavoro*, pp.148–49.
47. Interview with Zeno Ramelli in Geneva.
48. Ramelli, *Campi Di Lavoro*, pp.148–49.
49. 'Britische Internierte', Swiss Federal Archives, E5791 1000 949 941.
50. Weinberg, *A World at Arms*, p.762.
51. 'Activities of War Correspondents on Swiss Border', 1944, the National Archives, Kew, England, FO 371/39875.
52. Weinberg, *A World at Arms*, p.695.
53. Interview with Edward Neville Mumford.
54. William Pennington, *Pick Up Your Parrots and Monkeys … and Fall in Facing the Boats* (Cassell, 2003).
55. 'Gli Indiani Sono Partiti', *L'Eco Di Locarno* (Locarno, 30 September 1944) p.2.
56. 'Hindou, Indische Internierte', Swiss Federal Archives, E5791 1000949 991.
57. 'Corriere Locarnese', *Corriere Del Ticino* (Lugano, 4 October 1944) p.3.
58. 'Gli Indiani Sono Partiti', *L'Eco Di Locarno* (Locarno, 30 September 1944) p.2.
59. Salvisberg, 'Final Report Ticino Sector', 1945, Swiss Federal Archives, E5791 1000949 2370.
60. *Ibid*.
61. Interview with Edward Neville Mumford.
62. 'H.Q. Allied P.W. Repatriation Unit', the National Archives, Kew, England, WO 170/3746.
63. Von Arx, 'Internierte Aus Einer Fremden Welt'.
64. '22 Ind RFT Camp War Diary for Dec 1944', 1944, National Archives of India, Misc/359/H; '17 Ind Reinforcement Camp War Diary Dec 44', 1944, National Archives of India, Misc/364/H.
65. 'Disposal of Ex PWs from Western Theatre of War', p.95, National Archives of India, PP_000002999124.
66. *Ibid*., p.122.

Chapter 12

1. Reuters, 'Repatriated Indian Prisoners in Britain', *Times of India*, 2 September 1944, p.3.
2. Vourkoutiotis, *The Prisoners of War and German High Command*, pp.172–73.
3. 'Bombing of Prisoner of War Camps – Germany', the National Archives, Kew, England, FO 916/1184.
4. Horner, *For You the War Is Over*.
5. A.A. Filose, *King George V's Own Central Indian Horse*, Vol. II (Edinburgh: Blackwood, 1950) p.409; 'Rest Camps', India Office Records at the British Library, IOR L/WS/1/916.
6. 'Allemagne WK XII Stalag XIIA, XIID, XIIF', ICRC Archives, Geneva.
7. 'Censors Reports for Middle East June 1944–March 1945', India Office Records at the British Library, IOR/L/PJ/12/656.
8. MacKenzie, *The Colditz Myth*, p.359.
9. *Long March to Freedom*, directed by Stephen Saunders (Netflix, 2011).
10. Virk, *Indian Army Post Offices in the Second World War*, pp.347–49.
11. Claire Makepeace, *Captives of War: British Prisoners of War in Europe in the Second World War* (New York: Cambridge University Press, 2017) p.186.
12. Wylie, 'Muted Applause?', p.263; 'Bombing of Prisoner of War Camps – Germany', the National Archives, Kew, England, FO 916/1184.
13. *Long March to Freedom*.
14. Laurence William Hitchcock, 'In German Hands', *RIASC Journal*, XIV (1946) pp.8–17 (p.17).
15. *Ibid*.
16. Virk, *Indian Army Post Offices in the Second World War*, p.349.
17. 'Medal Recommendation for Sapper Natarajan', the National Archives, Kew, England, WO 373 101 544.
18. 'Indian P.O.Ws Freed via Russia', *Fauji Akhbar*, 3 April 1945, p.20, United Services of India.
19. MacKenzie, *The Colditz Myth*, p.391.
20. 'Part I to XIII – CSDIC(I) Red Fort Delhi Report No. 902–1000', p.15, National Archives of India, PP_000002998624.
21. 'Allemagne Marlag Ilag Nord', ICRC Archives, Geneva.
22. 'Camp History Milag Marlag', the National Archives, Kew, England, WO 208/3270.
23. Virk, *Indian Army Post Offices in the Second World War*, pp.349–50.
24. 'Indian Army Clerk Outwits Gestapo', *Times of India*, 2 May 1945, p.4.
25. 'PRISONERS OF WAR: Repatriation (Code 91(F)): Rehabilitation of Repatriated Prisoners of War', the National Archives, Kew, England, WO 32/10757.
26. 'Indian POWs' Reception Headquarters: Personnel and Administration, Part 1, 1944–1947', 1945, India Office Records at the British Library, IOR L/WS/1/709.
27. Diwan Chand Bhaskar, 'Indian Ex-P.O.Ws in England', *Fauji Akhbar*, 12 June 1945, p.10, United Services of India.

28. Oliver Clutton-Brock, *Footprints on the Sands of Time: RAF Bomber Command Prisoners of War in Germany 1939–45* (Grub Street, 2003) pp.238–39.
29. Macdonald Hastings, 'The POWs Fly Home', *USI Journal* (1945) pp.304–06.
30. 'POWs Reception HQ Part 1', India Office Records at the British Library, IOR L/WS/1/709.
31. Philip Kindersley, *For You the War Is Over*, p.187.
32. 'Rapports de Visite Müller Losone et Leysin', ICRC Archives, Geneva, B G 002 185; 'Hindou, Indische Internierte', Swiss Federal Archives, E5791 1000949 991.
33. Interview with Birendra Nath Mazumdar.
34. Letter from Jai Bahadur to Mrs Bell, 17 January 1945, Imperial War Museum, London, 23628.
35. 'Heimschaffungen', Swiss Federal Archives, E5791 1000 949 922.
36. 'Indian POWs Reception Headquarters Personnel and Administration Part 2', 1945, p.2, India Office Records at the British Library, IOR L/WS/1/710.
37. 'POWs Liberated by Russians', 1945, the National Archives, Kew, England, FO 916/1201; one is remembered on the Cassino memorial, one (oddly) at Rangoon, but the third could not be found on the Commonwealth War Graves Commission website.
38. 'POWs Liberated by Russians', National Archives, Kew, England, FO 916/1201.
39. 'Indian Prisoners of War: Charente', the National Archives, Kew, England, WO 229/73/13.
40. Mahal Singh, letter to Emile Bonhotal, 28 November 1944, Claude Demet collection.
41. 'Monthly Reports of Indian Military Mission in Germany', India Office Records at the British Library, IOR/L/WS/1/1593.
42. *Ibid.*
43. 'Reception HQ Part 2', p.2, India Office Records at the British Library, IOR L/WS/1/710.
44. Report by Captain Warren November 1944 in 'Indian Prisoners of War: Charente', the National Archives, Kew, England, WO 229/73/13.
45. Benbow, 'Indian PWs', the National Archives, Kew, England, WO 229/73/15.
46. Perret and Vallotton, *Ceux D'Étobon*, p.67.
47. *Ibid.*, p.83.
48. *Ibid.*, pp.84–85.
49. *Ibid.*, p.95.
50. *Ibid.*, p.97.
51. Fernand Auberjonois, 'Tristresse d'Étobon', trans. by Hannah Michel-Bowman, *Les Lettres Françaises* (Paris, 17 February 1945).
52. Perret and Vallotton, *Ceux D'Étobon*, pp.154–55.
53. *Ibid.*, pp.163–65.
54. 'POWs Reception HQ Part 1', p.1, India Office Records at the British Library, IOR L/WS/1/709.

55. 'HQ POW Reception Camp War Service Diary', 1944, the National Archives, Kew, England, WO 179/5929; Virk, *Indian Army Post Offices in the Second World War*, p.197.
56. 'Rest Camps', India Office Records at the British Library, IOR L/WS/1/916.
57. 'Indian POWs and CSDIC', India Office Records at the British Library, IOR/L/WS/1/1516.
58. 'Indian POW Reception HQ', 1945, India Office Records at the British Library, IOR/L/WS/1/704.
59. 'War Diaries Indian POW Reception Headquarters Part 2', 1945, p.2, India Office Records at the British Library, IOR L/WS/1/705.
60. 'HQ POW Reception Camp War Service Diary', the National Archives, Kew, England, WO 179/5929.
61. 'Indian POW Reception HQ', India Office Records at the British Library, IOR/L/WS/1/704.
62. 'Rest Camps', India Office Records at the British Library, IOR L/WS/1/916.
63. '55 Indian General Hospital War Service Diary', 1941, the National Archives, Kew, England, WO 177/2223.
64. Commonwealth War Graves Commission.
65. 'Indian POW Reception HQ Liaison Letters', India Office Records at the British Library, L/WS/1/1396.
66. 'Mrs Bartaby Pearson & POW Reception Camps', 1945, India Office Records at the British Library, IOR/L/WS/2/68.
67. Rumer Godden, *Bengal Journey* (Calcutta: Longman, 1945) p.40.
68. 'Indian POW Reception HQ', India Office Records at the British Library, IOR/L/WS/1/704; 'Mrs Bartaby Pearson', India Office Records at the British Library, IOR/L/WS/2/68.
69. 'Indian POW Reception HQ', India Office Records at the British Library, IOR/L/WS/1/704; for more on Gooneratne, see Bowman, *The Indian Contingent*, p.44.
70. 'War Diaries Indian POW Reception Headquarters Part 2', India Office Records at the British Library, IOR L/WS/1/705.
71. 'Shivaji Jayanti Utsav in England', *Fauji Akhbar*, 7 August 1945, p.12, United Services of India.
72. 'Indian POW Reception HQ', India Office Records at the British Library, IOR/L/WS/1/704.
73. *Ibid.*
74. *Ibid.*
75. 'Mrs Bartaby Pearson', India Office Records at the British Library, IOR/L/WS/2/68.
76. 'The Id El Adzha in England', *Islamic Review* (1945) p.70.
77. 'POW Rec Camps', India Office Records at the British Library, IOR/L/WS/2/43.
78. 'Indian POWs and CSDIC', India Office Records at the British Library, IOR/L/WS/1/1516.
79. Letter from Sardar Khan to Kay Hukam Dad, Hukam Dad Khan collection.

80. Bas Kybird, 'Memories of Methwold', Joe Masons Page, 2013: joemasonspage. wordpress.com/2013/07/16/ [accessed 16 December 2022].
81. 'Indian POW Reception HQ', India Office Records at the British Library, IOR/L/WS/1/704; 'Staunch Indian Troops', *The Times*, 18 June 1945, p.2.
82. 'Rest Camps', India Office Records at the British Library, IOR L/WS/1/916.
83. Report on 'Visit to Indian Prisoner of War Camp in Norfolk, 21 May 1945', in 'Rest Camps', India Office Records at the British Library, IOR L/WS/1/916. Interestingly, these ranks still exist in the armies of South Asia, now referred to as 'junior commissioned officers'.
84. Report by Lieutenant Colonel Sundian-Smith on VCOs in Olfag 79, in 'Rest Camps', India Office Records at the British Library, IOR L/WS/1/916.
85. *Ibid.*
86. Secret and most immediate note dated 25/5/45, in 'Rest Camps', India Office Records at the British Library, IOR L/WS/1/916.
87. 'Rest Camps', India Office Records at the British Library, IOR L/WS/1/916.
88. *Ibid.*
89. 'Indian Acquitted of Girl Attack Charge', *Bury Free Press & Post*, 27 July 1945, p.9.
90. *Ibid.*
91. Reports from Gooneratne on incidents with RPOWs in Thetford, in 'Rest Camps', India Office Records at the British Library, IOR L/WS/1/916.
92. Letter from GHQ Delhi 9/3/46 in 'Rest Camps', India Office Records at the British Library, IOR L/WS/1/916.
93. 'Prisoners of Wars – NAI', 1945, National Archives of India, Misc/3830/H.
94. 'Rest Camps', India Office Records at the British Library, IOR L/WS/1/916.
95. 'Ex-POWs Thank Red Cross', *Fauji Akhbar*, 4 September 1945, p.12, United Services of India.
96. 'Embarkation HQ Bombay', 1943, National Archives of India, Misc/3975/H.
97. 'Former Indian War Prisoners Return', *Times of India*, 29 June 1945, p.1.
98. 'Indian Prisoners of War Return', *Times of India*, 17 April 1944, p.4.
99. A.S. Naravane, *A Soldier's Life in War and Peace*, pp.175–76.
100. Interview with Dr Qausar, 2022.
101. Gupta, *India in the Second World War*, p.42.
102. 'Prisoners of Wars - NAI', National Archives of India, Misc/3830/H.

Epilogue

1. @nomhossain, 'Tweet: Fascinating', 16 March 2022.
2. 'Royal Artillery Depot Deolali, Monthly Intelligence Reports', National Archives of India, Misc/1936/H.
3. *Ibid.*
4. *Ibid.*
5. *Ibid.*
6. *Ibid.*
7. Hamid, *Sahabzada Yaqub Khan: Pursuits and Experiences as Prisoner of War*, p.179.

8.   Mohan Singh, *Soldiers' Contribution to Indian Independence*, p.366; Yasmin Khan, *The Great Partition: The Making of India and Pakistan* (New Haven: Yale University Press, 2007) pp.29–30.
9.   Raghavan, *India's War*, p.448.
10. 'Rapports de Visite Müller Losone et Leysin', ICRC Archives, Geneva, B G 002 185.
11. Interview with Leila Sen.
12. Email from Leila Sen to Ghee Bowman, 4 November 2022.
13. Speech by Muneeza Shamsie at the launch of Major General Syed Ali Hamid's book *Sahibzada Yaqub Khan: Pursuits and Experiences as Prisoner of War* (Islamabad, 2022).
14. Vaughan, *A History of the 2nd Royal Lancers*, p.190.
15. Jit Singh Sarna, 'Indian Army History Thread', Bharat Rakshak (2007): forums.bharat-rakshak.com/viewtopic.php?f=3&t=2623&start=40 [accessed 26 July 2019].
16. Interview with Aaliyah Gilani, Fizza Bibi, Saboor and Ghayur Gilani, 2018.
17. Pearson, *Brief History of the K.G.V's Own Bengal Sappers and Miners Group, R.I.E.* (Roorkee, 1947) p.148.
18. Dileep Padgaonkar, *Under Her Spell: Roberto Rossellini in India* (New Delhi: Viking, 2008).
19. Perret and Vallotton, *Ceux D'Étobon*.
20. Vandana Joshi, 'The Making of a Cosmopolitan Jangi Qaidi: A Leaf from Sohan Singh's Prison Notebook', Das Moderne Indien in Deutschen Archiven (2020): www.projekt-mida.de/reflexicon/the-making-of-a-cosmopolitan-jangi-qaidi/ [accessed 18 December 2021].
21. Hamid, *Sahabzada Yaqub Khan: Pursuits and Experiences as Prisoner of War*, p.192.
22. Salvi, *Whom Enemies Sheltered*, p.146.
23. *Ibid.*, p.151.
24. Commonwealth War Graves Commission.
25. Vartier, *Histoires Secrètes de l'Occupation En Zone Interdite*, p.285.
26. Satish K. Issar, *General S.M. Shrinagesh* (New Delhi: Natraj, 2009), pp.123–24; 'Monthly Reports of Indian Military Mission in Germany', India Office Records at the British Library, IOR/L/WS/1/1593.
27. 'Monthly Reports of Indian Military Mission in Germany', India Office Records at the British Library, IOR/L/WS/1/1593.
28. Email from George Hay and Nick Bristow to Ghee Bowman, 10 July 2023.
29. Levi Verbauwhede, 'Grafsteen van Noord-Indische soldaat uit WO I gevonden naast bouwwerf: "Geen idee hoe dit hier terechtkomt"', 18 August 2023: www.nieuwsblad.be/cnt/dmf20230818_94968918
30. Interview and tour of Épinal with Jacques Grasser.
31. Interview with Claude Canard and Raymond Berdah.
32. 'India's Gift to France', *Times of India*, 31 August 1945, p.7; 'Monthly Reports of Indian Military Mission in Germany', India Office Records at the British Library, IOR/L/WS/1/1593.
33. 'Proposal for Pakistan Memorial at Épinal', the National Archives, Kew, England, FO 371/69748; for the 1947 memorial, see Bowman, *The Indian Contingent*, pp.157–58.

34. Perret and Vallotton, *Ceux D'Étobon*.
35. Jules Perret: I am grateful to Claude Canard for sending me this version.
36. Amitav Ghosh, 'The Slave of MS H6', in *Subaltern Studies VII* (New Delhi: Oxford University Press, 1992) pp.159–214 (p.161).
37. 'Listes Des Effectifs Des Camps de Prisonniers En Mains Allemandes Envoyées Par l'OKW', Swiss Federal Archives, B G 017 04-01.
38. Virk, *Indian Army Post Offices in the Second World War*.
39. See the epilogue of my previous book for some thoughts on collective memory: Bowman, *The Indian Contingent*, pp.199–202.
40. Aleida Assmann, 'Forms of Forgetting', Herengracht 401 (2014): h401. org/2014/10/forms-of-forgetting/ [accessed 1 September 2023].
41. *Ibid.*
42. Quoted in Raphael Samuel, *Theatres of Memory*, Vol. 1 (London: Verso, 1994) p.viii.
43. Pat Reid, *The Colditz Story* (London: Hodder & Stoughton, 1952); *The Colditz Story*, directed by Guy Hamilton (British Lion Films, 1955); *Colditz*, directed by Brian Degas (BBC, 1972); Macintyre, *Colditz: Prisoners of the Castle*; Anita Singh, 'New *Colditz* TV Series Highlights "appalling Racism" of British Officers', *The Telegraph*, 3 June 2023: www.telegraph.co.uk/news/2023/06/03/ tv-series-dismantle-colditz-mythology-racism-brit-officers/
44. Lynne Gray-Ross, 'Jack Date War Log', 27 October 2022.
45. Barnett, *Hitler's Digger Slaves*, p.279.
46. Interview with Claude Canard and Raymond Berdah.
47. Interview with Aaliyah Gilani, Fizza Bibi, Saboor and Ghayur Gilani.
48. Omer Tarin, 'Research into Ex-POWs Families in Hazara', August 2023.
49. Tweet from Savie Karnel, 16 March 2022.
50. Interview with Aaliyah Gilani, Fizza Bibi, Saboor and Ghayur Gilani.
51. Interview with Nighat, Waqas Ahmed and Robina, 2018.
52. Interview with Muhammed Yunis and Gul Mubarak.
53. Aanchal Malhotra, *Remnants of a Separation: A History of the Partition through Material Memory* (Gurugram: Harper Collins, 2017) pp.8, 16.
54. Jagdish and Suresh, interview with Jai Lall's family, trans. by Dilbag Dabas, 2023.
55. Interview with Dilbag Dabas, 2023.
56. 'Indian Order of Merit Certificate for Jai Lall', 1945, collection of Jai Lall family, *Gazette of India* No 208.H.
57. Interview with Jean-Noël Naidet.
58. Jules Perret diary, p.101.
59. A.J. Grewal to Ghee Bowman, 'Lakha Singh Grewal', 13 May 2023.
60. 'Netaji's Statue Unveiled in Palampur', *Tribune*, 23 January 2021: www. tribuneindia.com/news/himachal/netajis-statue-unveiled-in-palampur-202810.
61. K.S. Thimayya, quoted in Apurba Kundu, *Militarism in India: The Army and Civil Society in Consensus* (London: Tauris, 1998) p.56.
62. Raghu Karnad, *Farthest Field: An Indian Story of the Second World War* (Noida, Uttar Pradesh: William Collins, 2015) p.xvi.
63. Tarin, 'Research into Ex-POWs Families in Hazara', August 2023.
64. Raghavan, *India's War*, p.2.
65. *Ibid.*, p.461.

66. Zareer Masani, *Indian Tales of the Raj* (London: BBC, 1987) p.5.
67. 'The Chattri Memorial': www.brighton-hove.gov.uk/libraries-leisure-and-arts/parks-and-green-spaces/chattri-memorial; 'The Woking Peace Garden': www.visitsurrey.com/things-to-do/the-peace-garden-p1463921; 'Sikh Soldier Statue in Smethwick Honours WW1 Dead', BBC News (2018) www.bbc.co.uk/news/uk-england-birmingham-46083728; Vidushi Tiwari, 'Why Is Scotland Building a Memorial for Indian and Pakistani Soldiers?', STV (2023): news.stv.tv/scotland/why-is-scotland-building-a-memorial-for-indian-and-pakistani-soldiers-at-glasgows-kelvingrove-museum
68. Harbakhsh Grewal, 'Lt-Col CS Dhillon – A Brief Biography'.
69. 'Trois Itinéraires Didactiques Pour Trois Siècles d'histoire': www.boncourt.ch/files/424/Curiosit%C3%A9s/210705_RISp_IT_80x110-Vdef.pdf

Index

Note: *italicised* page references denote illustrations.